MW01202142

Reading Contemporary Environmental Justice

This volume investigates 11 contemporary environmental justice narratives from Kerala, the south-western state in India. Introducing a detailed review of environmental literature in Malayalam, the selected eco-narratives are presented through two key literary genres: life narratives and novels, conveying the socio-environmental pressures, problems, and anxieties of modern, globalising Kerala. This text also entails primary investigations of 'toxic fictions' and 'extractivist fictions,' including Malayalam novels that narrate the disastrous consequences of the permeation of toxic pollutants in human and ecosystemic bodies, and novels that chronicle the impact of exploitative mining activities on the environment. All eco-narratives analysed in the book exhibit the familiar pattern of the Global South environmental narratives, namely, a close imbrication of the ecological and social spheres. *Reading Contemporary Environmental Justice* argues that these selected eco-texts offer inspiring scenarios where the subaltern people show *thantedam*, or courage, to claim *thante idam*, one's own space in society and on the Earth. This volume will be essential for those looking to expand their understanding of environmental justice and the harmful effects of development and modernisation.

R. Sreejith Varma earned his PhD from the Indian Institute of Technology Madras in 2018, and also holds an MPhil in Comparative Literature and an MA in English from the University of Hyderabad. He currently works as an assistant professor in the Department of English, Vellore Institute of Technology, Vellore.

Routledge Studies in World Literatures and the Environment
Series Editors: Scott Slovic and Swarnalatha Rangarajan

For more information about this series, please visit: www.routledge.com/Routledge-Studies-in-World-Literatures-and-the-Environment/book-series/ASHER4038

Reading Contemporary Environmental Justice

Narratives from Kerala

R. Sreejith Varma

NEW YORK AND LONDON

First published 2024
by Routledge
605 Third Avenue, New York, NY 10158

and by Routledge
4 Park Square, Milton Park, Abingdon, Oxon, OX14 4RN

Routledge is an imprint of the Taylor & Francis Group, an informa business

© 2024 R. Sreejith Varma

ISBN: 978-1-032-29370-7 (hbk)
ISBN: 978-1-032-29371-4 (pbk)
ISBN: 978-1-003-30131-8 (ebk)

DOI: 10.4324/9781003301318

Typeset in Sabon
by Newgen Publishing UK

Contents

Acknowledgements

This book evolved from my PhD dissertation at the Indian Institute of Technology Madras. I am immensely thankful to my PhD supervisor Professor Swarnalatha Rangarajan for initiating me into the field of the environmental humanities and for her scholarly guidance which shaped my arguments and thoughts. I consider it a real privilege and honour to have worked with her.

I am grateful to Professor Scott Slovic who first spotted the potential of a book in my dissertation and who, along with Professor Swarnalatha, edits the Routledge series 'World Literatures and the Environment' through which this book is coming out.

I would like to also thank the members of my doctoral committee Dr Srilata K., Dr Suresh Babu M., and Dr Chitraa Venkataachalam for their generous encouragement and valuable feedback. I am grateful to Dr R. Azhagarasan, Department of English, University of Madras, who showed keen interest in my project and offered insightful comments.

At Routledge, I would like to express my thanks to Michelle Salyga and Bryony Reece for their competent editorial assistance.

My thanks are also due to the office staff and technical staff at Kerala Sahitya Akademi Library, Thrissur, and Jawaharlal Nehru University Library, New Delhi, from where I gathered part of the resources for my research; Samik Malla for his friendship, meticulous reading of my drafts, and incisive comments; Lakshmi Chithra Dilipkumar for her careful proofreading and constructive criticism; and Anchitha Krishna for her friendship.

I am grateful to the publishers who have granted me permission to reuse my previously published works: parts of Chapter 2 appeared as a chapter in the book, *Women and Nature?: Beyond Dualism in Gender, Body, and Environment* edited by Douglas A. Vakoch and Sam Mickey and published by Routledge. Chapter 4 uses material from my published article titled 'Resource Extractivism and Environmental Damage: An Analysis of Two

Extractivist Fictions from Kerala' in the journal *ISLE: Interdisciplinary Studies in Literature and Environment*.

Finally, I would like to place on record my deep thanks to my parents, grandmother, sister, wife, and parents-in-law for their unfailing love, care, and encouragement.

1 Introduction

Contemporary India faces many pressing environmental issues, ranging from deforestation to air and water pollution, caused predominantly by human activities, which are increasingly becoming entangled with environmental justice concerns. This book examines 11 contemporary environmental justice narratives from Kerala, a south-western state in India. The selected narratives are written in Malayalam, the main language spoken in Kerala, and fall under two different literary genres, namely, life narratives and novels. These 11 texts convey, in varying degrees, the socio-environmental pressures, problems, and anxieties of the modern, globalising Kerala. Thirty-one years ago, in 1991, when India was reeling under a financial crisis, the Narasimha Rao–led Union government announced the economic liberalisation that opened up the Indian markets to global corporate investors and marked India's entry into the era of globalisation. India's switch to LPG (Liberalisation, Privatisation, and Globalisation) policy significantly boosted the country's industrial sector. Khan and Tarique point out that 'the total industrial output increased six times between 1990 and 2010' which, unfortunately, also meant that '[i]n the post reform period … pollution level has increased by nearly six times' (187). With regard to rising pollution levels and mounting concern among the citizens, Ravi Agarwal observes:

> The crisis of the environment really escalated after 1990, when India liberalized its economy, moving from a socialist to a market based one. The subsequent increase in industrial activity was beyond the capacity of the environmental regulatory infrastructure to manage and this led to the many citizens filing cases in the Courts against the pollution and its impacts on health. Many new industrial projects were stalled as a result. The system had come under a severe strain, which continues to this day. Also political interference and the lack of independence of the regulator made it virtually ineffective.

DOI: 10.4324/9781003301318-1

In December 1984, the world's worst industrial disaster happened in Bhopal, the capital of Madhya Pradesh, when 40 tonnes of toxic methyl isocyanate (MIC) gas leaked from the US-based Union Carbide's pesticide plant tragically killing more than two thousand people in a single night. A combination of factors including 'operating errors, design flaws, mainten- ance failures, training deficiencies and economy measures that endangered safety' caused this colossal tragedy (Diamond). A major repercussion of this calamity was the amplification of distrust among the public towards megacorporations running environmentally risky factories and businesses. Christopher Key Chapple compellingly argues:

> Modern environmentalism in India ... began with the disaster in Bhopal in 1984. This event, which killed thousands and permanently injured millions of people, signaled that India's Green Revolution had come full circle. The magic chemicals that increased agricultural production and filled India's granaries beyond capacity, staving off the possibility of famine even during an extended drought, exploded into weapons of unimaginable destruction. India, which prior to this time had only a vague awareness of the environmental movement in the United States, suddenly became a lightning rod for grassroots environmental activity.
>
> (19)

The Bhopal disaster raises pointed questions of socio-environmental justice, corporate accountability, compensation rights, and safe waste disposal. Reports indicate that at least three hundred tonnes of toxic waste are still lying about the disaster site posing serious public health risks in addition to contaminating the groundwater sources (Bhaduri; Narain and Bhushan).

With the arrival of polluting industries, dams, and other developmental projects in their vicinities, the indigenous populations are the worst affected. They are often displaced and deprived of their livelihood sources, resulting in their further marginalisation. According to Rajkishor Meher, 8.54 million (40%) of the 21.3 million people displaced in India between 1951 and 1990 were tribals (458). He also points out that tribal displacement is accentuated by the establishment of mineral-based industries by trans- national corporates in the tribal regions of the country which is triggering increasing tussles between 'ecosystem-dependent peoples and the elites' (458–459). Madhav Gadgil and Ramachandra Guha memorably refer to such displaced tribal communities as 'ecological refugees' and the resource- consuming, city-dwelling elites who 'devour[] everything produced all over the earth' as 'omnivores' (4).

There has been a slew of tribal resistances against land alienation, espe- cially in central and western Indian states, like the infamous 2007 Nandigram incident in West Bengal, when 14 villagers were killed in a police shooting when they protested against land acquisition by the Left government for a chemical hub to be set up by an Indonesian company; the villagers' protests holding the banners 'We need food, not steel' against a possible takeover of their agricultural land by the global steel conglomerate ArcelorMittal; the potential displacees' protest against the Koel–Karo hydroelectric project over the Koel and Karo Rivers in Jharkhand; and the tribal protests against the proposed power plant in Prem Nagar in Chhattisgarh ('Tribal' 2–18). The *Narmada Bachao Andolan*, led by Medha Patkar against the proposed Sardar Sarovar Dam across the Narmada River in Gujarat that would render about 250,000 people homeless, is another striking example from India of development-induced displacement.

Another significant repercussion of the LPG policy is the widening poor–rich divide in India. Debunking the myth that globalisation helps in the reduction of Global South poverty, Vandana Shiva, a powerful anti-globalisation voice from India, points out:

> The main mantra of globalization is 'international competitiveness.' In the context of the environment, this translates into the largest corporations competing for the natural resources that the poor people in the Third World need for their survival. It is often argued that globalization will create more trade, which will create growth, which will remove poverty. What is overlooked in this myth is that globalization and liberalized trade and investment create growth by destroying the environment and local, sustainable livelihoods. They, therefore, create poverty instead of removing it.
>
> ('Ecological' 570)

Farmer suicides, the substitution of traditional seed varieties by new, high-cost seeds supplied by private seed companies, erosion of indigenous farming traditions, and biopiracy of biological resources and indigenous knowledge are a few other problems rocking the Indian agricultural sector that is increasingly becoming globalised. Profit is prioritised over environmental conservation in globalised India which seeks to increase its economic growth rate while simultaneously also striving for global superpower status.

Like in the rest of India, economic reforms and globalisation have had a deep impact on Kerala as well. The last two decades have seen rapid urbanisation and speeding up of the transition from an agriculture-dependent society to a consumerist one. In her study of paddy land cultivation in Kerala, Sheeba Abraham alerts us to the rapid disappearance of paddy farms in Kerala which is threatening the state's food security. She observes that flouting the existing rules regarding wetland conservation, paddy fields are levelled to raise residential and commercial buildings and ominously predicts that '[i]f necessary actions are not taken immediately by the authorities concerned, there will be nothing to hand over to the coming generations.'

A chief marker of the post-globalisation phase of Kerala is the rise of 'indigenist politics' (Steur 59). Dalits comprise 9.8% of Kerala's total population and adivasis form 1.14% (Mohan). While the entrenched casteism traditionally prohibited land ownership rights to the Dalits, the adivasis were alienated from their lands due to 'encroachments, land grabbing, forest notifications and the formation of private plantation companies' (P. T. George). The watershed land redistribution reforms, launched in 1958 by the first communist government of Kerala to end large land holdings by the feudal *zamindars*, were followed by the historic Kerala Land Reforms Act 1963 (during the United Front government) and a major amendment in 1969. Kerala's land reforms had disastrous consequences for both adivasis and Dalits because the settler-farmers received landowning rights which dispossessed the adivasis who were the original holders of the land (Swamy 74) while the small pieces of land distributed to the Dalits were 'too inadequate even to put up a house' (Radhakrishnan via Yadu 7). On 19 February 2003, a group of adivasis, led by the tribal activist C. K. Janu, occupied the Muthanga forestland from where they had been forcibly evicted during the 1970s and 1980s for setting up a wildlife sanctuary (Janu 76). The tribal occupation of Muthanga forest was to protest against the state government that failed to solve the tribal land issue. During the protest, Janu was beaten up and arrested by the police while two people (including a policeman) were killed in police firing. C. K. Janu entered Kerala's public consciousness with this landmark Muthanga protest.

Chapter 2 of this book studies C. K. Janu's life narrative titled *Mother Forest: The Unfinished Story of C. K. Janu* (2004) which describes her remarkable socio-ecoactivist interventions. *Mother Forest* is a powerful narrative that demonstrates how the autochthonous tribal communities were left bereft of their land ownership rights by the state that incessantly operates in cahoots with corrupt private interests. This unholy nexus has pushed the tribal communities of Kerala into multiple agitations for land and livelihood. Chapter 2 titled 'Oiko-autobiographies: Subaltern Environmentalism in the Life Narratives of Five Ecoactivists,' also examines four other life narratives, namely, *Mayilamma: Oru Jeevitham* [Mayilamma: A Life] (2006) by Mayilamma, a member of the Eravallar tribe and the leader of the uprising against water mining by the cola giant Coca-Cola in Plachimada village; *Jeevadayini* [The LifeGiver] (2011) by the Kasaragod anti-endosulfan protest leader Leelakumariamma; and the two life narratives titled *Kandalkkadukalkkidayil Ente Jeevitham* [My Life Amidst Mangrove Forests] (2002) and *Ente Jeevitham* [My Life] (2010) by Kallen Pokkudan, a Dalit ecoactivist from the Kannur district of Kerala, who engaged in the planting and preservation of mangroves across Kerala. These life narratives critically bring into focus a host of important socio-environmental issues in Kerala, like the tribal land question (*Mother Forest*), health risks of deadly pesticides (*Jeevadayini*), the depletion and contamination of groundwater by global corporate forces (*Mayilamma*), and the need to preserve endangered mangrove forests (*Kandalkkadukalkkidayil Ente Jeevitham* and *Ente Jeevitham*). 'Oiko-autobiography' is a term that I coin in Chapter 2 to refer to these life narratives whose subjecthoods are firmly etched on the canvas of their *oikos*—the Greek word meaning 'house' which, by extension, also means nature/earth. These oiko-autobiographies are significant ecotexts that deal with the lives of four important grassroots 'oikos-carers' who have given expression to subaltern environmentalism in the context of Kerala. To analyse these texts, the chapter draws on concepts like 'relational autobiography,' 'slow violence,' 'partnership ethics,' 'ecofeminism,' 'ecomasculinism,' 'material ecocriticism,' and 'earth democracy,' among others. The selected oiko-autobiographies are also a part of the growing body of subaltern life narratives emerging from Kerala that includes *Oru Laingikathozhilaliyude Atmakatha* (2005) by Nalini Jameela, translated into English by J. Devika as *The Autobiography of a Sex Worker* (2007); *Amen: Oru Kanyasthreeyude Atmakatha* (2009) by Sister Jesme (and self-translated into English as *Amen: The Autobiography of a Nun* (2009)) which recounts the gender inequality and corruption in the Catholic churches that prompted her to leave the Congregation of Mother of Carmel; and *Ormakkurippukal* [Memoirs] (1994) by the ex-Naxalite K. Ajitha, translated into English by Sanju Ramachandran as *Kerala's Naxalbari: Ajitha, Memoirs of a Young Revolutionary* (2008).

Chapter 3, titled 'Toxic Fictions: Environmental Toxicity in Three Malayalam Novels,' takes up for analysis three novels, namely, Ambikasuthan Mangad's *Enmakaje*[1] (2009), Sarah Joseph's *Aathi*[2] (2011), and Balakrishnan Mangad's *Bhoomiyude Kannu* [The Eye of the Earth] (2004). I use the term 'toxic fiction' to foreground the thematic thread of pollution and toxicity that runs through all three novels. *Enmakaje* narrates the somatic and ecological threats of the use of the deadly pesticide called 'endosulfan' in the cashew plantations in the eponymous village of Enmakaje and surrounding areas. Interspersing myths, local beliefs, and facts and presenting the horrors of toxified oikos, the novel makes a powerful case for the right of every living being to a healthy and safe environment. Sarah Joseph's *Aathi* discusses multiple environmental issues like poor sanitation, improper human waste disposal, garbage dumping, and pesticide toxification in Aathi and Chakkam Kandam. *Bhoomiyude Kannu*, probably the first environmental justice novel in Malayalam, dramatises the mass ecojustice movement against the operation of a diesel power plant that trigged multiple toxic concerns, health risks, and water scarcity in a north Malabar village. The chapter employs a variety of theories like material ecocriticism, toxic discourse, excremental ecocriticism, and so on, and uses the works of ecocritics ranging from Lawrence Buell to Heather Houser and John Blair Gamber to study these novels. The chapter contends that the three novels studied are representative texts of the emerging genre of toxic fiction in contemporary Malayalam literature. A couple of other Malayalam toxic fictions of note include *Bhopal* (2009) by K. Aravindakshan, which narrates the story of a Malayali family living in one of Bhopal's disaster-affected localities, and *Kanyadhaivangal* [Virgin Gods] (2013) by Anni Andrews, which chronicles how the death of her daughter, after being exposed to the toxic fumes emitted by a factory, prompted an Uttar Pradesh–based school teacher named Maheswari to fight for environmental causes and participate in the anti-endosulfan protests in Kerala. Employing powerful apocalyptic rhetoric, these toxic fictions advocate an immediate and uncompromising switch to sustainable and environmentally considerate developmental activities as the only solution.

Chapter 4, titled 'Extractivist Fictions: Anti-Mining Struggles in Three Malayalam Novels,' ecocritically reads three novels: *Manal Jeevikal* [Sand Creatures] (2013) by G. R. Indugopan, *Manalazham* [The Depths of Sand] (2015) by Hari Kurisseri, and *Kalpramanam* [Proof Etched in Stone] (2014) by Rajeev Sivasankar. These are lesser-known novels by writers who have received sparse or nil critical attention. Hence, this chapter also serves as an introduction to these novels and novelists for both Malayalam *and* Anglophone readership. *Manal Jeevikal* is inspired by the real environmental justice concerns surrounding extensive black sand mining activities in the Kollam district of Kerala. Places like Aappadam and Chalithura are depicted as facing sea surges and under the threat of submergence. *Manalazham* problematises sand extraction from paddy fields and the ecojustice resistance started in Mannida village by the differently abled school teacher named Satchidanandan. This is a new mining practice as opposed to the long-term practice of exploitative river sand extraction that has already damaged the health and existence of several rivers in Kerala. The novel addresses numerous socio-environmental problems like the fatal open sinkholes left by sand mining, groundwater depletion, and the unholy political–bureaucratic–police nexus that turns a blind eye to unbridled sand extraction activities. *Kalpramanam* discusses the environmental impact of excessive quarrying of stone and the consequent disappearance of hills in the fictional village named Pazhukka. Much of the novel's narrative space is also devoted to chronicling the villagers' environmental justice protests to preserve their hills. The novel grapples with a raft of socio-environmental issues like the misuse of agricultural land, careless handling of explosives in the quarries, air and water pollution, and the displacement of people.

In this chapter, I introduce the term 'extractivist fiction' to highlight the common theme of resource extractivism that runs through all three novels. These extractivist fictions narrate powerful 'ecomaterial tales' (Cohen x) and deal with the politics of mining and developmentalism in Kerala's context. The ecocritical and extractivist theories of Joan Martinez-Alier, Rob Nixon, Heather Sullivan, and Richard M. Auty, among others, are employed in this chapter to examine these novels.

All works that I study in this book share a common concern for environmental justice and give expression to the significant changes in human–environmental relations in the post–LPG Kerala society. Through a close reading of the selected texts, I will bring to the fore the highly entangled nature of the social and environmental concerns in contemporary Kerala. The selected texts are remarkable for their depiction of scenarios where the subaltern people show *thantedam*, which stands for 'courage' in Malayalam, to claim *thante idam*, one's own space in society and on the earth (Zacharia 109).

A major accomplishment of this book is its attempt to help these significant Malayalam ecotexts reach the international Anglophone audience as this is probably the first work written in English about contemporary environmental writings in Malayalam. As most of the texts used in this book have not been translated into English before, I have also undertaken the translation of the excerpts from the texts for the purpose of citation.

Ecocriticism: The Origins

The overarching framework used to analyse the texts in this book is 'ecological criticism' or 'ecocriticism' as it is more commonly called. The term 'ecocriticism' was first used by William Rueckert in his 1978 essay 'Literature and Ecology: An Experiment in Ecocriticism' to suggest 'the application of ecology and ecological concepts to the study of literature' (Glotfelty xix–xx). However, ecocriticism, as an organised theoretical field, was launched by the publication of *The Ecocriticism Reader* (1996) edited by Cheryll Glotfelty and Harold Fromm. *The Ecocriticism Reader* comprises 25 essays by authors ranging from William Howarth and Lynn White Jr. to Scott Slovic. Glotfelty's introduction titled 'Literary Studies in an Age of Environmental Crisis' traces the origins of the field besides offering a succinct definition of ecocriticism. Glotfelty defines ecocriticism as 'the study of the relationship between literature and physical environment' (xviii). Ecocriticism dismisses the speciesist assumptions of human superiority as fallacious and advocates an ecocentric egalitarian vision where every life form is valued for possessing an intrinsic worth. The terms 'interrelationship' and 'interdependence' are, hence, key to ecocritical inquiry. In his book *The Ecological Thought* (2010), Timothy

Morton relevantly notes, 'The ecological thought realizes that all beings are interconnected. This is the mesh. The ecological thought realizes that the boundaries between, and the identities of, beings are affected by this interconnection' (94).

In her famous 'Introduction' to *The Ecocriticism Reader*, Glotfelty also differentiates between ecocriticism and other streams of literary theory. She notes: 'Literary theory, in general, examines the relations between writers, texts, and the world. In most literary theory, "the world" is synonymous with society—the social sphere. Ecocriticism expands the notion of the "world" to include the entire ecosphere' (xix). The question of what makes up an environmental text is answered by the eminent ecocritic Lawrence Buell in his 1995 book, *The Environmental Imagination*. In his book, Buell gives a useful list of four 'ingredients' that characterise an environmental text:

1   The nonhuman environment is present not merely as a framing device but as a presence that begins to suggest that human history is implicated in natural history.
2   The human interest is not understood to be the only legitimate interest.
3   Human accountability to the environment is part of the text's ethical orientation.
4   Some sense of the environment as a process rather than as a constant or a given is at least implicit in the text. (7–8)

The literary moorings of the US strand of nature writing that accord with Buell's conception of environmental texts can be found in the works of three nineteenth-century writers: Ralph Waldo Emerson (1803–1882), Margaret Fuller (1810–1850), and Henry David Thoreau (1817–1862), together known as the 'Transcendentalists,' 'whose work celebrates nature, the life-force, and the wilderness manifested in America' (P. Barry 240). Among the triumvirate, Thoreau has been especially influential: his *Walden; or, Life in the Woods* (1854) is consistently considered as a staple text for environmental literature courses taught at universities across the globe. The preoccupation with the wilderness that nineteenth-century writers like Thoreau showed finds its distinct echoes in the works of the twentieth-century ecopoet Gary Snyder. In *The Practice of the Wild* (1990), Snyder usefully differentiates between nature and wild:

Nature is the subject, they say, of science. Nature can be deeply probed, as in microbiology. The wild is not to be made subject or object in this manner; to be approached it must be admitted from within, as a quality intrinsic to who we are. Nature is ultimately in no way endangered; wilderness is. The wild is indestructible, but we might not see the wild.
(182)

Snyder's works are also deeply influenced by Zen Buddhism and Native American myths. In his 'Introductory Note' to his Pulitzer Prize–winning collection of poems and a few non-fiction writings, *Turtle Island* (1974), Snyder writes:

> Each living being is a swirl in the flow, a formal turbulence, a 'song.' The land, the planet itself is also a living being—at another pace. Anglos, Black people, Chicanos, and others beached up on these shores all share such views at the deepest levels of their old cultural traditions—African, Asian, or European. Hark again to those roots, to see our ancient solidarity, and then to the work of being together on Turtle Island ['the old new name' for the North American Continent].

The British counterpart of nature writing had its origins even further back in time, during the Romantic period (1785–1830) and in the works of writers like William Wordsworth (1770–1850), Dorothy Wordsworth (1771–1855), S. T. Coleridge (1772–1834), John Keats (1795–1821), and George Gordon Byron (1788–1824) (Barry 241). The UK anthology, *The Green Studies Reader: From Romanticism to Ecocriticism* (2000), in which the editor Laurence Coupe announces that 'we may be said to entering "the ecocritical age"' (4) is significant for its presentation of environmentally oriented writings by authors ranging from William Blake and William Wordsworth to Greg Garrard and Patrick D. Murphy. *The Country and the City* (1973) by Raymond Williams and *Romantic Ecology: Wordsworth and the Environmental Tradition* (1991) by Jonathan Bate are easily the two pioneering works of British environmental literature (P. Barry 241).

The Waves of Ecocriticism

Lawrence Buell, in his seminal text *The Future of Environmental Criticism* (2005), uses the 'wave metaphor' to demarcate the history of ecocriticism. He identifies the development of ecocriticism as being marked by two 'waves.' The first wave originated around 1980 whereas the second wave was launched around 1995.[3] In 2009, Joni Adamson and Scott Slovic announced the emergence of a new third wave since post-2000. More recently, Scott Slovic proposed that a further fourth wave of ecocriticism is underway since around 2012. Other metaphors like the 'rhizome' (Deleuze and Guattari) and 'palimpsest' (Buell17) have also been used by critics to indicate the non-linear, horizontal, and layered trajectory of ecocriticism.

The 'first wave' of ecocriticism was dominated by a focus on wilderness narratives and works that essentially celebrated the natural environment. The first-wave ecocritics primarily studied the work of writers like the

Transcendentalists and the English Romantics. Some of the notable first-wave ecocritics are Raymond Williams, Joseph Meeker, Carolyn Merchant, and Terry Gifford (Borlik 12). One of the most influential strands of the first-wave ecocriticism was 'ecofeminism' which emerged in the 1980s and explored the connection between women and nature in terms of the male domination they both suffered. Karla Armbuster explains that ecofeminism critiques the 'dominant ideologies of dualism and hierarchy within Western culture that construct nature as separate from and inferior to human culture (and women as inferior to men)' (98). The French feminist Françoise d'Eaubonne coined the term 'ecofeminism' in her book *Le Féminisme ou la Mort* [Feminism or Death] (1974) in which she argued, as Carolyn Merchant points out, 'pollution, destruction of the environment, and run-away population growth [are] problems created by male culture' and 'called upon women to lead an ecological revolution to save the planet' (Merchant, *Radical Ecology* 194). The ecofeminist movement originated in the United States following the conference on 'Women and Life on Earth: Ecofeminism in the 1980s' organised by Ynestra King et al. at Amherst in 1980 (Sturgeon 26). India's Chipko Movement in which village women of Uttarakhand hugged trees to stop the trees from being felled and the Kenyan afforestation campaign called the Green Belt Movement led by Wangari Maathai are notable examples of ecofeminist activism (Merchant, *Radical Ecology* 193).

The English chemist James Lovelock's 1979 book, *Gaia: A New Look at Life on Earth* which advances the influential 'Gaia hypothesis' and the idea of a living earth, has inspired ecofeminist scholars. Drawing on the eponymous Greek goddess of earth, Lovelock writes, 'Gaia is the superorganism composed of all life tightly coupled with air, the oceans and the surface rock' (xii). Lovelock posits that the earth has a self-regulating mechanism that maintains the equilibrium of temperature and climate (homeostasis) and argues that although anthropogenic interventions can modify the planet and make it unfit for *human* inhabitation, life will continue in the form of lower organisms like ants and algae (Grey). Carolyn Merchant, in her chapter titled 'The Death of Nature: Women and Ecology in the Scientific Revolution' included in *Earthcare* (1996), argues that the idea of the earth as an organism was present 'in ancient systems of thought' and points out that while the identification of earth/nature with 'a nurturing mother' was at the heart of the organic theory, a contrasting image of nature as a havoc-wreaking female was also in circulation—that of a 'wild and uncontrollable nature that could render violence, storms, droughts, and general chaos' (77). Merchant contends that with the onset of the Scientific Revolution, the image of the 'nurturing mother' disappeared, and the latter image of 'nature as disorder' that man should keep in check gained wider acceptance. She asserts that the 'rational control over nature, society, and self,' facilitated by the 'submergence of the organism by the machine' has led to, what she famously terms, 'the death of nature' (85–86).

The best-known Global South[4] ecofeminist is perhaps the Indian physicist Vandana Shiva whose works find ecofeminist inspiration in the ancient Hindu spiritual traditions. Ecofeminism is an active field of inquiry with a rapidly growing body of literature. However, texts like *Woman and Nature: The Roaring Inside Her* (1978) by Susan Griffin, *Ecofeminism* (1993) by Maria Mies and Vandana Shiva, *Gyn/Ecology: The Metaethics of Radical Feminism* (1978) by Mary Daly, and *Feminism and the Mastery of Nature* (1993) by Val Plumwood continue to have much sway over a lot of contemporary ecofeminists.

Another prominent theoretical strand in the first wave of environmental thought is 'deep ecology.' It foregrounds the interconnectedness of all organisms and dismisses anthropocentrism in favour of biocentrism/ecocentrism. Deep ecology recognises the intrinsic, as opposed to the instrumental, value of all life forms. The Norwegian philosopher Arne Næss coined the term 'deep ecology' in his 1973 essay titled 'The Shallow and the Deep, Long Range Ecology Movements: A Summary.' The chief tenets of deep ecology are as follows:

1 The well-being and flourishing of human and nonhuman life on earth have value in themselves (synonyms: inherent worth, intrinsic value, inherent value). These values are independent of the usefulness of the nonhuman world for human purposes.
2 Richness and diversity of life forms contribute to the realisation of these values and are also values in themselves.
3 Humans have no right to reduce this richness and diversity except to satisfy vital needs.
4 Present human interference with the nonhuman world is excessive, and the situation is rapidly worsening.
5 The flourishing of human life and cultures is compatible with a substantial decrease of the human population. The flourishing of nonhuman life requires such a decrease.
6 Policies must therefore be changed. The changes in policies affect basic economic, technological, and ideological structures. The resulting state of affairs will be deeply different from the present.
7 The ideological change is mainly that of appreciating life quality (dwelling in situations of inherent worth) rather than adhering to an increasingly higher standard of living. There will be a profound awareness of the difference between big and great.
8 Those who subscribe to the foregoing points have an obligation directly or indirectly to participate in the attempt to implement the necessary changes. (Næss and Sessions)

However, deep ecology has attracted criticism from Third World ecocritics like Ramachandra Guha. In his essay titled 'Radical American Environmentalism and Wilderness Preservation: A Third World Critique,' Guha famously argues that deep ecology's emphasis on biocentrism and wilderness is unviable in Third World contexts as they clash with the needs and survival issues of the local human population. As an example, he cites India's tiger conservation programme, Project Tiger, which he justly asserts, 'sharply posits the interests of the tiger against those of poor peasants living in and around the reserve' (75). Calls for the preservation of pristine wilderness raised by the deep ecologists are realisable, according to Guha, only in places like North America that 'possess[es] a vast, beautiful, and sparsely populated continent' in contrast to the densely populated Global South nations.

The 'second wave' of ecocriticism acknowledges that both natural and built environments have 'long since all mixed up' and argues for greater inclusivity in ecocritical inquiry. It calls for the accommodation of the study of the 'landscape of metropolitan sprawl' on an equal footing with that of wilderness as well as the development of an environmental justice perspective (Buell, *The Future* 21–22). One of the pioneering texts in the second wave of environmental writing is Rachel Carson's classic *Silent Spring* (1962). It is an environmental science book that raised awareness about the harmful effects of pesticides like DDT (dichlorodiphenyltrichl oroethane). The book was so influential that it even brought about the ban on the agricultural use of DDT in the United States in 1972 (and later in many other countries). Greg Garrard opens his book *Ecocriticism* (2004) by noting that 'modern environmentalism begins with "A Fable for Tomorrow," in Rachel Carson's *Silent Spring* (1962)' (1). The fictive chapter from *Silent Spring* that Garrard cites offers a searing image of an Edenic village sinking into an environmental collapse wrought, not by any supernatural actors, but by the people themselves. Lawrence Buell, in his essay 'Toxic Discourse,' asserts that '[c]ontemporary toxic discourse effect-ively starts with Rachel Carson's *Silent Spring*' (645). The toxic discourse focuses on human and social health issues and addresses the anxieties about the human-induced toxification of the planet-oikos by industrial chemicals, pesticides, and nuclear fallout. According to Buell, 'the campaigns against toxic dumping have been the catalyst and remain the centerpiece' of envir-onmental justice movement (642).

Giovvanna Di Chiro explains the origin and current relevance of the term 'environmental justice,' thus:

> The term 'environmental justice' emerged from the activism of the com-munities of color in the United States in the latter half of the twentieth century and is now used by many to describe a global network of social

movements fiercely critical of disparities and depredations caused by the unchecked expansion and neocolonial logic of fossil fuel-driven modern industrial development. Activists and scholars of environmental justice challenge the disproportionate burden of toxic contamination, waste dumping, and ecological devastation borne by low-income communities, communities of color, and colonized territories.

(100)

Another useful definition of 'environmental justice' is given by Joni Adamson, Mei Mei Evans, and Rachel Stein in their introduction to the important collection titled *The Environmental Justice Reader* (2002) that they edited. They note, 'We define environmental justice as the right of all people to share equally in the benefits bestowed by a healthy environment. We define the environment, in turn, as the places in which we live, work, play, and worship' (4). Blending environmental justice with the ecocritical praxis, T. V. Reed talks about 'environmental justice ecocriticism' in his essay titled 'Toward an Environmental Justice Ecocriticism.' He proposes this term to 'further develop the environmental justice strand of ecocriticism' and to 'foster new work that understands and elaborates the crucial connection between environmental concerns and social justice in the context of ecocriticism' (145). In his essay, Reed also relevantly presses for the inclusion of the questions of race and class in ecocritical discussions and identifies 'environmental racism' as an important ecocritical concern.[5]

In their 1997 book titled *Varieties of Environmentalism: Essays North and South*, Ramachandra Guha and Joan Martinez-Alier draw attention to the environmentalism of the Global South which they term the 'environmentalism of the poor.' In their book, Guha and Martinez-Alier famously distinguish between a 'full-stomach environmentalism of the North' and the 'empty-belly environmentalism of the South' (xxi) and argue that the Global North environmentalism 'relies rather heavily on "social movement organization"—such as the Sierra Club or the Friends of the Earth—with its own cadre, leadership and properly audited sources of funds' (17). By contrast, they point out that environmental movements in Global South countries like India are characterised by nature-based conflicts that adopt *dharna* and *bhook hartal* as their forms of protest[6] (17). The term 'environmentalism of the poor' is used to emphasise environmental justice struggles waged in the Global South by the poor indigenous communities to protect their livelihoods 'against mining companies, hydroelectric dams, biomass extraction and land grabbing, and oil and gas exploitation' (Martinez-Alier, 'The Environmentalism of the Poor' 239). Examples of the environmentalism of the poor include Sunderlal Bahuguna's indefinite hunger strike as part of the Chipko movement, the *Narmada Bachao Andolan* (Save the Narmada Movement) led by Medha Patkar against the construction of the Sardar Sarovar Dam on the Narmada River in India which would displace about 250,000 people, and the protests against the operations of Karnataka Pulpwoods Limited (KPL) which planted eucalyptus trees in thirty thousand hectares of common land in Karnataka that had previously been used by the villagers for fuel wood, fodder, small timber, and other materials (Guha and Martinez-Alier 6–14).

Rob Nixon's 2011 book titled *Slow Violence and the Environmentalism of the Poor* remarkably builds on Guha and Martinez-Alier's works and, as the book's title suggests, makes connections between what he calls 'slow violence' and the environmentalism of the poor because, as he argues, people bereft of resources are 'the principal casualties of slow violence'(4). By 'slow violence,' Nixon means 'a violence that is neither spectacular nor instantaneous, but rather incremental and accretive, its calamitous repercussions playing out across a range of temporal scales' (2). Examples of slow violence include 'thawing cryosphere, toxic drift, biomagnification, deforestation, the radioactive aftermaths of wars, [and] acidifying oceans' (2). In his book, Nixon, building on Benedict Anderson's influential conceptualisation of the 'imagined communities,' also proposes the concept of 'unimagined communities' which comprise mostly rural or ecosystem people who are both physically and imaginatively displaced in the name of development, thereby removed from 'the idea of both a national future and a national memory' also (151).

An important emerging field within the second wave of ecocriticism is 'postcolonial ecocriticism' which sits at the intersection of postcolonial and environmental studies. 'Postcolonial ecocriticism' is sometimes synonymously used with 'green postcolonialism' and 'postcolonial green' (for example, in the 2010 book *Postcolonial Green: Environmental Politics and World Narratives* edited by Bonnie Roos and Alex Hunt). In his important essay titled 'Environmentalism and Postcolonialism,' Rob Nixon astutely observes that the intellectual remit of ecocriticism has been limited due to the disengagement of postcolonial literary studies with environmental concerns. Similarly, the field's preponderant American studies' focus has restricted ecocritics to see broader connections as well (206). *Postcolonial Ecocriticism: Literature, Animals, Environment* (2006) by Graham Huggan and Helen Tiffin is an important text in this field wherein they significantly point out how postcolonial ecocriticism is 'broadly *eco-socialist* in inspiration' and that it appropriately censures the global-capitalist forces which function like the modern-day manifestation of colonialism (15). In his remarkable essay, 'Postcolonial Studies and the Challenge of Climate Change,' Dipesh Chakrabarty demonstrates 'how postcolonial thinking may need to be stretched to adjust itself to the reality of global warming' (1). In the essay, he calls attention to three images of 'human,' viz. the 'rights-bearing' human of the Enlightenment; the postcolonial–postmodern conception of human characterised by the differences of class, sexuality, gender, and history; and the human in the epoch of the Anthropocene. These are not mutually exclusive categories as they remain operative at the same time. Chakrabarty emphasises how humans have become a geophysical force which invites us to think of our species non-ontologically. He notes,

> [I]n becoming a geophysical force on the planet, we have also developed a form of collective existence that has no ontological dimension. Our thinking about ourselves now stretches our capacity for interpretive understanding. We need nonontological ways of thinking the human.
>
> (13)

Timothy Morton, years later, uses the term 'Hyperobjects' to refer to 'this human thing' *(Dark Ecology* 15) that is spread across the planet and exerting a transformative effect.

A few other notable titles in the field of postcolonial ecocriticism include *Postcolonial Environments: Nature, Culture and the Contemporary Indian Novel* (2010) by Upamanyu Pablo Mukherjee; *Postcolonial Ecologies: Literatures of the Environment* (2011) edited by Elizabeth DeLoughrey and George B. Handley; and *Caribbean Literature and the Environment: Between Nature and Culture* (2005), edited by Elizabeth M. DeLoughrey, Renée K. Gosson, and George B. Handley.

Although ecocriticism did expand from being a 'predominantly ... white movement' (xxv) as acknowledged by Cheryll Glotfelty in her introduction to *The Ecocriticism Reader* (1996), it was still lingering, even in its 'second wave' in the dichotomy of white and non-white voices (Adamson and Slovic 6). Thus, in their Introduction to the 2009 special issue of *MELUS* on 'Ethnicity and Ecocriticism' which they guest-edited, eminent ecocritics Joni Adamson and Scott Slovic sought to redress the balance by calling for a '*new* third wave [of environmental writing], which recognizes ethnic and national particularities and yet transcends ethnic and national boundaries' (6). Ursula Heise is an important third-wave ecocritic who, in her 2008 book *Sense of Place and Sense of Planet*, talks along the lines of the environmental slogan 'Think globally, act locally' (85) about 'the urgency of developing an ideal of "eco-cosmopolitanism," or environmental world citizenship' (10). With 'eco-cosmopolitanism,' Heise expands the global communitarian thinking of cosmopolitanism to include both human *and* more-than-human beings. She notes, 'Eco-cosmopolitanism ... is an attempt to envision individuals and groups as part of planetary "imagined communities" of both human and nonhuman kinds' (61). Scott Slovic usefully explains that, in the third wave of ecocriticism, 'global concepts of place are being explored in fruitful tension with neo-bioregionalist attachments to specific locales, producing such neologisms as "eco-cosmopolitanism," "rooted cosmopolitanism," "the global soul," and "translocality"' (7).

'Ecomasculinism' is one of the prominent 'new gendered approaches in ecocriticism' (Slovic, 'The Third' 7). It explores the connections between men and nature and looks for instances where men express an 'ethics of care' for the earth. Mark Allister's *Eco-man: New Perspectives on Masculinity and Nature* (2004), consisting of 20 essays, is an important volume in this field. Scholars like Catriona Sandilands, Simon Estok, and Greg Garrard write on green queer theory, which is another important theoretical field in the third wave of ecocriticism (Slovic, 'The Third' 7). Other important developments in the third wave of ecocriticism include an 'intensified focus on the concept of "animality,"' and the 'expansion of the scope of environmental justice to encompass non-human species and their rights' (Slovic, 'The Third' 7).

In his 'Editor's Note' to the 2012 Autumn issue of the journal *Interdisciplinary Studies in Literature and Environment*, Scott Slovic significantly announced the 'fourth wave of ecocriticism':

> It now seems to me, as we near the end of 2012, that the material turn in ecocriticism is broadening to the extent that it may well represent a new 'fourth wave of ecocriticism.' I see a proliferation of studies and courses emphasizing the fundamental materiality (the physicality, the consequentiality) of environmental things, places, processes, forces, and experiences. Ranging from studies of climate change literature to examinations of the substance of ecopoetic language, there is a growing pragmatism in ecocritical practice.
>
> (619)

The 2014 book titled *Material Ecocriticism* edited by Serenella Iovino and Serpil Oppermann, containing 19 essays, is a cornerstone of the fourth wave of ecocriticism. According to Iovino and Oppermann, '*material* ecocriticism examines matter both *in* texts and *as* a text, trying to shed light on the way bodily natures and discursive forces *express* their interaction whether in representations or in their concrete reality' (2; emphasis in the original). They argue that material ecocriticism upholds the 'theory of distributive agency' that views the human agency as entangled in a web of 'apersonal agencies' (3). A related idea is that of 'trans-corporeality' proposed by Stacy Alaimo in *Bodily Natures: Science, Environment, and the Material Self* (2010), an important work that looks at the intersection of matter and environment. Trans-corporeality refers to 'the material interconnections of human corporeality with the more-than-human world' (Alaimo 2). Besides *Bodily Natures*, Iovino and Oppermann's *Material Ecocriticism* builds on a few other earlier works also, such as

New Materialisms: Ontology, Agency, and Politics (2010) edited by Diana Coole and Samantha Frost, *Becoming Animal: An Earthly Cosmology* (2010) by David Abram, *Meeting the Universe Halfway: Quantum Physics and the Entanglement of Matter and Meaning* (2007) by Karan Barad, *Vibrant Matter: A Political Ecology of Things* (2009) by Jane Bennett, and *The Whole Creature: Complexity, Biosemiotics and the Evolution of Culture* (2006) by Wendy Wheeler (11).

The Waves of Environmental Literature in Malayalam

In this section, I propose that the Malayalam ecoliterary tradition could be periodised into two waves according to the 'wave metaphor' suggested by Buell. Malayalam is the native language of Kerala and the Lakshadweep islands with 29 million speakers in India (Asher and Kumari xxiv). In 2013, the Indian government recognised Malayalam as one of its classical languages. Noted Malayalam literary scholar Ayyappa Paniker states, 'According to the most dependable evidence now available to us, Malayalam literature is at least a thousand years old. The language must certainly be older' (*A Short* 11).

Kerala's remarkably picturesque natural beauty sets it apart from other Indian states. Going by the tag line of 'God's Own Country,' Kerala attracts thousands of tourists, both domestic and foreign, annually thanks to the extensive campaign spearheaded by the Kerala Tourist Development Corporation (KTDC). The emergence of capitalist forces is generally looked at with suspicion by a large section of laypeople and writers in Kerala, especially because of the prevailing intellectual climate nurtured by the long political tradition and popularity of communism. The high literacy rate that Kerala maintains has translated into a wider readership, which in turn has facilitated the emergence as well as extensive circulation of a variety of newspapers and other media.

According to the 2002 National Readership Survey, the highest readership of dailies is in Kerala (Bunsha). This has fostered a more politically savvy and environmentally aware citizenry vis-à-vis other states in India that are, therefore, more receptive to the emergence of environmentally oriented writings. Malayalam literature has a strong ecocritical tradition as well. The field of 'harithaniroopanam' ('haritha(m)' means 'green' and 'niroopanam' means 'criticism') has produced landmark texts such as *Harithaniroopanam Malayalathil* [Green Criticism in Malayalam] (2002), edited by G. Madhusoodanan, which is an ecocriticism reader of Malayalam literature comparable to *The Ecocriticism Reader* (1996) edited by Cheryll Glotfelty and Harold Fromm.

The Romantic period of Malayalam literature was launched by the publication of N. Kumaranasan's (1873–1924) elegiacal poem *Veenapoovu*

[A Fallen Flower] in 1907,[7] which finds parallels between human life and the life cycle of a flower (S. Rajasekharan 63), and declined after the death of the poet Changampuzha Krishna Pillai in 1948 (Palakeel 187). The Romantic period with the likes of Kumaranasan and Chengampuzha Krishna Pillai constitutes the 'first wave' of environmental writing in Malayalam. Chengampuzha Krishna Pillai's *Ramanan* (1936), a pastoral elegy and still a bestseller in Malayalam, is one of the landmark texts of this period. P. Kunhiraman Nair is another important first-wave ecopoet. Ayyappa Paniker notes,

> P. Kunhiraman Nair (1905–1978) is primarily a poet of nature, tirelessly eulogizing the beauty of the landscape of Kerala—often in terms of the rituals and festivals as well as the images associated with the beliefs, customs and traditions of the people. In 'Kaliyacchan' we can trace most of the characteristics of his poetry.
>
> ('Modern' 245)

The post-Romantic poets like G. Sankara Kurup (1901–1978), Edasseri Govindan Nair (1906–1974), Vailoppilli Sreedhara Menon (1911–1985),[8] Vayalar Rama Varma (1928–1975), O. N. V. Kurup (1931–2006), P. Bhaskaran (1924–2007),[9] and Sugathakumari (b. 1934) carried on with the lyrical style of their predecessors (Palakeel 188) showing a significant influence of the Romantic poets in their taking up of environmental themes in their writings. G. Sankara Kurup, a major poetic voice in Malayalam, translated Rabindranath Tagore's *Gitanjali* (1910) into Malayalam and was also the first recipient of the Jnanpith Award for his collection of poems titled *Odakkuzhal* [The Bamboo Flute] (1950). K. Ayyappa Paniker remarks that Kurup 'passed through various stages of evolution marked by movements such as mysticism, symbolism, realism and also socialist realism' (*A Short* 81). Kurup's most famous poem is *Sooryakanthi* [The Sun Flower], which presents the sunflower as in love with the Sun.

Witnessing Kerala's rapid transition from a premodern agrarian society to an industrialised and consumerist one, the league of post-Romantic poets sounded a note of alarm at the myriad ways in which humans ventured to control and exploit nature in the name of development. Edasseri Govindan Nair, for instance, evinced the ecological prudence to foresee the environmental costs of unsustainable development. In his famous poem, 'Kuttippuram Palam' [The Kuttippuram Bridge], he wrote about the plight of Perar River which plodded on under the newly built Kuttippuram Bridge and asked worriedly, 'Mother Perar, will you also turn into a sewage ditch?' (qtd. in Mangad, 'Sheevothi' 199). O. N. V. Kurup, who is much younger than Edasseri and has a strong leftist leaning, wrote the classic 'Bhoomikkoru Charamageetham' [A Requiem for the Earth] (1984), which reinvoked the 'Mother Earth' trope and emphasised how humans' ecocidal activities are guilt-worthy exercises in matricide.

Eminent Malayalam ecocritic G. Madhusoodanan states:

> The ecological reading of Malayalam novels should begin by rereading the early realist novel *Vishakanyaka* written by S. K. Pottekkatt and first published in 1948. This novel sheds light on the original sources of conflicts regarding the conservation of Western Ghats forests that have presently reached a crescendo in Kerala in the context of the Gadgil and Kasturirangan Reports.
>
> (24)

Pottekkatt's *Vishakanyaka* [The Poisonous Virgin] (1948) deals with the migration of Christian peasant families from Travancore to Malabar (North Kerala).[10] According to Ambili Anna Markose:

> *Vishakanyaka* is the first popular novel which contextualizes migration and the politics of land and religion. *Vishakanyaka* begins with a very elaborate narration detailing how Christian families prepare for migration. Towards the end of the novel, almost everyone loses their lives and property in the forests. Anthony and the rest of the group return to Travancore, thinking that the land of Malabar is nothing but a seductive '*vishakanyaka*,' a poisonous virgin.
>
> (188)

In the pre-globalisation era, it was also the immensely popular travelogues by S. K. Pottekkatt that introduced the unfamiliar landscapes of Africa, Nepal, Indonesia, the Soviet Union, England, and so on to the Malayalis.

Acclaimed Malayalam novelist and short story writer Vaikom Muhammed Basheer's (1908–1994) short story titled 'Bhoomiyude Avakashikal' [The Inheritors of the Earth] is important as it speaks for the right of every living being to the earth. To his wife and her cousin who want to shoot bats that were destroying coconuts, the story's narrator memorably declares:

> [Bats] are one among God's many creatures. Let coconuts be destroyed. That doesn't matter. Let us be satisfied with what we get after they have taken their share. They certainly have a right to coconuts. They too are part of the Almighty's creation, as are the palms.
>
> Remember the ancient right that God bequeathed at the auspicious moment of creation—all living beings are the rightful inheritors of the Earth.
>
> (83–84)[11]

The river Nila, also known as Bharathappuzha, is a constant presence in most of the works by M. T. Vasudevan Nair (b. 1933), a noted Malayalam novelist, short story writer, playwright, screenwriter, and film director. About his affinity for Nila, Nair writes: 'I have often wandered in search of various geographically different places. But, I always come back here. Perhaps it could be my limitation. Rather than great seas that hold unknown wonders in their wombs, I like my familiar Nila' (qtd. in Leelakrishnan 26).[12] In his essay 'Mad Dreams,' Nair significantly addresses the need for the ethical treatment of circus animals. He writes:

> For God's sake, be considerate. These are our animals, they belong to you, to everybody in the world; it is not for the entertainment of men that they have been left in the world. They came first. We should be protectors, not callous persecutors to them.
>
> (qtd. in T. K. George 141–142)

The social realist Thakazhi Sivasankara Pillai (1912–1999) was 'a chronicler of Kuttanad,' which was his native village also known as the 'rice bowl of Kerala' (K. M. George, *Best*). His powerful novel, *Randidangazhi* [Two Measures] (1948) dramatises the Dalit agricultural workers' struggle for land ownership in Kuttanad. The slogan 'land to the tillers' used by the revolting agricultural labourers in the novel invokes the political scenario of 1958 when the first communist government of Kerala led by E. M. S. Namboodirippad introduced the Land Reforms Ordinance to end large land holdings in Kerala (P. K. Rajasekharan 454). The Ordinance issued a limit to the extent of land a family could own and distributed the excess land to the tenants composed mostly of peasants from Dalit and Scheduled Caste communities. This theme is dealt with on an elaborative canvas in his Jnanpith Award–winning novel, *Kayar* [Coir] (1978), also set in Kuttanad. Ayyappa Paniker notes:

> The documentary aspect of *Kayar* is brought out by the very topography of Kuttanad, which is Thakazhi's home *tinai* (region). Land had then functioned as the counter for all financial transitions, and continued to dominate all human concerns and relationships, till the Land Reforms Act changed everything. This historic transformation of man's relationship with land, as also between man and man, men and women and even man and God, forms the staple theme of *Kayar*.
>
> ('The end')

Amstrong Sebastian argues that ecofeminist themes can be found in the works of Kamala Das, alias Madhavikkutty (1934–2009), and calls her 'the ecofeminist pioneer of Kerala.' This generation of fiction writers, especially M. T. Vasudevan Nair, S. K. Pottekkatt, and Uroob (Parutholli Chalappurathu Kuttikrishnan, 1915–1979) employed a lyrical style of writing with most of their novels and short stories firmly rooted in the familiar cultural milieu and locales of Kerala. By contrast, the immediate next generation of novelists, categorised as the 'Modernists,' showed explicit signs of Western inspiration in their writings and often located their novels in big cities like New Delhi (for example, novels *Delhi* (1969) and *Delhi Gadhakal* [Delhi Songs] (2011) by M. Mukundan (b. 1942) and *Bovine Bugles* (1978) by V. K. N. (Vadakkke Koottala Narayanankutty Nair, 1932–2004)). The Modernists include, in addition to Mukundan and V. K. N., O. V. Vijayan (1930–2005), (George Varghese) Kakkanadan (1935–2011), Anand (b. 1936), and Zachariya (b. 1945).

The award-winning philosophical book *Jaiva Manushyan* [The Organic Man] (1991) by Anand is an important work that deals with 'the organic nature of human condition' (Anand 11).

He argues that prehistoric man regarded himself as a slave of nature, which he considered more powerful than him. But with the growth of science, he began to consider himself the master of nature. Anand notes:

> Man confronted nature first as an opponent, and then, as an enemy. He wanted to defeat nature's forces like water, fire, light and wind. Ultimately, he wanted to shackle nature itself and make it his slave. He showed this domineering attitude to other [nonhuman] living beings in nature. If they fulfilled his need, they should live. If not, they are a nuisance or enemies ... With greed typical of the masters, he started to take possession of the natural resources and deplete them.
>
> (11–12)

O. V. Vijayan's first novel, *Khasakkinte Ithihasam* (1969), which he self-translated into English as *The Legends of Khasak* (1994) and is widely considered as a Modernist classic in Malayalam literature, evocatively captures the landscape and culture of Palakkad. Vijayan's later novel, *Madhuram Gayathi* [Sweetly Sings] (1990), set in a post-apocalyptic world, is an ecospiritual tale with a Peepal tree as the protagonist. The novel opens with a description of how the earth was broken and separated into two halves following a 'big explosion at the end of a terrible war' (10). A guru who has been meditating, along with his disciple, for one hundred years in the Southern Hemisphere wakes up to announce that the nuclear winter has ended. The novel goes on to depict the machines in the northern half of the earth that create plants, animals, and men with 'artificial life' who, therefore, remain slaves of the machines (10). V. V. Balakrishnan summarises the novel thus:

Vijayan's short story 'Renuka' reveals in a nutshell what *Madhuram Gayathi* is on a larger canvas. *Madhuram Gayathi* is about a journey undertaken by Sukanya and the great Pipal tree in search of the former's Parents, Sumangala and Mrithyunjayan. This journey reveals to them the complex mysteries of creation and existence. The world of this novel is divided into two hemispheres—the northern hemisphere of machines and rationality and the southern hemisphere of peace, tranquillity [sic], and ecological equilibrium. The futile effort of man to find solace in the world of modern science and industries is powerfully dramatized in the novel.

(134–135)

Vijayan's environmental vision finds expression in *Oru Sindoorappottinte Orma* [The Memory of a Vermilion Dot] (1987) when he writes:

We severed the human-nature bond and mechanised and chemicalised nature. As a result of the wave beams that were invented against the justice of creation (shall I say the justice of God?), dreadful diseases were born and released into the world. The problem of our age is not communism or anti-communism. We are engulfed by the problems of life and life-threatening abnormalities, and also that of the environment and [human] attitudes that are anti-environmental.

(qtd. in Jacob, 'Novelile' 474)

Mayyazhippuzhayude Theerangalil (1974),[13] arguably the magnum opus of M. Mukundan, is set in Mayyazhi (the present-day Mahé), also Mukundan's place of birth, which was under French colonial rule for two centuries. Although Mahé is geographically located within Kerala, administratively it is part of the Union Territory of Puducherry. About the novel, noted critic P. K. Rajasekharan perceptively comments,

Mayyazhippuzhayude Theerangalil is a meditation on place. The history of Mayyazhi is the history of conflicts of the land searching for identity. Mayyazhi ... is located virtually in a *trishanku* between 'France' and 'India.' *Mayyazhippuzhayude Theerangalil* is, thus, a story of the rewriting of place.[14]

His 1989 Malayalam novel titled *Daivathinte Vikruthikal* is also set in Mayyazhi.[15]

The post-Romantic period in Malayalam forms the second wave of environmental writing when environmental literature is complemented by explicit environmental justice movements like the Silent Valley agitation. The Silent Valley agitation in the 1970s and early 1980s against the damming of the Kunthi River, a tributary of Nila, in the Silent Valley ever-green forest in Palakkad district, can easily be considered one of India's most high-profile environmental campaigns in the twentieth century. The proclaimed objective of setting up the dam was to end power shortage in northern Kerala by producing 50 MW of electricity and providing water to irrigate twenty-five thousand hectares of farmland. Located in the Nilgiri Hills, the Silent Valley forest 'contains India's last substantial stretch of tropical evergreen forest' (Parameswaran 1117) and is home to a number of rare species of plants, ferns, and endangered species of fauna like the lion-tailed macaque (Karan 39; Parameswaran 1117). The Save Silent Valley Movement gained considerable momentum and popularity after the Malayalam writers—chiefly poets—like N. V. Krishna Warrier (1916–1989), Sugathakumari, O. N. V. Kurup, Vishnu Narayanan Namboothiri (b. 1939), Vaikom Muhammad Basheer, and S. K. Pottekkat joined hands and formed a *Prakriti Samrakshana Samithi* [Nature Preservation Committee] to campaign against the ecocidal hydroelectric project. They also organised a 'Kaviyarangu' [Poetry Seminar] and talks by influential intellectuals such as Sukumar Azhikode (1926–2012) and scientists like Satheesh Chandran Nair, Thomas Varghese, and others (Athmaraman 35). Mocked by the pro–Silent Valley Project people as '*marakkavikal*' (tree-poets), the poets who sympathised with the fate of the endangered rainforest published an anthology of environmental poems called *Vanaparvam* (1983) which included, among others, Kurup's 'Bhoomikkoru Charamageetham,' Sugathakumari's 'Marathinu Sthuthi' [Hymn to Trees], and Ayyappa Paniker's (1930–2006) 'Nadevide Makkale?' [Where Is the Country, My Children?] which begins with the famous line, 'Kadevide Makkale?' [Where are the Forests, My Children?]. G. Madhusoodanan notably observes that 'the environmental art in Malayalam was officially inaugurated with the publication of *Vanaparvam*' ('Vimarshanathile' 11). In November 1983, Indira Gandhi, the then Prime Minister of India, ordered to stop the con-struction of the Silent Valley Hydroelectric Project and, in 1985, declared Silent Valley a national park (Raman 38; S. J. Nair 9). The Silent Valley Movement gave a new impetus to environmental writing in Malayalam.

In her preface to the book *Kaavu Theendalle* [Don't Desecrate the Sacred Grove] (1993), Sugathakumari writes in retrospect:

> Nature conservation is faith; a religion. Once you fall in love with the forest, there is no escaping it. It will dissolve you in a firm embrace. A lot of us have had such an experience during the Silent Valley controversy in 1979. Suddenly, there was a big change in our lives, lifestyles and also in our life goals. That really shook us. Coming out of it after walking through the heat of that period, we felt we had changed completely from our previous selves. We became people who could embrace the earth

in our minds. We begin to look at the birds, babies and butterflies not only with love but also with anxiety in our eyes. In the perimeter of my vision, I see a lot of faces. That of ailing women, the dispossessed tribals, the face of every evicted animal. I try to be the voice of the voiceless.

(7)

Her famous article 'Kaavu Theendalle, Kudivellam Muttum' [Don't Desecrate the Sacred Grove, Drinking Water Will Dry Up] draws attention to the ecological service rendered by the sacred groves, dedicated to serpent gods, that are part of ancestral *tharavad*s in Kerala. These sacred groves are biodiverse forest environments that house snakes, mongoose, bats, honeybees, skinks, squirrels, different varieties of frogs, birds like pigeons, parrots, cuckoos, and so on. The *kaavu* also included a pond. The article is written in the form of an ecoparable describing the narrator and his/her young peers chopping down the trees of the *kaavu*, unmindful of the grandmother's wise words, 'Don't desecrate the grove! ... If the *kaavu* is ravaged, the well will dry up!' (11). They go on to build a bungalow after drying up the pond. Soon, the well runs dry. They send petitions to the government demanding drinking water supply to the village and convene protest gatherings. At night, when the narrator lies down sleepless under the spinning ceiling fan that blows hot air, s/he hears the voice of the *kaavu*'s deity that says:

> You didn't realise that each *kaavu* is a piece of evergreen forest. We collected the rain and brought it to the water sources of your well. We instantly purified the air that you poisoned with every breath of yours. We preserved the light of the infinite chain of life. O human who destroys everything! It's not just *you* who have to live on this earth. Each blade of grass, every dragonfly, snake and eagle is invaluable to the earth. You, the world conqueror, are just a ring in this chain. Remember, the road of destruction leads to total annihilation!
>
> (14)

Post-1990 and more spiritedly after 2000, several critical studies on the green thread in Malayalam literature made their appearance, drawing insights from some of the major environmental writers like Rachel Carson, William Rueckert, and Cherryl Glotfelty, among others.

G. Madhusoodanan credits P. P. K. Poduval's 'Paristhithivicharam Malayalam Kavithayil' [Environmental Thought in Malayalam Poetry] published in 1990 as the first major study that attempted to look at Malayalam literature from an environmental perspective (Madhosoodanan 19). P. P. K. Poduval later published *Paristhithikkavithakku Oraamukham* [An Introduction to Ecopoetry] (1995) and *Paristhithibodhavum*

Samskaravum [Environmental Thought and Culture] (2007). The publication of *Harithaniroopanam Malayalathil* [Ecocriticism in Malayalam] (2002) and *Kathayum Paristhithiyum* [Short Story and the Environment] (2000) by G. Madhusoodanan and *Paristhithidarsanam Malayala Kavithayil* [Ecological Vision in Malayalam Poetry] (2010) by S. Rajasekharan have also immensely contributed to the establishment of environmental criticism in Malayalam.

Malayalam literature, in this period, is marked by the publication of a swell of life writings from the subaltern ranks, where the frail adivasis[16]/ Dalits/minority communities/women asserted their agency and spoke in the first person about the immiserating effects of their subaltern existence. Most of these memoirists are also activists engaged in significant socio-environmental resistance movements in Kerala. A few significant titles, in addition to the five oiko-autobiographies examined in Chapter 2 of this book, include *Chengara Samaravum Ente Jeevithavum* [The Chengara Struggle and My Life] (2013) by Seleena Prakkanam, the Dalit woman leader of the Chengara land struggle when about one thousand landless people, mostly Dalits, encroached on the rubber estate owned by Harrison Malayalam Plantations Ltd on August 4, 2007; *Chorinte Manamulla Cheru* [Sludge that Smells like Rice] (2010) by Pallikkal Bhavani, a housewife who wages a 15-year-old lone battle against sand mining activities in the Kallada river in Kollam;[17] and *Vishamazhayil Pollyia Manassu* [A Mind Singed by Toxic Rain] (2010) by Sri Padre who is one of the leaders of the anti-endosulfan campaign in Kasaragod.

In addition to these life narratives, many novels and plays dealing with environmental themes—mostly based on the friction between the landless/displaced/victims of ecocidal developmental activities and the government–corporate nexus—are also being published in Malayalam. Six important environmental justice novels are discussed in Chapters 3 and 4 of this book. They are the three 'toxic fictions'—Ambikasuthan Mangad's *Enmakaje* (2009), Sarah Joseph's *Aathi* (2011), and Balakrishnan Mangad's *Bhoomiyude Kannu* (2004)—and the three 'extractivist fictions'—G. R. Indugopan's *Manal Jeevikal* (2003), Hari Kurusseri's *Manalazham* (2015), and Rajeev Sivasanker's *Kalpramanam* (2014).

An important ecodrama published in the last decade is Francis T. Mavelikkara's play titled *Swapnangal Vilkkanundu* [Dreams for Sale] (2013) which is based on the Kasaragod endosulfan disaster. The multiple-award-winning novel *Alahayude Penmakkal* [Daughters of Alaha] (1999) by Sarah Joseph draws attention to the marginalised lives of the residents of the village named Kokkanchira in Thrissur. Kokkanchira is a place where 'those who are expelled from the city' (Joseph 33), like scavengers, arrack distillers, petty thieves, prostitutes, and so on, come to. The place was once the cremation site of anonymous dead bodies. The novel's eight-year-old narrator Annie, whose family migrated to Kokkanchira after being evicted from their land in the city, realises that even her teachers view the residents of Kokkanchira with disgust and derision. Critic Mariamma Panjikkaran argues:

> *Aalahayude Penmakkal* is a unique novel in Malayalam, that fully transmits the marginalised history and experience of a subaltern group of people, in their own socio–linguistic milieu. The novel deals with the waxing and waning of 'world's cheapest people' living at a place, 'full of the dead, decayed and desecrated'. One cannot escape from one's own past or predicament. So every man, woman and child, living at 'Kokkanchara' has [sic] to live and die as the dispossessed—as the dirtiest people in the dirtiest suburb.
>
> (31)

The novels *Kocharethi* (1998) (translated into English as *Kocharethi: The Araya Woman* (2011) by Catherine Thankamma) and *Ooralikkudi* [The Oorali Dwelling] (1999) by Narayan, the first adivasi fiction writer from Kerala, are deeply embedded in the unique socio-environmental relationship of the adivasi communities in Kerala. Although Malayalam literature still seems to linger mostly in the second wave of environmental writing that is preoccupied with the overarching theme of socio-environmental justice, the writings produced during this latter period are remarkable for the spike in authentic indigenous voices that concomitantly raise the subaltern question and assert their right to land and livelihood.

While segmenting the ecocritical tradition using the 'wave metaphor,' Lawrence Buell put forward, it must be remembered, a caveat as well:

> This first-second distinction should not ... be taken as implying a tidy, distinct succession. Most currents set in motion by early ecocriticism continue to run strong, and most forms of second-wave revisionism involve building on as well as quarreling with precursors.
>
> (*The Future* 17)

He went on to even state that the image of a 'palimpsest' might be more appropriate than that of 'waves' (*The Future* 17). This caveat, needless to add, holds true for environmental writing in Malayalam also. Along with the 'second wave' of environmental writing in Malayalam, 'first-wave'esque green writing is also still happening. P. Surendran (b. 1961), known for his leftist predilection, for instance, writes prolifically on environmental themes and is representative of the 'first-wave' trend. His first published novella *Mahayanam* [The New Path] (1987) traces an episode wherein five Naxalites on the run after a murder are guided by a poet, who is a sympathiser of their cause, to an ancient fort located in the heart of a forest. The novella ends with the leader of the disbanded group fleeing to the adivasi hovels in the forest after leaving his gun in 'a green flame hanging above the trees that took the shape of a palm reaching out for the weapon' (58). *Haritha Vidyalayam* [The Green School] (1989), Surendran's well-known short story, is also remarkable for the strong ecosophic message it carries. The story features an unnamed boy as the protagonist who leaves his dysfunctional school to explore nature and learns more important lessons that open his 'eyes of *njnana*' (88). When later confronted by schoolmates, the boy finds that he has even grown in size compared to them and refuses to go back to his old school.

The rhizomatic development of the environmental literary tradition in Malayalam exudes ample promise and potential and has earned a stature similar to other major literary trends in Malayalam like Modernism and Postmodernism. While studying the selected contemporary environmental justice writings, this book will address the following research questions, in addition to the general questions that the central planks of ecocriticism are concerned with:

1 How are human–nature relations depicted in the selected Malayalam ecotexts?
2 How do these texts explore the connection between gender and the environment?
3 How is the material embeddedness of human bodies depicted in the narratives studied in this book?
4 How do the texts taken up for analysis in this book approach and narrate environmental pollution, socio-environmental violence, and toxification?
5 What are the ecological problems of resource extractivism represented in the texts analysed in this book?

The chapters that follow offer an ecocritical reading of the selected ecotexts while probing the aforementioned research questions.

Notes

1 J. Devika's English translation of *Enmakaje*, titled *Swarga*, was published in 2017.
2 Rev. Valson Thampu's English translation of *Aathi*, titled *Gift in Green*, was published in 2011.
3 The timeline of the first, second, and third waves was provided by Scott Slovic in his 'The Third Wave of Ecocriticism: North American Reflections on the Current Phase of the Discipline' published in the journal, *Ecozon@*, vol. 1, no. 1, 2010, pp. 4–10. The time frame of the fourth wave of ecocriticism can be found in Scott Slovic's 'Editor's Note' to the Autumn 2012 issue of *ISLE*, pp. 619–621.

4 The 'Global South' refers to the developing countries in Asia, Africa, and Latin America that lie to the south of the Brandt Line named after the former German Chancellor Willy Brandt, who suggested the North–South division in terms of economic development. Australia, New Zealand, and the countries in Europe, North and Central America comprise the Global North and are considered 'rich' and with high living standards.

5 Environmental racism superposes the variable of 'race' onto the gender–nature connection forged by ecofeminism, owing to their shared experience of exploitation.

6 As Guha and Martinez-Alier themselves point out elsewhere in the text, *dharna* means a 'sit-down strike' and *bhook hartal* means 'indefinite hunger strike' (*Varieties* 14).

7 Though the first Malayalam novel, *Kundalatha* by T. M. Appu Nedungadi, was published in 1887 and the first Malayalam short story, *Vasana Vikruthi* by Vengayil Kunhiraman Nayanar, was published in 1891, poetry was the dominant literary genre in the first half of the twentieth century.

8 Though G. Sankara Kurup, Edasseri, and Vailoppilli Sreedhara Menon were not post-Changampuzha poets, they are categorised under 'post-Romantic' period based on their poetic style that treats non-human nature in a less romanticised way.

9 P. Bhaskaran, Vayalar Rama Varma, and O. N. V. Kurup are known as the 'red trio' in Malayalam literature suggesting their engagement with communist themes in their poetry. They have also been criticised in some quarters for imitating the poetic style of Changampuzha Krishna Pillai, even dubbing them '*mattoli kavikal*' (echo-poets).

10 *Orotha* by Kakkanadan (1935–2011), a novelist quite younger than Pottekkatt, is another novel that also narrates the theme of the migration of Christians from Travancore to Malabar.

11 English translation by Vanajam Ravindran.

12 All translations from Malayalam used in this book, unless otherwise mentioned, are mine.

13 An English translation of the novel titled *On the Banks of the Mayyazhi* by Gita Krishnankutty was published in 1999.

14 Quoted in the blurb of *Mayyazhippuzhayude Theerangalil* (DC Books, 2013).

15 The English translation of *Daivathinte Vikruthikal* titled *God's Mischief* by Prema Jayakumar was published in 2002.

16 *Adivasi*, literally 'original inhabitant' in Hindi, is widely used in the Indian subcontinent to refer to the tribal populations. I use the terms 'adivasi' and 'tribal' interchangeably throughout this book.

17 The life narratives of C. K. Janu, Leelakumariamma, Mayilamma, and Kallen Pokkudan are studied in Chapter 2 of this book.

2 Oiko-autobiographies

Subaltern Environmentalism in the Life Narratives of Four Ecoactivists

Kerala is often compared to developed countries in the Global North on account of the state's impressive social indicators like high literacy, low population growth, and low mortality rate. Lauding the 'Kerala model' of development, the Nobel Prize–winning economist Amartya Sen states that '[t]he Indian government should try to emulate the Kerala experience' (70). Notwithstanding such social developmental parameters, Kerala faces numerous ecological problems like the death of rivers due to deforestation and construction of dams; water extraction; discharge of effluents from industries; indiscriminate aerial spraying of pesticides and fertiliser use leading to changes in the diversity of species and organisms; poisons seeping into food chains resulting in serious physical deformities in humans; uncontrolled sand mining that not just hinders natural purification of water but also lowers water levels in wells and lakes; and a burgeoning ecotourism industry that compromises both the fragile coastal ecosystem and the values and traditions of indigenous communities. This chapter takes up for analysis the life narratives of four prominent contemporary grassroots socio-ecoactivists from Kerala, namely, *Mother Forest: The Unfinished Life of C. K. Janu* (2004) by the tribal land rights activist C. K. Janu; *Mayilamma: Oru Jeevitham* [Mayilamma: A Life] (2006) by the eponymous tribal woman leader of the Plachimada anti–Coca-Cola campaign; *Jeevadayini* [The Life-Giver] (2011) by the Kasaragod anti-endosulfan protest leader Leelakumariamma; and the two life narratives titled *Kandalkkadukalkkidayil Ente Jeevitham* [My Life Amidst Mangrove Forests] (2002) and *Ente Jeevitham* [My Life] (2010) by Kallen Pokkudan, a Dalit ecoactivist from the Kannur district of Kerala who engaged in mangrove planting and protection activities. Through a reading of these four ecotexts, this chapter brings into focus the moving accounts of the lives of these prominent subaltern oikos-carers, who participated in socio-ecoactivism in contemporary Kerala, in an attempt to restore their expropriated, damaged, or threatened oikic spaces.

DOI: 10.4324/9781003301318-2

The word 'subaltern' is derived from the Latin terms *sub* (under) and *alter* (other) (P. Barry 237) and was first used as a critical term by the Italian Marxist thinker Antonio Gramsci to refer to 'those *classes* of people with little political and cultural power' (Nayar, *The Postcolonial* 143). The term is used expansively in subaltern studies and other contemporary critical theories 'as a name for the general attribute of subordination in South Asian society whether this is expressed in terms of class, caste, age, gender and office or in any other way' (Ranajit Guha 35). This chapter will show that the selected five Malayalam life narratives are energised by a kind of 'subaltern environmentalism' which runs counter to mainstream environmentalisms. Laura Pulido usefully distinguishes between mainstream environmentalism and subaltern environmentalism thus:

> Mainstream environmentalism typifies an NSM [New Social Movement] in that it attracts people concerned with an issue who have only a limited personal connection to it. In contrast, subaltern environmental struggles draw people who already exist as a social or spatial entity in some way– perhaps as workers, a village, or a racialized class.
>
> (25)

The socio-ecoactivism exemplified by the subaltern subjects of the five life narratives is in marked variance from the 1970s' Save Silent Valley agitation in Kerala which was an environmental justice campaign spearheaded by activists who were largely already famous writers. Laura Pulido further points out:

> Many grassroots activists have attacked the mainstream for focusing on what are perceived to be elitist or racist concerns, such as endangered species and wilderness preservation … "The narrowness of the mainstream movement, which appears to be more interested in endangered animals (nonhuman) species and pristine undeveloped land than at-risk humans, makes poor minority people think that their concerns are not 'environmental'" (Austin and Schill 1991, 72).
>
> (25)

This critique of the elitist tendency of 'deep ecology' as well as the Northern variety of environmentalism is characteristic of 'the environmentalism of the poor,' a comparable concept put forward by Ramachandra Guha and Joan Martinez-Alier (95–96). The five subaltern life narratives studied in this chapter call for human-sensitive environmentalism and are examples of the environmentalism of the poor.

While autobiography, in general, remains the predominant form of subaltern expression in India, I prefer to call the life narratives of Janu,

Leelakumariamma, Mayilamma, and Pokkudan 'oiko-autobiographies' to emphasise the 'emplaced subjectivities' of these writers and to contrast them with the 'regular' autobiographical writings wherein the individual selves are rendered variously in terms of their caste, gender, colour, religion, or sexual orientation. Being an 'ecocentric' narrative, with the individual's environment claiming a prominent narrative space rather than functioning as, in the words of Christopher Manes, 'a hazy backdrop against which the rational human subject struts upon' (16), an oiko-autobiography is the least solipsistic of all autobiographies. The oiko-autobiographers discussed in this chapter clearly express what the American environmental writer Edward Abbey calls 'loyalty to the earth' (147), and they also significantly question the interventionist technologies that ruin the health of the land, water bodies, and forests. In the next section, I define the autobiography and give a brief overview of some of the key autobiographical texts as well as position these five oiko-autobiographical texts alongside other relevant oiko-autobiographies in world literature. In the subsequent section, I will undertake a detailed textual analysis of the five oiko-autobiographies.

Autobiographies: Definitions and the Nature Writing Traditions

Autobiographies or life narratives could probably be best defined by what they are *not*, that is fiction. Autobiography is usually categorised as 'non-fiction'[1] as it is associated with a *lived* reality charted through the acts of 'truth-telling' and direct 'self-representation' while fiction concerns itself with an *imagined* reality whose original provenance may or may not be the author's real-life experiences. Invoking this binary opposition, Barett Mandel, therefore, rightly proclaims that 'Every reader knows that auto-biographies and novels are finally totally distinct' (qtd. in Anderson 6). Philippe Lejeune's popular definition of autobiography is as follows: 'A retrospective prose narrative produced by a real person concerning his own existence, focusing on his individual life, in particular on the development of his personality' (qtd. in Anderson 2). Autobiography is different from a 'memoir' in that, in the latter format, as Abrams puts it, 'the emphasis is not on the author's developing self but on the people and events that the author has known or witnessed' (22). The English Romantic poet Robert Southey (1774–1843) is credited with the coinage of the term 'autobiography,' when, in the *Quarterly Review* (1809), he lauded the life of Portuguese poet and painter Francisco Vieira as a 'very amusing and unique specimen of auto-biography' (qtd. in Parekh 274; Anderson 7). The term became popular and became 'a matter of established usage' by the 1830s (Nussbaum via Anderson 7).

Saint Augustine's *Confessions*, comprising 13 books and believed to be written circa AD 397, is widely held as 'originary, the first autobiography of any kind in our modern sense of the term' (Jeffrey 286). Spiritual in tone and intention, *Confessions* is an account of Augustine's conversion to Christianity. As Augustine explains, it 'praise[d] the good and just God for whatever [was] good and bad in me' and was written primarily to 'encourage humanity's understanding and love for [God]' (qtd. in M. S. Williams 235). Rousseau's *Confessions* (1782), modelled after Augustine's *Confessions*, is also a rightful contender for the status of the first modern autobiography (Coleman vii). Rousseau's *Confessions*, unlike Augustine's work, is secular in nature and notable, especially for the repeated assertions of the virtue of honesty and 'being totally frank' (Ogrodnick 22) to the reader. He writes,

> I should like in some way to make my soul transparent to the reader's eye, and for that purpose I am trying to present it from all points of view, to show it in all lights, and to contrive that none of its movements shall escape his notice, so that he may judge for himself of the principle which has produced them.
>
> (qtd. in Anderson 45)

Other key early autobiographical works with a dominant philosophical/spiritual theme include John Bunyan's autobiographical work *Grace Abounding to the Chief of Sinners* (1666) which is a saga of spiritual conversion and the English Romantic poet William Wordsworth's *Prelude* (1850) which is a significant 'autobiographical epic poem' that depicts 'the narrator's development as a poet, the forces that shaped his imaginative powers, and his spiritual crisis and recovery' ('The Prelude').

This familiar trope of 'self as synonymous with spiritual quest' (Neuman 294) is perpetuated in some of the classic oiko-autobiographies like *Walden* (1854) by Thoreau and *A Sand County Almanac* (1949) by Aldo Leopold. The personal self, in these life writings, is always presented as immersed in the larger metaphysical and sacred physical environment. The quasi-spiritual markers in *Walden* are many—like the self-imposed seclusion to 'a cabin just twelve feet by fifteen feet,' beside the remote eponymous pond, simple living ('Simplicity, simplicity, simplicity!' (Thoreau 81)) and the character called 'The Hermit' whom critics associate with Thoreau. Cecilia Konchar Farr distinguishes between early works like *Walden* 'where nature serves as a backdrop for more central human endeavors' and the later oiko-autobiographies 'where nature and human endeavors are less easily separated' (95). She further explains:

> In the late twentieth century, with the rise of environmental consciousness and postmodern thinking, the borders between nature and self blur; indeed, both nature and self become contested territories. In

ecobiographies, nature becomes us, and we begin to question who is constructing whom. As a colleague and I wrote, 'the narrative "I's ... are as much constructed by Nature as they are construction *of* Nature it is impossible to tell where the Self ends and Nature begins or where Nature ends and the Self begins: ego and eco are inextricably intertwined." '

(95; emphasis in the original)

The intersection of self-narration and nature writing in works like Terry Tempest Williams' *Refuge* (1991) and Sue Hubbell's *A Country Year* (1986) is explored by Mark Allister in *Refiguring the Map of Sorrow* (2001) by employing the framework of 'relational autobiography.' Allister defines 'relational autobiography' as the 'writing about one's self in relation to someone else' (3). This notion of relationality, according to Allister, extends from 'human attachments, persons connected as parents and children, siblings, friends, co-workers, and so forth' to the more-than-human nature (3). Thus, while the 'regular' autobiographies are limited by their singular focus on the 'individual identity,' the relational autobiographies engage in a reconsideration of the writers' lives as well as other people and places (19). Allister goes on to argue:

If autobiography critics shift the focus from 'autonomous selves' to how humans change and grow 'relationally,' then autobiography need not focus on the writer's 'life.' The 'self' of autos might well change to 'self/others,' and the linear narrative of one person's life, as is typical in autobiography, might well be altered to include structures that are more ecological than chronological, figuratively more like an interconnected web.

(18)

Closely related to Allister's conceptualisation is the concept of 'ecological self' advanced by the deep ecologist Arne Næss which involves a 'widening and deepening of the self' ('Self-Realization' 82). An ecological self, according to Næss, is a 'mature self' underpinned by empathy and identification with other living beings in nature. Freya Mathews' works, like the book titled *The Ecological Self* (1991) and the article 'Community and the Ecological Self' (1995), explore this concept and usefully distinguish between a 'relational self' and 'a holistic, ecological self.' According to Mathews, while the relational self retains some individual identity albeit being in a 'system of relations' with other beings as in a nexus, the 'ecological self' refers to a 'wider web' where 'individuals are constituted by [an] identification with the biotic community as a whole, and accordingly lack any independent ontological status' ('Community' 81). The trouble with Næss's and Mathews's conceptualisations is that they are couched in metaphysical terms. The interconnectedness of the self with other ecosystemic bodies, for Næss and Mathews, is a path to self-realisation. The conjunction of the self and the environment in the subaltern environmentalisms of Janu, Leelakumariamma, Mayilamma, and Pokkudan, by contrast, is never about self-actualisation and transcendence, but rather, very much grounded in the material issues of livelihood and survival. The subaltern environmentalism expressed by these four oiko-autobiographers, therefore, is also in sharp variance with other oiko-autobiographies like *Walden* that place a high premium on wilderness preservation efforts. In his influential essay 'Radical American Environmentalism and Wilderness Preservation: A Third World Critique' (1989), the Indian environmental historian Ramachandra Guha pertinently notes:

> [T]he emphasis on wilderness is positively harmful when applied to the Third World. If in the U.S. the preservationist/utilitarian division is seen as mirroring the conflict between 'people' and 'interests,' in countries such as India the situation is very nearly the reverse. Because India is a long settled and densely populated country in which agrarian populations have a finely balanced relationship with nature, the setting aside of wilderness areas has resulted in a direct transfer of resources from the poor to the rich. … Until very recently, wildlands preservation has been identified with environmentalism by the state and the conservation elite; in consequence, environmental problems that impinge far more directly on the lives of the poor—e.g., fuel, fodder, water shortages, soil erosion, and air and water pollution—have not been adequately addressed.
>
> (75)

The selected five subaltern oiko-autobiographies that evince a clear enmeshing of the ecological and social offer exemplary samples of Southern environmentalism.

The imbrication of the eco and the ego, in the American oiko-autobiographical tradition, is markedly pronounced in renowned works like *Desert Solitaire* (1968) by Edward Abbey and *Refuge* (1991) by Terry Tempest Williams (Farr 95–96). These later works, according to Farr, 'represent the successful hybrid of memoir and nature writing that is unique to, and characteristic of, the late twentieth century' (96). An eloquent critique of industrial tourism that threatens the environment of national parks finds expression in *Desert Solitaire*; the moving tale of the flooding of the Great Salt Lake and the health hazards of living in proximity to the nuclear testing site is recounted in *Refuge*, while the significance of afforestation efforts upheld by Wangari Maathai's becomes apparent in *Unbowed* (2006). These three texts are thematically consonant with the survival and anti-toxic struggles chronicled in the Malayalam oiko-autobiographies of the subaltern ecoactivists studied in this chapter.

Raising the Land Question: C. K. Janu's *Mother Forest* and Tribal Struggles in Kerala

In *Varieties of Environmentalism* (1997), Ramachandra Guha and Joan Martinez-Alier argue that environmentalisms of the Global North and the Global South differ considerably. They explain: '[P]oor counties and poor individuals are not interested in the mere protection of wild species or natural habitats but do respond to environmental destruction which directly affects their way of life and prospects for survival' (xx). Guha and Martinez-Alier's statement points to two principal features of the Global South environmentalism, namely, the intermeshing of the ecological and social realms and an amplified prioritisation of human survival issues. India's former Prime Minister Indira Gandhi's 1972 speech at the United Nations Conference on Human Environment in Stockholm also draws attention to how human livelihood concerns tend to take precedence over wilderness conservation and animal welfare in Global South contexts like India:

> [U]nless we are in a position to provide employment and purchasing power for the daily necessities of the tribal people and those who live in or around our jungles, we cannot prevent them from combing the forest for food and livelihood; from poaching and from despoiling the vegetation. When they themselves feel deprived, how can we urge the preservation of animals? How can we speak to those who live in villages and in slums about keeping the oceans, the rivers and the air clean when their own lives are contaminated at the source? The environment cannot be improved in conditions of poverty.
>
> (15)

The oiko-autobiography, *Mother Forest: The Unfinished Story of C. K. Janu* (2004) by C. K. Janu (b. 1970), a tribal activist hailing from the Wayanad district of Kerala, adequately gives expression to the 'environmentalism of the poor' unique to the Global South context. In *Mother Forest*, nature does not appear as a pristine wilderness untouched by human presence. The forest, instead, is presented as a provider of resources that are vital for human sustenance as well as a place of human/more-than-human cohabitation. The overarching question that the oiko-autobiography of C. K. Janu raises is that of a 'dwelling,' or rather the lack of it due to deforestation and expropriation of tribal lands by the non-tribals. 'Dwelling,' according to Greg Garrard, is one of the prominent tropes of environmental writing. In *Ecocriticism* (2004), he expounds on its significance: ' "Dwelling" is not a transient state; rather, it implies the long-term imbrication of humans in a landscape of memory, ancestry and death, of ritual, life and work' (108).

Janu's text marks the transition of the forest from a meaningful bioregional dwelling inhabited by the tribals to an alienated, cordoned-off place that is off-limits to them.

According to the 2011 census, the tribal population of Kerala constitutes 1.45% of the total with a majority of them residing in Wayanad, Idukki, and Palakkad districts. The Kerala tribals who traditionally lived off the land were thrown into abject poverty when the migrant non-tribals encroached upon and appropriated their lands through persuasion tactics and coercion. G. S. Jayasree argues that the tribals 'did not even have the notion land was "property" and that they could be alienated from it' (xvi). Hence, the adivasis did not assume they could have individual rights to the land. The land was, as Jayasree puts it, 'not separable from their sense of collective identity' (xvi). As per the statistics in 2002, 24.7%, that is, 22,491 families, of Kerala tribals are landless while 34.02% or 30, 981 families own less than one acre of land, making, as Bijoy indicates, 'the overwhelming majority landless or near-landless' (4332).

Set against this social context of Kerala, Janu's oiko-autobiography offers striking images of poverty and hunger in addition to the horrendous exploitation that the tribal agricultural workers were subjected to. She writes:

> when we worked in the rainy season we could leave only after planting the whole field. it would be quite dark by the time we reached our hovels. even after reaching them we would not be able to sleep immediately. we would be so hungry and cold. it was impossible to kindle the fire in the hearth. we would eat some *chakka* or *thina*. the little ones would sleep even without that. we wouldn't be able to see each other since we had no lights. Anyway everyone must look the same when hungry.
>
> (14)

Mother Forest is composed of two chapters. The first chapter offers descriptions of Janu's life in the forestscapes of Wayanad district, the feudal system, the agricultural work done by her community members, as well as Janu's steps towards attaining literacy. The second chapter traces the societal and lifestyle changes that have come over the tribal community; Janu's association, and her later disillusionment, with the Communist Party; as well as her early attempts at land agitation in Mananthavaadi and Munnar through which she emerged as an activist. About the two-fold division of the text, the book's translator N. Ravi Shanker comments, '[The first chapter is] closer to Janu's inner world, while the second chapter [is] more polemical and belong[s] to the outer world' (xii). Swarnalatha Rangarajan, in her reading of *Mother Forest*, draws on Jean-François Lyotard's concepts of *oikeion* and *politikon* to analyse the structural uniqueness of the text. She writes:

> Lyotard's (2000) definition of ecology as the 'discourse of the secluded' is particularly appropriate to this text. Lyotard points out that in ancient Greece, there existed a clear opposition between oikeion, the home space and politikon, the public space where all action took place. The secluded (women, slaves and children) were confined to the 'oikeion' or home space, which is 'the shadowy space of all that escapes the light of public speech, and it is precisely in this darkness that tragedy occurs' (Lyotard 2000, 135). *Mother Forest* marks the rites of passage from the oikeion to the politikon and the articulation of an environmental justice ethic of care both for the indigenous people and the environment.
>
> (445)

However, the *oikeion*, in the tribal context, has an added complexity since, for the forest-dwelling tribals, the notions of 'domesticated' and 'wild' hardly exist. In *Mother Forest*, C. K. Janu evocatively describes her life amid 'unending forests' and how, at night, everyone used to gather in the courtyard and spend 'hours listening to what the forests mumbled' (3). Thus, for the tribals who 'lived in and with nature' (Kapoor 44), the lessons in ecological literacy were obtained early and first hand:

> Nature lay open for little ones to learn from. Time and seasons could be told from the chirping of certain birds. The months could be counted when the leaves fell from the trees. From the darkening clouds descending on the hilltops and the forests we could gauge the direction of the wind. Our lives were so strongly interlinked with Nature, the earth and the trees.
>
> (Bhaskaran 51)

The deep topophilic connection that Janu, as a girl, experienced towards the land and the 'mother' forest as documented in the first chapter is juxtaposed with the growing estrangement and topophobia that the younger generation of her community experience. In the opening of the second chapter, Janu observes: 'Mother Forest had turned into the Departmental Forest. It had barbed wire fences and guards. Our children had begun to be frightened of a forest that could no longer accommodate them' (30). The alienation from the land that the younger generation tribals feel happens as a consequence of the implementation of ill-conceived government projects. Janu refers to this when she argues:

The life cycle of our people, their customs and very existence are bound to the earth. This is more so than in any other society. When projects are designed without any link to this bond, our people suffer. This may be wrong if looked at from the point of view of civil society. But it is self-evident when we go to newly formed colonies. We who dug the earth and found water at will are now reduced to agitating for drinking water supplied through pipes.

(47)

The attachment to the forest environment that Janu's oiko-autobiography accentuates is typical of 'New forest texts,' an analytical category suggested by Swarnalatha Rangarajan. Distinguishable from the *Aranyakas* (literally, 'forest books') of the Vedic period which are 'wisdom texts,' these new forest texts are 'volatile spaces in which texts of turbulence are written' (Asokan 47). Rangarajan notes:

Unlike the 'aranyaka' texts that advocated the pursuit of oneness with the universe in the wilderness unhindered by the tensions that characterize life in society, the new forest texts ... bring to the foreground a bricolage of themes which uncover the subsistence and survival-based issues of Indian environmentalism faced by forest dwellers who have been traditionally dependent on local natural resources.

(442)

The 'livelihood ecology' (Gari qtd. in Martinez-Alier, *The Environmentalism of the Poor* 2002, 10) that the new forest texts like *Mother Forest* foreground points to the unviability of adopting the 'antihuman environmentalism' (Nixon, *Slow Violence* 5) of the Global North in the Global South contexts. Thus, C. K. Janu's anxieties about deforestation and her plea for forest conservation are imbued by an ecological consciousness that is hurt by the dwindling wilderness as by the material concerns of a tribal woman who depends on the forest for resources for sustenance.

Mother Forest documents how the majority of the tribals, with the changes in the traditional lifestyle involving sustainable agricultural practices, turned themselves into mere wage labourers (Bhaskaran 30). The transition proved unfavourable to the tribals as the wages they got were not adequate to stave off hunger. They helplessly witnessed the disintegration of agricultural lands that were allowed to lie fallow by their paper-owners who, then, used the excuse 'agriculture was not paying' to build concrete houses there. The loss of land and access to the forest brought the tribals into greater contact with the civil society which had deleterious repercussions for the tribal communities. Janu highlights the instances wherein young tribal girls were sexually exploited by the 'outsiders' who took the girls to tribal hostels in towns in the name of education. About the transformations that have come over the tribal community, Janu comments:

> [The girls] imbibed only the wrong aspects of civil society. The way they spoke and the way they behaved became a matter of shame and degeneration ... Unable to study or to pass the tests in new syllabi they lost their balance. They had to, [sic] for the cities to get their menial jobs done. Our people began to apply for such menial jobs. They became good-for-nothings by writing competitive tests and failing miserably in them. And the government ridiculed us further with figures that proved that our people were [ ] in a condition to compete with people from civil society. Certain ruling forces and power centres emerged who could stamp this society underfoot as a group of people who always failed.
>
> (48)

Thus, uprooted from their lands and estranged from the forest oikos yet unable to blend in with the civil society, the tribals became tragic liminal figures or 'nowhere people' (S. Nair).

Janu observes that all land struggles by the tribals in Kerala 'have been struggles to establish the ownership rights of the real owners of this land for the right to live on it' (55). Though *Mother Forest* does not cover the watershed Muthanga agitation on 4 January 2003 when thousands of tribals under the leadership of C. K. Janu and the *Adivasi Gothra Maha Sabha* (The Grand Assembly of Tribals) encroached on the deforested portions of Muthanga and erected tents after the state government failed to keep its promise of land distribution to the tribals (Bijoy and Raman, 1975–1976), it documents the circumstances that led to what climaxed in Muthanga. After describing a few land occupations by the tribals led by her in places like Appootti, Vellamunda, Chinieru, and Kundara in Munnar, where the agitating tribals were subjected to police action, Janu wryly notes: 'The only reason our people did not run away was that they had no place or land to run to. For that same reason they have been severely beaten up' (54).

Echoing Ben Chavis's observation that 'the issue of [socio-] environmental justice is an issue of life and death' (qtd. in Sze 175), Janu asserts, 'These were not just land encroachments. They were life and death struggles for our basic rights to live and die where we were born' (55). *Mother Forest* is at once a place-based, topophilic narrative and a writing about displacement. It offers a gendered perspective on the state of 'uninhabitance' experienced by the Kerala tribals and rescues the Kerala indigenes from a long-haul 'spatial amnesia' (Nixon, *Slow Violence* 151–152). *Mother Forest* and C. K. Janu's socio-environmental activism should be understood, evidently, as part of the larger picture of growing struggles and writings for indigenous rights around the globe.

Fighting the Toxin: Leelakumariamma's *Jeevadayini* and Kerala's Endosulfan Disaster

The Green Revolution during the 1960s and 1970s aimed primarily to tackle the food problem in India through the introduction of advanced technology, high-yielding crop varieties, and extensive use of pesticides. Adopting improved agrotechnology was expected to overcome the Malthusian prophecy of an impending population–resources imbalance, while material abundance was sought to be achieved by combating scarcity through an unprecedented control of the environment (Shiva, *The Violence* 14). India's agricultural experiment yielded remarkable returns in its early years, but the ecological ramifications of the Green Revolution soon became apparent as the chemical fertilisers reduced the soil fertility and insect-pests developed immunity to the pesticides. Agriculture became more commercialised, and the introduction of new seed varieties replaced the common, traditional ones. The oiko-autobiography of Leelakumariamma, *Jeevadayini* [The Life-Giver], foregrounds the ambiguity of an Agricultural Officer who was raised in a traditional Gandhian farmer family in Kannur in northern Kerala but had to campaign for the environmentally unfriendly programmes of Green Revolution as part of her job. Pappiyamma, Leelakumariamma's mother, led the way for her daughter by toiling hard in the fields using traditional organic farming methods. Using cow dung as the main fertiliser, she cultivated various crops such as paddy, tapioca, *thina*, and *chaama* on their 15-acre farmland.

While pursuing agricultural science in college, Leelakumariamma had to unlearn the traditional farming methods that she had picked up at home and learn the names of different chemical fertilisers and pesticides like Malathion and the need to produce high yields in agriculture. It is with deep contrition that she writes about her work at the Agricultural Office in Kasaragod district when she was entrusted to distribute chemicals like DDT and Sevin (which was manufactured by Union Carbide India Limited's pesticide plant in Bhopal) to the local peasants. Leelakumariamma also deplores the loss of many traditional varieties of paddy seeds after the introduction of Green Revolution's High-Yielding Varieties (HYVs). She had to face her colleague's antagonism when she revealed to the unsuspecting farmers that the pesticides they were taking home were poisons. At the end of chapter 6 of the book, Leelakumariamma poignantly notes, 'Within almost three years, we, Agricultural Officers, killed a rich heritage of the local farmers' (Ajeesh 38).

Leelakumariamma's initiation into environmental justice activism was galvanised by the premature death of her elder brother Ramakrishnan, who, at her request, had come to stay with her to oversee the construction of her house in Periya village where she was transferred to. The livelihood of the villagers of Periya largely depended on the vast swathes of cashew orchards owned by the Plantation Corporation of Kerala (PCK), a public company run by the Kerala state government, where they either worked as labourers or obtained firewood. To ward off tea mosquitoes, PCK used helicopters to aerially spray the highly toxic endosulfan over the plantations. Endosulfan belongs to the group of 'persistent organic pollutants' (POPs) and is classified by 'the US Environmental Protection Agency as a category Ib (highly hazardous) chemical, since it is easily absorbed by the stomach, lungs and through the skin' (Rajendran 2206).

C. Jayakumar Thanal, the founding director of 'Thanal,' an environmental organisation based in Thiruvananthapuram, lists cancer, various mental and physical disabilities, psoriasis, blindness, aborted pregnancies, as well as reproductive disorders as the common health risks associated with endosulfan exposure (88). The seriousness of the health impacts of endosulfan that Jayakumar Thanal illustrates throws into sharp relief the extreme callousness shown by PCK towards human and other-than-human lives in these villages by its criminal nonadherence to the standard norms prescribed when endosulfan is aerially sprayed. The stipulations with regard to the aerial spraying of endosulfan include the following:

1 The spraying of endosulfan should be publicly announced through microphones two days before.
2 Endosulfan should be sprayed only five feet above the saplings.
3 Aerial spraying of endosulfan should be done only during early mornings and late evenings.
4 All water bodies should be covered before the spraying begins.
5 Cattle should not be allowed to enter the plantation up to twenty days after the spraying (Ajeesh 43; Padre, *Endosulfan Samaram* 47).

None of these steps was followed by PCK. As a result, the sprayed pesticide percolated into the uncovered water bodies in the area, making them unfit for both domestic and agricultural consumption (Rajendran 2207). Crows and other birds getting killed after consuming the poisoned water soon became a common sight (Ajeesh 39). Periya and a few other endosulfan-affected villages in Kasaragod began to witness 'the strange stillness' that Rachel Carson (2) famously described in the first chapter of *Silent Spring* (1962). Leelakumariamma's brother fell ill within a year of his stay in Periya; his eyes frequently became watery, and his sight also began to fail. Even doctors were unable to pin down the nature of his disease. The death of her perfectly healthy brother, whom she was very close to, just after a year of stay in Periya amply demonstrated to Leelakumariamma not only the physical health threats of pesticide use but also the 'emotional harm' that it could cause (Stein 194).

Leelakumariamma, who is credited as 'the first person ever to come forward against the aerial spraying of endosulfan by the Plantation Corporation of Kerala' (Ajeesh 5), launched her crusade to end this 'toxic rain' by sending out petitions to the state's Chief Minister, Health Minister, Agriculture Minister, the District Collector, and the chief authority of PCK in Kottayam. Her constant appeals to halt the spraying of endosulfan, however, did not evoke any response from them. She, then, started to sensitise the local public about the dangers of endosulfan and sent mass-signed petitions to ministers for three consecutive years (1994–1997). When she realised that it was pointless to wait any longer for governmental intervention in the issue, she decided to take the legal course.

Leelakumariamma's petition was considered by the *Munsiff* Court which ordered a stay on the spraying of endosulfan in the plantations. The morning after the court judgement, PCK's Kasaragod district manager, along with a small group of people, came to Leelakumariamma's house and threatened her that she would suffer hardships if she did not withdraw her complaint. Raising the gender question, Leelakumariamma asks if they would dare to turn up at her doorstep and threaten her if she were a man (Ajeesh 50). Rob Nixon has convincingly demonstrated how Rachel Carson and Wangari Maathai, two important female ecoactivists of the twentieth century, 'On all fronts, had to weather ad feminam assaults from male establishments whose orthodoxies were threatened by their autonomy' (*Slow Violence* 145). However, for Leelakumariamma, just as it was in the case of Carson and Maathai, her 'marginality was wounding but emboldening' (Nixon, *Slow Violence* 145). Much to the astonishment of the PCK authorities, she decided not to withdraw the complaint as she had the full support of the local villagers.

PCK moved the Subordinate Court (which is superior to *Munsiff* Court) for vacating the stay but lost as it upheld the earlier ruling. Following this, PCK approached the High Court of Kerala demanding Rs. 75 lakhs as compensation from Leelakumariamma for the losses incurred by the company. At this crucial juncture of her campaign, Leelakumariamma was helped by T. P. Padmanabhan, director of the environmental group called 'Society of Environmental Education in Kerala' (SEEK), who arranged a lawyer named Daisy Thampi to appear for her in the High Court. After hearing both sides, the Kerala High Court asked PCK to wait for the *Munsiff* Court's judgement. On 28 October 2000, the *Munsiff* Court passed the landmark judgement to stop the aerial spraying of endosulfan. Although she met with a life-threatening accident and is on crutches, Leelakumariamma continues her crusade for the ban of endosulfan across the country.

The damage that the 24 years of toxic exposure did to the local eco-system of these villages is immense. A study by Dr V. S. Vijayan of Salim Ali Foundation, for instance, reveals 'a decline in plant diversity between 40 and 70 percent, particularly for native species' in these villages where endosulfan was used (R. Mathew). The toxic spraying of endosulfan has also left in its wake a very large disabled community in Kasaragod. While endosulfan-related deaths in Kasaragod have crossed the five hundred mark (B. John 14), the long-term casualties of the toxin are staggering. Y. S. Mohan Kumar, a Kasaragod-based physician who first associated the proliferation of health problems in the villages with endosulfan use, predicts that the after-effects of pesticide use are likely to haunt generations in Kasaragod for the next 50 to 60 years (67). What unfolds in Kasaragod is an example of what Rob Nixon calls 'slow violence.' Nixon rightly argues that in the incidents of slow violence—just as in the endosulfan-impacted villages in Kasaragod—the 'post is never fully post' since '[v]iolence, above all environmental violence, needs to be seen—and deeply considered—as a contest not only over space, or bodies, or labor, or resources, but also over time' (*Slow Violence* 8). Thus, with the 'attritional lethality' (Nixon, *Slow Violence* 8) of endosulfan lingering over these villages, there is no 'post-endosulfan' phase to speak of.

Considering the plight of the indigent villagers who could not afford to flee from their villages to other safer locations, Leelakumariamma decided to stay back in Periya (Ajeesh 44–45). Her ecofeminist ethics obliterates the binary oppositions of privileged/oppressed and self/other and debunks the speciesist assumptions regarding human superiority. This is evident in her response to the menace of wild boars that wander at night into her back-yard organic farm to feed on the vegetables. Leelakumariamma reasons that it is the food crunch in the degraded habitats that impels wild animals to trespass into agricultural spaces and asks, 'What is the point in saving my crops by killing them?' (Ajeesh 25). Her inclusive vision is congruent with the ecofeminist thought that assumes 'sexism, racism, classism, spe-ciesism, and naturism (the oppression of nature) [as] mutually reinforcing systems of oppression' and gestures towards the 'liberation of *all* oppressed groups' (Gaard 5; emphasis added).

Leelakumariamma's oiko-autobiography is as much an 'ecoprotest' (Nayar, 'Indigenous Cultures' 292) writing as it is a trauma narrative triggered by environmental disturbance and personal loss. Her protracted battle to end endosulfan use in her village underscores the typical Global South scenario where the matters of environmental impoverishment are embedded in 'basic human rights and social justice' issues (Tarter 224; Comfort 229). The Kasaragod endosulfan disaster has also been fodder for creative writings in Malayalam. In Ambikasuthan Mangad's acclaimed novel *Enmakaje* (2009), Leelakumariamma makes a brief appearance and engages in a candid conversation with the novel's activist-protagonist Neelakantan about her anti-endosulfan campaign. This novel is studied in detail in this book's Chapter 3. Francis T. Mavelikkara's play *Swapnangal Vilkkanundu* [Dreams for Sale] (2013) is another remarkable literary narrative inspired by the toxic tragedy of Kasaragod.

The Struggle for Water Democracy: *Mayilamma: Oru Jeevitham* and the Plachimada Anti–Coca-Cola Campaign

Post the economic liberalisation in India in the 1990s, The Coca-Cola Company returned to the Indian market after an interval of 16 years (1977–1993) and established, in March 2000, a bottling plant in the small village of Plachimada under Perumatty Panchayat in the Palakkad district of Kerala. The plant came up on 34.64 acres in what were previously paddy fields and held out the promise of bringing 'development' to a 'backward' region (see Aiyer 643). Intended to produce its popular brands such as Coca-Cola, Fanta, Sprite, Limca, Kinley Soda, Maaza, and Thums Up, the plant started functioning in 2000–2001 (Bijoy 4333; Aiyer 643). The population of Plachimada, located at the border with the state of Tamil Nadu, comprises predominantly Dalit, tribal, and Muslim communities that are dependent on the cultivation of crops like paddy, coconut, bananas, and maize (Bijoy 4333). The prospect of jobs in the company was broken once it started functioning. Just a handful of the local people were given employment and citing their lack of education, the employed locals were asked to do menial tasks like cleaning bottles. C. R. Bijoy describes the operations of the company thus:

> About 85 lorry loads of beverage products containing 550–600 cases each with each case containing 24 bottles of 300 ml capacity left the factory premises daily. Six borewells and two open wells in the factory compound sucked out some 0.8 to 1.5 million litres of water daily. Within two years, the people around the plant experienced problems that they had never encountered before, the receding of the water table and the drastic change in the quality of water spread around 1 to 1.5 km radius of the plant. Water shortage upset the agricultural operations. Water became unfit for human consumption and domestic use.
>
> (4333)

Mayilamma: Oru Jeevitham, the oiko-autobiography of Mayilamma (1940–2007), an unlettered woman belonging to the Eravallar tribe in Plachimada, begins with an episode where the tribal community comes to grips with the falling quality of drinking water and the different health problems posed by it. Children at the local *anganwadi* centre fell sick after consuming food prepared with contaminated water, raising anxiety in their parents and the community at large. Water from the local sources, which was traditionally used for drinking and cooking, is found unfit for use, and the village faces signs of impending drought. Women who washed dishes with contaminated water complain of itching and painful sensation in their hands. As ailments begin to proliferate, the local tribals, who previously avoided hospital treatment even at the time of pregnancy and childbirth, become frequent visitors to hospitals. With water scarcity and pollution beginning to upset the health and daily activities of the local population, the Panchayat starts distributing water in tankers. The water distributed by the Panchayat is no better either; Mayilamma states it is rumoured that the water is being collected from somewhere below a crematorium near the Chittoor River (27).

Vandana Shiva, in her celebrated work *Staying Alive*, rightly emphasises that groundwater is not a limitless resource and affirms that '[v]iolence to the water cycle is probably the worst and most invisible form of violence because it simultaneously threatens the survival of all' (*Staying Alive* 175). According to the 'Global Risks 2015 Report' by the World Economic Forum, 'water crisis is "the #1 global risk based on impact to society" ' (qtd. in 'Facts about Water and Sanitation'). In the Global South context, women are the key players in domestic water management ('Gender and Water') as well as the 'water providers' of the families ('Gender and Water'; Shiva, *Staying Alive* 171). Thus, disappearing water sources create 'new burdens and new drudgery' for women (Shiva, *Staying Alive* 171). Mayilamma makes note of the predicament of the tribal women in Plachimada who, after the water mining by The Coca-Cola Company started, have to walk long distances in search of drinking water and wait, while carrying their pots, in long queues even during the monsoon months (23–26). She also indicates how it is often a trade-off between going to work and fetching water (26). For the underdeveloped rural tribal women, water scarcity poses a concomitant risk to personal sanitation and hygiene compounded by the non-existence of toilets and difficulties during menstruation and pregnancy. The issue of groundwater depletion in Plachimada was so severe that by 2005, the region was found to be a 'water impoverished zone' (Aiyer 645).

The mass campaign against The Coca-Cola Company's water abuse in Plachimada was formally launched on Earth Day, 22 April, 2002 by the *Coca-Cola Virudha Janakeeya Samara Samithy* [Anti-Coca-Cola People's Struggle Committee] with the participation of over 1300 people, most of whom were local tribals (Pariyadath 27; Bijoy 4334). The campaign was inaugurated by C. K. Janu who situated the Plachimada agitation within the larger picture of tribal protests for land and livelihood happening across the state which, Mayilamma states, instilled confidence in the gathered tribals. The protestors of Plachimada used the Gandhian 'Satyagraha' style of peaceful sit-ins and 'hunger strikes' to assert their water rights and livelihood issues. After a brief period of indifference and opposition, the anti–Coca-Cola campaign in Plachimada garnered support from environmentalists across the country and the globe and Mayilamma became the recognisable face of the agitation. The Plachimada struggle also attracted the attention of the national and international press. *Mayilamma: Oru Jeevitham* offers the history of the Plachimada movement in which the frail tribal-Dalit women engaged in a Goliath–David kind of struggle against a global corporate power for water democracy and whose eventual victory bolstered similar struggles against Coca-Cola elsewhere in the country and the world. The 'ecosickness' narratives (Houser) like *Mayilamma: Oru Jeevitham* also highlight how the environmentalism of the poor becomes 'an environmentalism of survival and livelihood' (Ciafone 125–129).

The Coca-Cola Company's hubristic act of handing out its waste sludge as fertilisers to the gullible local peasants also comes under criticism in the text. Mayilamma compares the stink of the waste sludge to that of decomposing carcasses (26). A BBC Radio Program exposé dated 25 July 2003 on the Plachimada waste dumping points out:

> Of the three solid wastes analysed, one showed relatively high levels of two toxic metals, namely, cadmium and lead. Some other heavy metals, including nickel, chromium and zinc, were also present at levels significantly above those expected for background, uncontaminated soil and sludge. The presence of high levels of lead and cadmium is of particular concern. Lead is a developmental toxin in humans, particularly noted for its ability to damage the developing nervous system. Cadmium is especially toxic to the kidney, but also to the liver—it is classified as a known human carcinogen.
>
> (qtd. in Bijoy 4334)

Driven by the dangerous assumption that 'natural resources and the poor [are] dispensable elements of ecosystems' (Shiva, *Staying Alive* 213), The Coca-Cola Company's activities reveal an environmental racist dimension as the marginalised subalterns are selectively targeted to live with toxic industrial waste ('Environmental Racism'). Coca-Cola's entanglement in the issues of toxicity in the Indian context is highly complex. The Centre for Science and Environment (CSE) in New Delhi published a report in 2003 that indicated unacceptably high levels of pesticides like Lindane, DDT, Malathion, and Chlorpyrifos in the products of The Coca-Cola Company and PepsiCo (Summerly; Aiyer 644). The pesticide residues in these products were toxic enough to cause health issues like cancer, nervous and reproductive system disorders, birth abnormalities, and immune system problems (Summerly). By contrast, the colas available in the United States were found to be pesticide-free (Ramesh). A few newspapers interestingly reported that the farmers of Chhattisgarh were successfully using Coca-Cola in lieu of costlier pesticides to protect their rice crops from pests (Putul). Ananthakrishnan Aiyer observes that it is the reports of pesticide content in the soft drinks that marshalled the Indian urban middle class's opinion against the Coke brand (646). In her oiko-autobiography, Mayilamma expresses her concern at the practice of some local people who consume toddy mixed with Coca-Cola for greater intoxication (16). In this manner, toxicity and its social and ecological health ramifications become a shared concern for both *Jeevadayini* and *Mayilamma: Oru Jeevitham.*

The tribal agitation against a Multinational Corporation (MNC) like The Coca-Cola Company should be situated in the broader history of tribal struggles for land and livelihood in Kerala. Mayilamma shares the history of Plachimada tribals' land holdings and distribution that involves painful stories of tribal exploitation (17–18). According to her, the lands where the tribals toiled from dawn to dusk were usurped by the non-tribals after paying them a meagre 100–200 rupees. The tribals were beaten up if they resisted to give up their lands. Mayilamma also documents a crisis faced by them not so long ago due to the unavailability of a proper burial ground for her community (21–22). When someone died, the tribals had to cross the Kerala–Tamil Nadu border to go to the Tamil Gounders' land to inter the deceased. This issue often escalated into violent conflicts between the two groups. The problem was finally solved when the district collector arranged a burial ground for the tribals at Nellimedu (Pariyadath 22).

The tribals' loss of land is interlinked with the high levels of illiteracy in the community.

C. K. Janu, for instance, notes how the tribals lost their lands since they 'were unable to find out or remember the survey numbers,' thus, failing to prove their ownership (Bhaskaran 40). Landless and displaced, the tribal communities who were self-sufficient 'producers' of grain were reduced to the state of 'consumers' who buy 'everything from the shops' (Bhaskaran 52). Ananthakrishnan Aiyer, therefore, indicates that the Plachimada struggle also 'needs to be analyzed as part of the unfolding agrarian crisis and not simply as a case of valiant community struggling against the rapacious practices of a transnational corporation like The Coca-Cola Company' (640).

Mayilamma's oiko-autobiography seems to also advocate what Pramod Parajuli famously referred to as 'ecological ethnicity.' 'Ecological ethnicity' is a form of 'knowing subalternity' (Nayar, 'Indigenous Cultures') that transcends the narrow definitions of ethnic politics (Parajuli, 'Ecological

Ethnicity'). It is cognisant of the reality that the nation-state, which ought to rescue the subaltern communities from exploiters, oppression, and under-development, often plays a crucial part in the processes of exploitation, subjection, and deprivation (Parajuli, 'Coming Home' 189). The notion of ecological ethnicity acknowledges the indigenous community as the 'purveyor of authentic knowledge of the terrain' and 'foregrounds human identity as intimately linked to the local land forms, ecology, weather and mineral, animal and plant life' (Nayar, *Postcolonial Studies* 56). Thus, the 'ecological ethnicity' entails the realms of both *oikeion* and *politikon*. This shift from *oikeion* to *politikon* in Mayilamma's oiko-autobiography, how-ever, is more of a continuum rather than an abrupt transition. The *politikon* of Mayilamma is always informed by *oikic* concerns. Mayilamma, for instance, says that when she gets an opportunity to meet Ms Sonia Gandhi, the Member of Parliament and the former president of the Indian National Congress, she has only one question to ask: 'There is a small well in front of my house. We were drinking water all these days from that well. Now the water is not good. We are not against you giving any company a permit or an award. But, can you bring the good water back to our well?' (66).

June 2016 saw a new development in the Plachimada movement as the Kerala Home Department, under pressure from the National Commission for Scheduled Castes (NCSC), filed a criminal case against The Coca-Cola Company at Meenakshipuram police station under the Scheduled Castes and Scheduled Tribes (Prevention of Atrocities) Act, 1989. The company was charged with the non-bailable offence of 'wilful pollution' of water resources in the locality chiefly populated by tribal communities (Shaji). It is noted to be the first major case to be filed against the company in India and is hoped to bring long overdue justice and compensation to the Plachimada victims.

Mangrove Man: The Ecoactivism of Kallen Pokkudan

The environmental significance of mangrove forests is foregrounded in the two oiko-autobiographies by the ecoactivist Kallen Pokkudan (1937–2015), namely *Kandalkkadukalkkidayil Ente Jeevitham* (2002) and *Ente Jeevitham* (2010). Pokkudan belongs to the Pulaya caste which is a part of the 'Scheduled Castes' of India. An elementary school dropout, he has planted over one lakh mangroves across Kerala and given more than five hundred lectures in schools and colleges across India about the importance of mangrove conservation. Pokkudan's remarkable ecoactivist efforts were acknowledged through numerous prominent awards including P. V. Thampi Environment Award (2001), Bhoomi Mithra Award (2003), and Vanamithra Award (2006) given by the Government of Kerala besides a special mention by UNESCO (*La*

Paz Group). His other published books, like *Choottachi*[2] (2010) and *Kandal Inangal* [Varieties of Mangroves] (2015), are illustrated accounts of different varieties of mangroves and the riparian biota that attest to Pokkudan's close observation of the local environment. Pokkudan has also played the role of a Dalit activist in the award-winning Malayalam film *Papilio Buddha* (2013) directed by Jayan K. Cherian which narrates Dalit land struggles and atrocities against Dalits. The 2011 Malayalam film *Sthalam* [Place] directed by Kaviyoor Sivaprasad is based on the life of Kallen Pokkudan.

There is a growing interest in the study of the ecological value of mangrove swamps, especially in the Asian countries that were affected by the 'Boxing Day tsunami' in 2004. A BBC news report dated 25 December 2005 and titled 'Tsunami: Mangroves "saved lives,"' for instance, draws attention to the remarkable findings of a study concerning the 2004 Indian Ocean earthquake and tsunami:

> The World Conservation Union (IUCN) compared the death toll from two villages in Sri Lanka that were hit by the devastating giant waves. Two people died in the settlement with dense mangrove and scrub forest, while up to 6,000 people died in the village without similar vegetation.
>
> (Kinver)

A 2008 research paper authored by Saudamini Das and Jeffrey R. Vincent that presents data collected from 'several hundred villages' in the eastern Indian state of Odisha about the 1999 'Super Cyclone' concludes as follows: 'villages with wider mangroves between them and the coast experienced significantly fewer deaths than ones with narrower or no mangroves' (Das and Vincent 7357). Evidence shows that mangrove forests that comprise salt-tolerant plants which grow in brackish coastal marshes in the tropical and subtropical regions of the world not only act as 'bioshields' against cyclonic storms and violent sea waves but could also help 'mitigat[e] future cyclonic risk' (Muraleedharan et al. 7; Emery 237; Das and Vincent 7357; Bahinipati and Sahu 186). A report by the Environmental Justice Foundation expounds on this process:

> The [mangrove] trees both shield the land from wind and trap sediment in their roots, maintaining a shallow slope on the seabed that absorbs the energy of tidal surges … Mangrove forests reduce the impact of tsunamis by reducing both the height and the velocity of the incoming waves, and by distributing water among the canals and creeks of the mangroves, thus decreasing the level of inundation.
>
> (3)

The post-disaster studies about the 2004 Indian Ocean tsunami describe how many concrete buildings and bridges had collapsed, unable to withstand the giant waves of the tsunami, which appropriately raises the question of whether 'man-made structures [can] ever be substitutes for nature?' ('Asian Tsunami'). Vimukthi Weeratunga, one of IUCN's biodiversity coordinators, opines that people's respect for natural barriers has grown since the tsunami experience (Kinver). Responding to such findings, the state government of Kerala has announced Rs. 35-crore project that involves planting mangroves to protect the Kerala coast from tidal surges (G. Barry).

While the popular and scientific interest in mangrove conservation is recent, Pokkudan had been engaging in this activity for over two decades. He started planting and preserving mangroves in his native village called Pazhayangadi in the Ezhome Panchayat in Kannur district of Kerala. In addition to the need to preserve the mangrove ecosystems, Pokkudan's oiko-autobiographies also address numerous other issues like Dalit rights, labour exploitation in a feudalist society, sexual exploitation of Dalit women, casteism in the communist movement, and the persisting, multitiered practice of untouchability in the hierarchical society of India. While Pokkudan's life narratives are significant in themselves for being the early Dalit autobiographies in Malayalam, I am interested in the ecopolitical dimensions of Kallen Pokkudan's life as depicted in his two life writings, *Kandalkkadukalkkidayil Ente Jeevitham* and *Ente Jeevitham*. The following analysis also aims to contribute to the discourse of ecomasculinities, which Scott Slovic justly acknowledges as an important trait of the 'third wave' of ecocriticism ('The Third Wave' 7), by presenting Pokkudan as an 'eco-man' from Kerala.

In the opening chapter of *Ente Jeevitham*, Pokkudan describes his life thus: 'My life, in short, is the transition from Kallen Pokkudan to Kandal Pokkudan' (9). *Kandal* is the Malayalam term for mangrove. The signboard that is erected in front of his house which bears the name 'Kandal Pokkudan' below his original name 'Kallen Pokkudan' also signals this remarkable transition. In *Kandalkkadukalkkidayil Ente Jeevitham*, Pokkudan makes clear that he wishes to be known as 'Kandal Pokkudan' (65). This wish of Pokkudan to turn his first name into 'Kandal' clearly emerges from a total identification of his self with the environment. It was following his disaffection with the Communist party as well as his community that Pokkudan turned to mangrove afforestation and conservation. He clarifies,

I was quite fed up. The Pulaya community was not generous enough then to approve of a Pulaya who was a Communist. I also feel that the Left Front is still not big-hearted to accommodate the members of Pulaya community. My community and party—the two groups that are dear to me–seemed to have become estranged from me.

(*Kandalkkadukalkkidayil* 65)

Pokkudan notes that he began planting mangrove seedlings with a humble aim—to protect children going to school along the Pazhayangadi River from the lashing wind. He says,

I have seen many children's umbrellas being lost in the wind and rain. It was the girls who suffered the most. I could remember a few deaths that happened as the children slipped, in the wind and rain, from the make-shift bridge wooden bridge across the river. I believed that it could be averted [if I grew mangroves].

(*Ente Jeevitham* 157)

He started by planting three hundred seedlings for about a kilometre on the riverside. It was during the 'second phase' of his mangrove cultivation when about one thousand mangrove plants had been raised that T. Pavithran, a faculty member of Payyannur College, took notice of his work. He brought in a photographer of the leading Malayalam daily *Mathrubhumi* which published the news on its front page. It elicited wide publicity for his ecoactivist work and thereafter, many researchers and environmentalists began approaching him to learn more about mangroves and his conservation efforts.

In the early days of his ecoactivism, Pokkudan faced intimidation, threats, and criticism which even made him declare to the media that he would not plant mangroves in Ezhome Panchayat (*Ente Jeevitham* 163). The obstacles in his path were many: on one occasion, some miscreants threw the mangrove seeds that he had collected on the banks into the river. He had to seek the help of Panchayat authorities when he saw that the mangrove plants that he had planted were being destroyed daily (*Ente Jeevitham* 157–158). The Kannur *tehsildar*[3] told Pokkudan that his planting of mangroves was a hindrance to 'developmental activities' (*Ente Jeevitham* 163). When he heard that about ten thousand, six-year-old mangroves that he had planted were chopped down, he had a nervous breakdown and had to seek professional help (Pokkudan, *Kandal Inangal* 160). However, thanks to the timely intervention of some environmental activists, the High Court of Kerala considered this issue and passed a judgement that six months' imprisonment along with a fine of two thousand rupees would be awarded to anyone who destroyed the mangroves. Pokkudan counts this judgement as a landmark in the legal history of Kerala.

The variety of mangrove that Pokkudan grows is *Rhizophora mucronata*. Its common name in Malayalam is *pranthan kandal*, meaning 'Mad Mangrove,' which Pokkudan jestingly identifies as a fitting symbol of himself because, on seeing him going about the 'useless' work of planting mangroves, many people have judged him to be crazy. 'This is an unstable state," he writes, 'A jolly craziness that I like. Sometimes, I feel I am a mad mangrove too' (*Kandalkkadukalkkidayil* 64). This sense of 'otherness,' a feeling that he is an 'outsider,' slightly *de trop*, is repeatedly hinted at in his both oiko-autobiographies.

Pokkudan describes his typical day as follows:

> I set out in search of the seeds early in the morning. I take drinking water and rice gruel and keep them in my boat. It will be dusk when I come back. I have gone to places like Dalil, Pallikkara, Neringinte Madu, Manappoyya, Boatkadu, and Manatti looking for mangrove seeds. I wrap the collected seeds [in a piece of cloth]. It will not rot for even three months. I plant them in places where cattle won't come. The seeds should be sowed after checking the nature of the soil and that of the highlands close to the mangrove swamps ... I have learnt most of these things by myself. Nobody has taught me anything.
>
> (*Kandalkkadukalkkidayil* 62)

Pokkudan's '(re)construction of nature,' as it were, is also an exercise in ecological restoration. His ecological restoration emanates from a concern for the health and future of the humans *and* the local ecosystem, as is typical of the Global South ecoactivisms where the ecological issues are closely interlocked with the survival struggles of the local human population. The picture that Pokkudan presents, however, is not that of conflict, but harmony and symbiosis. Pokkudan's narratives fascinatingly show how the bioregional dwelling of the indigenous Pulaya population literally begins with their hovels which are built quite close to the mangrove forests. He offers an insightful picture of the intermeshing of the traditional Dalit lives and the biodiverse mangrove wetlands:

> It was an altogether different world inhabited by the quiet lives of the mangroves, the Dalits and the fishes. The Pulayas consumed the fishes they caught from the wetlands. If they got big fish, they had to offer them to the landlords. It is in such places in the wetlands where the decayed leaves of the mangrove trees accumulated that medicinal fishes like *pottathanam, kakkathi,* and *anapothran* thrive. They were an important part of the diet of the Pulayas. That was why even a single person in the previous generation did not go to hospitals

for any medical treatment. We used to scout around and catch 101 different kinds of small fishes from the wetlands and dry them and eat them.

(*Ente Jeevitham* 170)

In *Kandal Inangal* (2015), Pokkudan explains,

During the times of famine, the raw fruits of this plant were consumed after cooking in steam. Maybe that is why it is called *Nalla Kandal* [Good Mangrove]. … In the olden times, people used to also eat both the raw and steam-cooked seeds of *Nalla Kandal* with a pinch of jaggery added. *Nalla Kandal* is also used as fodder for goat and cows.

(36–38)

Pokkudan's narratives are punctuated every now and then with exhaustive catalogues of the flora and fauna found in the mangrove forests; he provides the readers with information about 20 different varieties of mangroves, 9 different kinds of water birds, and 50 freshwater and 16 seawater fishes. His environmental sensibility and skills in observing nature are evident in the following sample descriptions: 'Fishes, just like people, have different clans, also different behavioural patterns—some are shy, a few others are fighters. There are extremists and moderates' (*Kandalkkadukalkkidayil* 54);

The bird, *Thavidikkocha* has lots of oil in its meat. Its oil is used as medicine for rheumatism and setting fractured bones. *Thavidikkocha* has black shades on the sides of its neck. Quail and owl are small birds. The meat of owl is given to children as it has medicinal qualities. The wings of the little cormorant are like an umbrella. The birds dive into the water and catch fish. The beak of this bird is red and its feet are like paddles! Crow, eagle, and *penakakka* are the birds that breed and build their nests on mangrove trees. That the mangroves should be preserved is important to these birds as well.

(*Kandalkkadukalkkidayil* 59)

Choottachi fish curry prepared by adding ground pepper is given to new mothers. This fish is an endangered species now. *Pottathan* is all black. It won't get big—only almost as big as a finger. It is nowhere to be seen now. It is a really tasty fish. Many such fishes have disappeared today.

In the olden days, one of the main jobs of the Pulaya women was prawn fishing. The women used to set out in groups, even at night. The catch was always good. This practice is carried on even now. But many varieties of prawns have become extinct. The catch is also not as good as it was in the past. All these things should be taken seriously.

(Kandalkkadukalkkidayil 56–58)

Similarly, he testifies to the water-purifying properties of mangroves via a description of a well situated in a sacred grove dedicated to snake gods and surrounded by 18 acres of mangrove forests. The well always has clear water. Pokkudan insightfully notes,

The local Hindu people of Mattur say that it is the place where celestial female beings meditated. They believe that the well has pure water because of that. But we [he and a few other environmentalists who visited the site] understand that it is because of the vast swathes of mangrove tress growing around it.

(Ente Jeevitham 163)

Pokkudan constantly uses suasory language and employs apocalyptic visions to promote an ethics of care for the mangrove ecosystem:

When nature's fury causes destruction, we cannot do anything. Didn't we recently see in newspapers and television the reports of the loss of lives following a typhoon (Odisha disaster)? It was caused by humans themselves. Without a second thought, modern man is destroying the coastal forests. Politicians, bureaucrats and contractors are of one mind about this. When rivers and marshes are levelled by dumping soil, it leads to floods as they cannot take in the additional water during the monsoons. Reports have begun to appear in newspapers that suggest that had the mangrove forests on the riversides not been destroyed, the ravages caused by the storms could have been averted. When all the green cover disappears, we are bound to lose everything in such violent storms. When are we going to realise this?

(Kandalkkadukalkkidayil 66)

In her article on mangrove conservation in Sri Lanka, Deepthi Wickramasinghe explains how mangroves help tone down the impact of storms:

Mangrove forests dissipate the force of tropical storms and reduce damage of coastal communities (IUCN 2011). These plants extend a crucial service in the context of climate change as they sequester even more carbon from the atmosphere than terrestrial forests, playing a key role in efforts to mitigate adverse impacts. Yet, globally, mangrove forests are diminishing in quality and [are] rated as among the most threatened habitats, with rates of loss exceeding those of rainforests and coral reefs.

(162)

According to a report prepared by the project team of Kerala Forest Research Institute, the mangrove cover in Kerala has declined from 700 sq. km to 17 sq. km and has attained a 'threatened status in Kerala' (Muraleedharan et al. 6–10). The fact that more than 80% of the mangrove stretch in Kerala is under private ownership further points to the extremely precarious state of mangroves (Muraleedharan et al. 6; Palott 77). Jaffer Palott, in his study of the significance of mangroves in Kerala, points out how the availability of water and transport facilities have made these 'ecotones' a favourite location to set up thermal power plants, sawmills, harbours, and so on and dump their debris, sewage, and other waste materials into these wetlands (79). According to him, '90% of mangrove forests have already been destroyed to create paddy and coconut fields' (79). Attesting to Palott's findings, Pokkudan also calls attention to how mangrove swamps have diminished to the state of a 'trash can' of the city:

It is now known to everybody that the roots of mangroves are not under the soil. To collect the seeds, one has to wriggle through the magnificent roots of the mangroves that hang down to the rivers. On your way, you will stumble upon syringes, needles, plastic utensils, decayed animal wastes from slaughterhouses, etc. that are brought from the cities and dumped into the river. So, it is almost an act of daredevilry to find the mangrove seeds from all the trash. Rivers, to us, have become trash cans to which all kinds of garbage can be dumped. Different varieties of fish die and float around in rivers on a daily basis. To whom should I say all this?

(*Kandalkkadukalkkidayil* 62)

Thus, the mangrove forests have become what Val Plumwood famously called the 'shadow places' which are the 'unrecognised … places that provide our material and ecological support, … [and] take our pollution and dangerous waste [and] exhaust their fertility.' One of the significant social impacts of the destruction of the mangrove ecology is the threat to the food sovereignty of the indigenous Dalits. The onslaught of the city on rural hinterlands seems to always create the twin problems of co-opting the indigenes into the homogenising processes of globalisation and eroding the autochthonous cultures, traditions, languages/dialects, and food habits.

Jaffer Palott, in his study, makes interesting connections between the public perception of swamp ecologies and the degradation of mangrove ecosystems. He remarks: 'Until recently the places containing mangrove forests were regarded as wastelands. They were known as shrubberies that house mosquitoes and other parasites' (74). William Howarth, in his article titled 'Imagined Territory: Writing of Wetlands,' has pointed out the negative significations long associated with wetlands and marshes. He explains:

> Antagonism towards wetlands governed most ancient civilizations … Early creation myths tend to form land out of water, describing the latter as a realm of demonic chaos. In Genesis I, the world is at first a shapeless void of waters until God moves upon their face, dividing light from dark, and then waters from waters, so that dry land may appear. The great Divider thus sets a course for generations of farmers: wherever men find low, water-saturated ground, they must drain and dry it, freeing themselves from 'the mud of the mire.'
>
> (521–522)

Repeated anthropogenic interventions in the mangrove forests that are taking a serious toll on the health of these fragile ecosystems substantiate the fact that the popular perception of swamplands as 'unattained capital' (Howarth 523) has still not died out. Although the Coastal Regulation Zone Act of 1991 has prohibited any developmental activities in the land up to five hundred metres from the High Tide Line, most construction work in places close to mangrove forests and wetlands is carried out unhindered in total defiance of the stipulations of the Act (Palott 81).

The 'victimisation' of the mangrove ecosystems resonates with the ghettoised, marginal lives led by the Dalits. The ten thousand mangrove trees chopped down by the 'developmentalists' call to mind the images of terrorised and exploited Dalit bodies under an oppressive societal structure. The analogy between Dalit bodies and the non-human components of nature is not recent; Dalit literature is replete with the trope of Dalit bodies being equated with that of animals.[4] Pokkudan himself emphasises the 'animalisation' of Dalit bodies by noting how 'the very names that are given to worms, birds, and animals' like *kakka* (Malayalam for 'crow'), *patta* (cockroach), and *kokkichi* (female crane) were reserved for the Dalit children by the upper-caste landlords while 'the names related to humans and gods were the monopoly of other castes' (*Kandalkkadukalkkidayil* 36). Even if a Dalit parent gave a 'good' name to his child, the landlords would give him/her a different name which would become his/her permanent name (*Ente Jeevitham* 18). Another incident where the dehumanisation of Dalit bodies manifests is when the feudal landlords place wagers on their labourers and make them fight. 'The wager,' Pokkudan says,

> was usually for two or three quarters of an *ana*. It would be a bloody fight … It was actually one of the ways in which the landlords created

and maintained rivalries among the labourers. The landlord and his servant used to enjoy watching their labourers fight.

(*Kandalkkadukalkkidayil* 36–38)

The practice of blood sports such as bearbaitings, cockfights, wrestling, and so on that involves a heavy dose of violence and aggressive behaviour is often understood as an expression of 'hegemonic masculinity.' In fact, the dominant models of masculinity and manhood, almost universally, are linked to, configured, defined, and enacted by 'destructive' or adventurous practices such as hunting and hiking as well as the operation of 'controlling big machines' like bulldozers and earth movers (Allister 2). An alternative model to such 'hegemonic masculinities' could be found in 'ecomasculinities' which emphasises 'the potential connections between masculinities and pro-environmental behaviour' (Kreps 2). Ecomasculinism has emerged as a useful counterpoint to ecofeminism that often identifies men as the 'problem people' while conceiving women as 'closer to nature' and the nourishers of the environment. Carolyn Merchant's foundational ecofeminist text *The Death of Nature: Women, Ecology and the Scientific Revolution* (1980), for instance, alleges 'nature-destructive masculinity as a prime cause of environmental problems' (Hultman). Ecomasculinism, by contrast, approaches the man–nature relationship by asking certain valid questions like 'How do fathers pass on environmental beliefs to children?' or 'How does experience in the natural world teach men about sorrow and loss?' and 'Can we construct a manhood around ecological principles and practices?' (Allister 7).

Ecomasculinities offer a convenient framework to analyse the ecoacitivism of Kallen Pokkudan. Pokkudan enacted ecomasculinity through his mangrove afforestation and preservation efforts which were exemplary instances of non-violent and life-preserving *man*–nature engagements. Pokkudan's words that 'today, we don't love nature. If we don't love nature, we can't love our fellow human beings … We have only this one earth to hand down to our children' (Keraleeyam 223–224) perfectly spell out the quintessence of his environmentalism. They also point to a vision of earth stewardship motivated by a paternal duty of taking care of the environment for future generations. It may be recalled here that it was his paternal concern for the school-going children distressed by the wind blowing from the Ezhimala side that first prompted Pokkudan to plant the mangrove seedlings. Not long before he died in 2015, Pokkudan had endeavoured to establish a 'Mangrove School' to propagate the need for mangrove conservation among the younger generation. After his death, Pokkudan's family and a few ecoactivists are carrying on with his efforts to actualise his dream ('Kozhikode').

C. K. Janu, Leelakumariamma, Mayilamma, and Kallen Pokkudan, whose oiko-autobiographies are studied in this chapter, fall under the category of 'grassroots activists' whose socio-environmental activism is 'lived' rather than merely 'spoken' (Devika 759). They belong to the rising number of subaltern ecoactivists from Kerala who dwell on the margins of the mainstream elite discourses on environmental justice activism— like Seleena Prakkanam, the female Dalit leader of the Chengara land struggle when over seven thousand landless Dalit families occupied a part of Harrisons Malayalam Plantations in Chengara (Rammohan 15); Pallikkal Bhavani and Darli *ammomma* (grandmother), both middle-class housewives waging isolated one-woman campaigns against sand mining in Kallada and Neyyar rivers, respectively; Sri Padre, the journalist whose early articles on the Kasaragod endosulfan catastrophe first captured the international attention on the affected villages; Cheruvayal Raman, the tribal farmer from the Wayanad district of Kerala and fondly known as 'Nellachan of Wayanad' [the paddy father of Wayanad] 'who [has been] resist[ing] the influence of Green revolution' by preserving 40 indigenous paddy seeds for 50 odd years (Pandathil and Raveendran); and Parayil Rajan, a fisherman from Kannur engaged in the planting and preservation of mangrove trees.

The four oiko-autobiographies analysed in this chapter significantly give voice to 'subaltern environmentalism' which brings into attention the sub-jugation of 'human others' (women, people of colour, [and in the Indian context, Dalits and adivasis], children, and the poor) and 'earth Others' (animals, forests, the land) in globalised India (Warren 1). In contrast to the 'regular' subaltern life narratives that tend to locate the autobiographic selves within their respective *social* communities, the five subaltern oiko-autobiographies studied in this chapter further expand these 'commu-nitarian, [and] collective' selves (Thankappan 196) to accommodate the fellow 'earth Others,' thereby causing obliteration of the self/setting binary. These oiko-autobiographies also function as significant bioregional writings effectively bringing to the fore important stories of the local socio-environmental struggles happening in the remote oikic spaces of Kerala. The 'partnership ethics' model proposed by Carolyn Merchant in her 1996 book titled *Earthcare* is appropriate to make sense of the entangled state of human subjects and non-human nature in these life stories. Merchant explains the notion of partnership ethics thus:

> A partnership ethic calls for a new balance in which both humans and nonhuman nature are equal partners, neither having the upper hand, yet cooperating with each other. Both humans and nature are active agents. Both the needs of nature to continue to exist and the basic needs of human beings must be considered.
>
> (218)

The partnership ethic is anchored in interdependence and synergy between the human community and the non-human community and critiques the Baconian ethic of human control over nature. A salient feature of the partnership ethic is its gender-neutral approach to earth care. Merchant points out, 'A partnership ethic of earthcare means that both women and men can enter into mutual relationships with each other and the planet independently of gender' (*Earthcare* 217). Merchant's words resonate with Scott Slovic's observation made in his essay 'Taking Care: Toward an Ecomasculinist Literary Criticism?' about the need 'to transcend both ecofeminism and ecomasculinism and concentrate on taking care, regardless of gender, to make our presence in the world as benign as possible' (78).

The oiko-autobiographies analysed in this chapter also uphold the vision of an 'earth democracy' which, according to the Indian environmental thinker Vandana Shiva, is a unique environmental consciousness underpinned by the idea of an 'earth family' that is the essence of the Indian saying, '*vasudhaiva kudumbakam*.' Shiva asserts that earth democracy is inclusive of 'diverse species, faiths, genders and ethnicities' and that it responds to the privatisation strategies adopted by corporate global forces with slogans like 'Our world is not for sale,' 'Our water is not for sale,' and 'Our seeds and biodiversity are not for sale' (Shiva, *Earth Democracy*). She argues, 'Privatization encloses the water commons. The enclosure of each common displaces and disenfranchises people which creates scarcity for many, while generating 'growth' for the few. Displacement becomes disposability, and in its most severe form, the induced scarcity becomes a denial of the very right to live' (*Earth Democracy*). Shiva specifically mentions the 'victorious' Plachimada movement as located 'at the heart of the emerging Earth Democracy' (*Earth Democracy*). However, the three other socio-ecoactivist efforts discussed in this chapter namely, the tribal land struggles led by C. K. Janu, the anti-endosulfan movement spearheaded by Leelakumariamma—both of which are fought using non-violent means—and the conservation activism of Kallen Pokkudan can also be taken as valid expressions of the vision of earth democracy as they accord with the 10 key principles of earth democracy, especially the fourth principle which states that:

[a]ll members of the earth community, including all humans have the right to sustenance—to food, water, to a safe and clean habitat, to security of ecological space. Resources vital to sustenance must stay in the commons. The right to sustenance is a natural right because it is the right to life. These rights are not given by the state or corporations, nor can they be extinguished by state or corporate action. No state or

corporation has the right to erode or undermine these natural rights or enclose the commons that sustain life.

(Shiva, *Earth Democracy*)

Notes

1 This is not to disacknowledge the hybrid genres like the 'fictional autobiography' and 'autobiographical fiction.' For a useful discussion, see the chapter, 'Lying Contests: Fictional Autobiography and Autobiographical Fiction' in Christy Rishoi's *From Girl to Woman: American Women's Coming-of-Age Narratives* (State U of New York P, 2003).
2 *Choottachi* is the Malayalam name for the Orange Chromide (*Etroplus maculatus*) fish.
3 A *tehsildar* is a tax officer of a 'tehsil,' an administrative division.
4 For instance, Sharankumar Limbale, in his autobiography *The Outcaste* (2003), recalls his forefather thus: 'Ithal Kamble was a farm worker on a yearly contract to a landlord … He worked hard, day and night, on the fields as well as in the house of the landlord. He was one of the beasts that toiled on the farm' (Limbale qtd. in Heering 213). For enlightening discussions of this trope, see 'Dalit Writing, Dalit Speaking: On the Encounters between Dalit Autobiographies and Oral Histories' by Alexandra de Heering (*Dalit Literatures in India*, edited by Joshil K. Abraham and Judith Misrahi-Barak, Routledge, 2016, pp. 206–223) and 'Indigenous cultures and the ecology of protest: moral economy and "knowing subalternity" in Dalit and Tribal writing from India' by Pramod K. Nayar in *Journal of Postcolonial Writing*, vol. 50, no. 3, 2014, pp. 293–303).

3 Toxic Fictions

Environmental Toxicity in Three Malayalam Novels

An environmental buzzword that comes up without fail in recent conferences, workshops, and critical texts on ecocriticism is the 'Anthropocene.' The term 'Anthropocene,' which is Greek for the 'recent age of man,' was coined by the American biologist Eugene Stoermer and made popular by the Dutch chemist Paul Crutzen (Rafferty). It emphasises the myriad ways in which humans influence and alter the earth's climate and ecosystem. Although the start date of the Anthropocene era is still debated, Crutzen, in his landmark essay 'Geology of Mankind' (2002), usefully points to a possible beginning point:

> The Anthropocene could be said to have started in the latter part of the eighteenth century, when analyses of air trapped in polar ice showed the beginning of growing global concentrations of carbon dioxide and methane. This date also happens to coincide with James Watt's design of the steam engine in 1784.

The period after 1945, when the atomic bomb was first tried, the so-called atomic era, is referred to as the 'Great Acceleration,' when there was a sudden and steep rise in the use of natural resources and the release of pollutants (Zalasiewicz et al. 15). The human impact on the earth's environment is enormous, yet often 'invisible'—like the increase in the atmospheric concentration of greenhouse gases like carbon dioxide and methane, which precipitates ecological problems like global warming as well as sea level rise due to the melting of polar ice caps (Zalasiewicz et al. 14). The international treaty, the Kyoto Protocol, adopted in December 1997 by the United Nations Framework Convention on Climate Change (FCCC) and signed by 191 nation-states in addition to the European Union, was a major step forward in marshalling and standardising the global efforts to reduce greenhouse gas emissions. The Kyoto Protocol acknowledged that global warming engenders severe

DOI: 10.4324/9781003301318-3

climate-associated problems like floods and droughts as well as 'an increased risk of extinction for 20 to 30 percent of all plant and animal species' ('Kyoto Protocol') and puts the onus on the developed countries— as they are historically the major contributors—to drastically decrease their greenhouse gas emissions.[1] The surging human population and the resultant rise in consumption levels are causing tremendous environmental stress. It is estimated that about two-fifths of the earth's land has been converted into agricultural fields, which invariably involves the destruction of forest, wetlands, and so on (Rafferty; 'Converting'). The extensive use of poisonous pesticides to increase agricultural yield, discharge of toxic industrial waste into rivers and water bodies, burning of fossil fuels, dangerous radioactive leakages, and so on have produced a toxified world and the resultant anxiety of an imminent environmental apocalypse.

In his book-length critical introduction to the field *Ecocriticism* (2004), Greg Garrard discusses pollution as the first key trope in environmental texts. He traces the etymology of the word 'pollution' to the Latin term *polluere*, which means 'to defile' (8). He further explains:

[The Latin word *polluere*'s] early English usage reflects its theologico-moral origins: until the seventeenth century it denoted moral contamination of a person, or acts (such as masturbation) thought to promote such contamination. This essentially interior or subjective definition was gradually transformed into an exterior or objective—in fact, specifically environmental—definition between the seventeenth and nineteenth centuries, to the point where today only its later definition is widely known.

(8)

Pollution has prominent class, race, and caste angles as most of the hazardous toxic industries and landfills are located at places where low-income, black, and lower-caste or minority communities reside. About the uneven 'social risk positions' (Beck 23), Ulrich Beck insightfully notes, 'like wealth, risks adhere to the class pattern, only inversely; wealth accumulates at the top, risks at the bottom' (Beck 35). The stratified social distribution of environmental risks, especially in terms of race, is referred to as 'environmental racism.'[2] Beck also draws attention to the multiple international and intra-national aberrations in the distribution of pollution when he writes, 'risks produce new international inequalities, firstly between the Third World and the industrial states, secondly among the industrial states themselves' (23). The international migration of toxic wastes happens when developed nations ship their hazardous industrial waste to developing countries like India for disposal which becomes 'environmental racism on a global scale' (Lipman). Material ecocritic Serenella Iovino, therefore, rightly asserts:

Considered in its complex framework of material and discursive elements, in fact, pollution has the power to reveal abuses and inequalities. Tracing pollution through the bodies of living organisms and living land as in a litmus test, this keyword signals the stories of political failures, socio-ecological decline, and the discriminatory practices that infiltrate uneven societies.

('Pollution' 168)

In his book *The End of Nature* (1989), hailed as 'the first book on global warming written for a general audience' (Skirble), Bill McKibben argues that the human impact on the planet ecosystem has been so prominent that the concept of 'nature' has become pointless. McKibben argues that because we changed weather, we have made the entire earth artificial. He states:

A child born now will never know a natural summer, a natural autumn, winter, or spring. Summer is going extinct, replaced by something else that will be called 'summer.' This new summer will retain some of its relative characteristics—it will be hotter than the rest of the year, for instance, and the time of year when crops grow—but it will not be summer, just as even the best prosthesis is not a leg.

(60–61)

Eaarth, McKibben's 2010 work where he extends his ideas contained in *The End of Nature*, is eerily subtitled, *Making a Life on Tough New Planet*. In *Eaarth*, McKibben argues that the human impact on the earth is so devastative that our old planet-oikos has vanished and has been replaced by what he calls the 'Eaarth.' He says that if we are lucky, we may be able to retain a planet that can support some form of civilisation, but there is no way of retrieving the old earth and civilisation (27).

The surge in apocalyptic narratives like McKibben's works signals an important development in environmental writings. Lawrence Buell, in his seminal work, *Environmental Imagination* (1995), famously observes that 'Apocalypse is the single most powerful master metaphor of the contemporary environmentalism' and goes on to suggest that imagination can be drawn upon to 'anticipate and, if possible, forestall actual apocalypse' (285). A few other important works that contribute to the apocalyptic rhetoric include the neo-Malthusian work titled *The Population Bomb* (1968) by Paul Ehrlich, which predicts mass starvation and other eco-social problems as a result of exponential growth in the human population; *Earth in the Balance: Forging a New Common Purpose* (2007) by Al Gore, which puts forward the 'Global Marshall Plan' comprising five compelling strategies including 'stabilizing world population' and 'educating the world's citizens about our global environment' to tackle the environmental problems, and numerous science fiction novels like *The Road* (2006) by Cormac McCarthy and *Parable of the Sower* (1993) by Octavia E. Butler (Gaard 93).

In 1998, Lawrence Buell offered a major impetus to the study of human-induced environmental apocalypse as represented in literary works by providing the framework of 'toxic discourse' in an essay of the same title. The essay points out that toxicity has seldom been 'discussed as a discourse' and sets out to 'define the forms, origins, uses, and critical implications of toxic rhetoric' (639). A succinct definition of 'toxic discourse' can be found in Buell's *Writing for an Endangered World* (2001) in which he explains it as an 'expressed anxiety arising from perceived threat of environmental hazard due to chemical modification by human agency' (31). According to Buell, this anxiety about environmental toxification is the 'catalyst' for, as well as the 'centerpiece' of environmental justice movements waged by subaltern communities since the latter half of the twentieth century (Buell, 'Toxic Discourse' 642). Buell credits Rachel Carson's environmental classic *Silent Spring* (1962) with the launching of the contemporary toxic discourse ('Toxic Discourse' 645). Carson's influential work brought to focus the deleterious environmental effects of the use of synthetic pesticides like DDT and played a crucial role in the nation-wide banning of DDT as well as revisioning of the laws concerning air, land, and water pollution in the United States. The toxic discourse and the antitoxic agitations follow the legacy of *Silent Spring* and contribute to the 'second wave' of ecocriticism (Buell, 'Toxic Discourse' 655).

An important recent study that builds on Buell's toxic discourse is John Blair Gamber's *Positive Pollutions and Cultural Toxins* (2012). In his introduction to the book, Gamber defines 'toxicity' as 'simply "the degree to which a substance is poisonous"' (6). Drawing on the chemist William H. Baarschers, he makes the crucial point that 'zero-level contamination' and environmental purity are 'impossible ideals' since finding spaces without a trace of toxins, be it biological waste or 'persistent organic pollutants,' would be difficult. The presence of small levels of toxins, he points out, will not make these spaces inhospitable or pose threats to the life forms contained in them. Gamber also appropriately draws attention to Baarschers's criticism of the 'environmental "hysteria"' regarding the existence of chemicals 'far below the levels of observable toxicity' in the environment. One's aim should be, Baarshcers pragmatically insists, for 'realizable goals of minimized toxicity' (Gamber 6).

The disastrous consequences of the penetration of toxic pollutants into the human and ecosystemic bodies constitute the binding theme of the three Malayalam novels taken up for analysis in this chapter, namely,

Ambikasuthan Mangad's *Enmakaje*[3] (2009), Sarah Joseph's *Aathi*[4] (2011), and Balakrishnan Mangad's *Bhoomiyude Kannu* [The Eye of the Earth] (2004). I use the term 'toxic fictions' to refer to these novels to acknowledge the central theme of toxicity that connects them. While *Enmakaje* dramatises the true story of the antitoxins movement in the titular village of Enmakaje against the use of endosulfan in the cashew plantations owned by the Plantation Corporation of Kerala (PCK), *Aathi* narrates multiple levels of toxic risks ranging from poor sanitation and improper human waste disposal to garbage dumping and pesticide poisoning in the island village of Aathi and Chakkam Kandam. *Bhoomiyude Kannu*, which can be credited as the first full-fledged toxic narrative attempted in Malayalam, narrates the ecological problems like air and water pollution of an unnamed, agriculture-dependent village in north Malabar after a diesel power plant is set up there. These toxic fictions are ecoapocalyptic narratives that indict corporate greed, skewed developmental policies, and the unholy political–bureaucratic–police–corporate nexus that push ordinary people into marathon struggles to protect their lives and livelihood.

These toxic fictions invite analysis by employing a 'politicized ecocriticism,' to invoke the subtitle of the 2014 book *Ecoambiguity, Community, Development* edited by Scott Slovic et al. A powerful, yet simple definition of politicised environments is provided by Terry Tempest Williams in *Red* (2001), which makes a passionate case for the preservation of the Redrock wilderness in southern Utah: 'It is a simple equation: place + people = politics' (3). The leaders and the participants of the antitoxic agitation in these novels are from local communities who are prompted into action by their love for the land. The leaders of political parties are presented as opportunists who either pay lip service to the environmental issues or take a downright oppositional stance against the protesting communities. The three novels taken up for analysis in this chapter can be read in conversation with other important toxic/environmental justice narratives like *Ceremony* (1977) by the Laguna Pueblo writer Leslie Marmon Silko, which draws attention to the degradation of Laguna reservations due to its proximity to an abandoned uranium mine; *Heroes and Saints* (1994), a play by the Chicana writer Cherríe L. Moraga inspired by the true story of the 'United Farm Workers' grape boycott in protest against pesticide poisoning' (89) in 1988 in McFarland, California, and narrates the story from the perspective of the child-victim Cerezita Valle who only has a head but no body; *So Far From God* (1993) by Chicana novelist Ana Castillo that deals with themes like pollution, occupational health risks, and chemical poisoning; *Solar Storms* (1995) by the Native American poet and novelist Linda Hogan which depicts the fight against the hydroelectric plant and damming which pose serious threats to the river ecology; *Tropic of Orange* (1997) by Karen Yamashita which deals with the grim realities of globalisation, human-induced global warming, and climate change; and *The Heart of Redness* (2000) by Zakes Mda, which narrates the environmental justice struggle against the environmental threats posed by a tourism project in South Africa.

Living with Toxins: Endosulfan Poisoning in Ambikasuthan Mangad's *Enmakaje* (2009)

Ambikasuthan Mangad (b. 1962) is a Malayalam short story writer, novelist, and critic whose writings evince a strong environmental commitment. His debut novel *Marakkappile Theyyangal* [The Theyyams of Marakkappu] (2003) dramatises the angst of the local fishing community—especially Umbichi, the novel's heroine—of coastal villages like Marakkappu and Azhithala as they face the prospect of displacement in the aftermath of the announcement of an ecotourism project in their villages. The novel depicts an invasive ecotourism project that ignores the place attachments of the local community and draws valid parallels between the violence inflicted on a woman's body and the earth. Mangad's *Kunnukal Puzhakal* [Hills and Rivers] (2009) is arguably the first single-authored collection of 'eco-short stories' in Malayalam. The 15 remarkable short stories in this collection successfully interweave the local *Theyyam*[5] legends into the narrative and deal with a variety of themes like the drying up of rivers, dwindling of forest cover and species diversity, biopiracy, commercialisation of ecotourism, toxification of the environment, and the disappearance of traditional jobs due to technological advancements. His short story titled 'Panchuruli,' written in 2002 and included in *Kunnukal Puzhakal*, merits special attention here since it engages with the theme of the Kasaragod endosulfan pesticide disaster to which he would return in his 2009 novel *Enmakaje*. 'Panchuruli' tells a revealing story of the double oppression of the pesticide victims of Maruthadakkam 'Colony' where they get involved in commercial kidney transplantation activities to meet their livelihood and medical expenses. The story's protagonist is Ithappan who, like his father Choman, used to earn his livelihood by collecting wild honey from the forest and selling it in the local market. But, when the Panchayat begins supplying beehives free of cost, he gets himself one and stops going to the forest for honey hunting. Before long, the forests also disappear, as the government cuts down the trees and starts setting up cashew plantations. Helicopters are brought in to aerially spray the pesticide in the plantations. Ithappan's honeybees die from toxic chemical exposure and his family slips into poverty. Ithappan's two daughters—the eight-year-old Minni and Cheniyaru (whose age is not mentioned)—and his wife Linki are also toxic victims. Minni has twisted feet and suffers from unremitting chest pain and headache while Cheniyaru is paralysed. Lonappan, the local moneylender, who is the kingpin of the local kidney donation racket, suggests that donating one of Ithappan's kidneys could fetch him a handsome sum of money. Ithappan agrees as he wants to treat Cheniyaru at the town hospital and take Minni to Chennai where she might be fully cured. In the climactic scene of the story, Lonappan reappears at Ithappan's doorstep accompanied by a white man in need of a kidney donor, it is striking that all the adult residents—including Linki—of Maruthadakkam Colony have 'sold' one of their kidneys. As Mangad writes, 'As if after the end of a big war, all adults bore scars on the lower sides of their chests' (34). The story ends with a moving scene in which Ithappan prostrates for a long time in front of the *Panchuruli Thara*, the sacred floor where the Panchuruli god is worshipped, to ask for forgiveness and then slips into the white man's car carrying an unsuspecting Minni who would donate one of her kidneys. The short story 'Panchuruli' has universal resonance as it draws attention to the never-ending misery of the communities affected by the contaminated oikos and also the domino effect of victimisation of impoverished toxic casualties.

The broader eco-social canvas of the Kasaragod endosulfan pesticide disaster unfurls in Mangad's acclaimed toxic fiction *Enmakaje* (2009). The novel is anchored in a mythical framework and is punctuated by the important events in the socio-environmental justice agitation in Enmakaje and other villages in the Kasaragod district. Enmakaje and the villages like Swarga and Padre are dotted with vast swathes of cashew plantations. These cashew plantations are managed by the PCK which had been using the deadly pesticide called endosulfan for about three decades in the plantations. As suggested in 'Panchuruli,' these cashew plantations were established by clearing large expanses of biodiversity-rich forests. The setting up of these cashew plantations has had a pronounced 'ecological imperial' dimension as well. 'Ecological Imperialism' is a term wielded by Alfred W. Crosby to refer to the 'biological [and] ecological component' behind the success of European imperialism (Crosby 7). Crosby argues that European imperialism thrived largely due to the successful introduction of plants, animals, and pathogens into the settler-colonies that altered the local ecosystems. The name *Parangi Mavu* by which the cashew trees are referred to in Malayalam betrays the tree's European origin as the word *Parangi* in Malayalam denotes the Portuguese people. The discovery of the sea route from Europe to India by the Portuguese explorer Vasco da Gama (1469–1524) who reached the Kappad beach in Kozhikode, Kerala, on 20 May 1498, ushered the Portuguese colonisation of the western coast of India. In 1504, the Portuguese allied with the then-king of Cochin to defeat Zamorin the ruler of Calicut. They built a fort in Cannanore and wrested the monopoly of the spice market from the Arabs. Dom Francisco de Almeida, headquartered in Cochin, was appointed the Portuguese's first

Viceroy in the East (Sadasivan 433). The Portuguese introduced a host of plant varieties like cashew, tobacco, custard apple, guava, pineapple, and papaya to Kerala (Bhatt and Bhargava 25). The ecological harm done by the establishment of cashew plantations to the Enmakaje ecosystem gets expression in the words of the ecoactivist named Jayarajan:

> The foreignness is in the very name [of the tree]! ... [B]ut that's not what I wanted to tell you ... it's about this terrible violence that the government's inflicted—the terror that it has perpetrated. They set up these monoculture plantations, destroying pricelessly biodiverse forests. And not in a negligible area. Six hundred hectares in Enmakaje alone!
>
> (154)

The world of Enmakaje is presented as a shared space of spiritual, ecological, and material energies. According to the 115-year-old tribal chief in the novel, Panji, Enmakaje had the largest number of snake temples in Kerala. Every family in the village had one or more snake temples. The cult of snake worship is an age-old religio-cultural practice in Kerala. As Notermans et al. point out, it is believed that 'the prosperity of the family depends on the blessing of snake gods because they are associated with fertility and life-giving power' (1). The snake temples were located within sacred groves called *kaavu* that performed significant nature preservation functions. These sacred groves were biodiverse ecosystems, home to a variety of medicinal herbs, snakes, other reptiles, butterflies, and birds. Nobody trespassed into these *kaavus* nor cut trees. The pond inside the grove functioned as a water harvesting mechanism and it never ran dry. In the novel, the heritage of snake worship is traced back to the ancient Jain worldview of *ahimsa* (non-violence) and reverence for all living beings. Enmakaje had been the land of Jains who were such strict adherents of non-violence that they had their dinner by dusk and went early to bed to avoid lighting lamps and thereby to prevent the death of moths (134).

The protagonists of the novel are Neelakantan and Devayani who lead socially withdrawn, monkish lives in a house atop the Jadadhari Hill. Although the duo lives under the same roof, they are not bound by marriage. Devayani is a former prostitute whom Neelakantan rescues. Their migration from the state capital Thiruvananthapuram to Enmakaje is, to borrow Michael R. Edelstein's expression, 'an escape from the city to a rural idyll' (qtd. in Buell, 'Toxic Discourse' 648). Drawing on Michel Foucault, Lakshmi Chithra Dilipkumar and Swarnalatha Rangarajan call the lush green world of Jadadhari Hill in the novel an 'ecological heterotopia.' They note:

[T]he fantasy of living in a state of pristine nature, whose contact enables disease-free living and able bodies, is negotiated through the complex idea of a heterotopia in the novel. A heterotopia, according to Foucault, is a 'placeless place,' something like a counter-site, 'an effectively enacted Utopia' in which all real sites contained in the culture can be found (Foucault 1986, 24). Mangad's novel posits an ecological heterotopia—the myth-laden Jadadhari Hill and the mysterious Speaking Cave in the jungles near Swarga where the central characters of the novel, Neelakantan and Devayani, take refuge after rejecting the corruptions of civilisation.

In the earlier chapters of the novel, Neelakantan and Devayani are referred to as simply *Purushan* [Man] and *Sthree* [Woman], respectively, suggesting a complete renunciation of their social identities, including their names. Neelakantan, who is usually clad in a piece of loincloth, feels irked even at being identified as a human since, in his opinion, 'Man is the most evil of animals' (46). When addressed as 'human' by a 'talking cave' located on the Jadadhari Hill, Neelakantan quips: 'I am not a human. Please don't call me that. I am an animal living in the forest. I have severed all ties with humankind' (24). Neelakantan's espousal of an animal identity is redolent of the repeated assertion 'I'm not a human being' by Animal, the 19-year-old protagonist of Indra Sinha's novel *Animal's People* (2007) which is based on the Bhopal gas tragedy.

Neelakantan has taken a vow that he will not talk to any human being other than Devayani. They feed on fruits and tubers grown in the forest. On rare occasions, they prepare some gruel. Once or twice a month, Devayani goes to the Swarga market and sells the bamboo baskets that they weave and use the money to meet the very few expenses they have. They are catapulted into a socio-environmental justice movement when they trace the death of Pareekshit, their seven-year-old foster son, to endosulfan exposure. Pareekshit's parents, who were also endosulfan victims, had committed suicide. It was Devayani who first brought Pareekshit to their house. When she first saw the boy, his body was covered with bleeding blisters. Although he looked like a year-old baby, his hair had already turned grey like that of an old man. He was also unable to speak or cry. When she brought the baby home, Neelakantan was angry at such an unwanted intrusion into his private life and even walked out of the house. However, he gradually took a liking to the child and consulted the tribal healer Panji for the child's ailments. Not knowing the boy's real name, Neelakantan named him 'Pareekshit' after the Hindu mythological character. In the *Mahabharata*, Ashwatthama targeted the deadly arrow Brahmastra at Pareekshit, the son of Abhimanyu and Uttara, during the final Kurukshetra War. Pareekshit was stillborn, but Krishna brought him to life. Krishna cursed Ashwatthama that he would suffer a skin condition with open sores and blisters for three thousand years. Narrating the legend of Pareekshit to his fellow ecoactivist Jayarajan, Neelakantan asks:

> Ashwatthama was cursed with a hellish life because he had committed an unspeakable sin. But this child who suffers like him, with sores all over, oozing pus, what sin did he commit to suffer this living death? Who is sending Brahmastras against so many children in Enmakaje?
>
> (149)

The act of naming the sick child 'Pareekshit' serves a symbolic function in the novel. It establishes an allegorical connection between contemporary health tragedies like the congenital abnormalities in the endosulfan-affected villages and the foeticide carried out by a lethal war weapon in the age-old mythological tale.

The extent of the environmental and health hazards posed by endosulfan use dawns on Neelakantan when Panji takes him on, what turns out to be, a 'toxic tour' of the neighbourhood comprising about 27 houses that have at least one suffering poison victim each. 'Toxic tour' is a term used by Phaedra C. Pezzullo in her 2007 book *Toxic Tourism*, wherein she defines the term as 'non-commercial expeditions into areas that are polluted by toxins' (5). Explaining the concept, she notes, 'More and more of these [affected] communities have begun to invite outsiders in, providing tours as a means of educating people about and, it is hoped, transforming their situation' (5). Neelakantan's toxic tour of the neighbourhood offers night-marish images of the ailing victims who teem these 'human sacrifice zones' (Pezzullo 5): like Shivappa Naik's teenage daughter Bhagyalakshmi whose abnormally long, protruding tongue makes it impossible for her to close her mouth; Narayana Shetty's bed-ridden daughter who has small legs and a head bigger than her torso; a calf with only three legs; the men-tally ill siblings who are kept shackled on the floor. A few other disabled people who appear in the novel are Abhilash, the monkey-shaped, men-tally challenged boy; the blind, 26-year-old Anwar whose long fingers and toes lie stretched out like an octopus's arms; Sukumaran, the headmaster of Vani Nagar school, who has a swollen belly and always pleads with others, 'pleas' will you kill me?'; the five-year-old Anju whose urinary bladder protrudes from her body. According to Dr Arunkumar, the neigh-bourhood adjacent to his clinic is a cancer cluster and has no less than 50 mentally ill patients. The toxic tour offered by Panji induces severe trauma in Neelakantan. At one point, he forbids Panji from visiting any more houses and returns home. Afterwards, Neelakantan loses sleep at night. His trauma is reflected in his description of the sick children he met on his toxic tour as 'neither animal nor human' (59). Later on in the novel, he likens his visit to a free medical camp organised by the Endosulfan Spray Protest Action Committee (ESPAC) for endosulfan victims to a 'walk amidst extraterrestrial beings' (104). The sense of bewilderment conveyed by Neelakantan's words at witnessing the teeming presence of the 'corporeal grotesque' (Nayar, *English* 57) invokes a kind of 'ecogothicism.' Ecogothicism is concerned with themes like monstrosity, 'social and environmental otherness,' and the fluid boundaries between human and non-human bodies. Explaining the concept, David Del Principe notes that an ecogothic approach adopts 'a nonanthropocentric position to reconsider the role that the environment, species, and nonhumans play in the construction of monstrosity and fear.' Enmakaje markedly exhibits ecogothic traits such as having a 'natural environment ... [that is] eerily ambient and [that] arouse[s] our anxieties,' especially in the narration of an episode when Neelakantan gets lost in an areca orchard that is devoid of all animal life:

> Suddenly something struck him. In this vast expanse, he could not sense the presence of a single living creature. Not even a lizard or a chameleon or a frog or snake or mongoose ...
>
> Neelakantan broke into a cold sweat, feeling as if he were stranded in the middle of a huge graveyard ... [T]he thought that not even a cockroach was to be seen was truly scary ...
>
> What a fatal silence, this!
>
> (122–123)

The intense experience of the loneliness felt by Neelakantan resonates with the idea of 'Eremozoic Era,' the Age of Loneliness, proposed by Edward O. Wilson to refer to the next geological era, characterised by an absence of biodiversity (E. O. Wilson 321). The excerpt significantly presents a postapocalyptic world and conveys anxiety at the severance of the chain of human–non-human coexistence that sustains life on this planet. 'Existence,' as eminent ecocritic Timothy Morton sagely reminds us, 'is coexistence. No man is an island' (*The Ecological Thought* 4). The image of pastoral disruption that *Enmakaje* accentuates evokes the ecoapocalyptic parable narrated in the opening chapter of Rachel Carson's *Silent Spring* (1962). Carson's famous 'A Fable for Tomorrow' is about an American pastoral town affected by an environmental blight caused by the mindless use of pesticides. 'There was a strange stillness,' writes Carson, 'The birds, for example—where had they gone? Many people spoke of them, puzzled and disturbed. The few birds seen anywhere were moribund; they trembled and could not fly. It was a spring without voices' (2). The chickens, cattle, sheep, pigs, fishes, and people died after having been affected by 'mysterious maladies.' Apple trees once laden with fruit now bore none; even streams appeared lifeless. Carson explains that 'No witchcraft, no enemy action had silenced the rebirth of new life in this stricken world. The people had done it themselves' (3). Rachel Carson's visionary text which, arguably, sounded the first note of caution about the toxification of the planet, continues to offer inspiration to numerous antitoxic battles waged across the world. The 'toxic injuries' that swarm the narrative of *Enmakaje* constantly remind us that, to borrow Alaimo's phrase, ' "nature" is always as close as one's own skin—perhaps even closer' (Alaimo 2).

The 'weirdly weird' consequences (Morton, *Dark Ecology* 7) of the pesticide use in Enmakaje point to the transformation of the village into a 'riskscape' (Cutter qtd. in Deitering 200). The river that flows down Jadadhari Hill was once home to a large number of fishes and frogs. The water of the river, like that of the river Ganges, was revered for its medicinal qualities. In the past, Panji's father, who was also a tribal healer, used to suggest taking a dip in the river for three consecutive days as a cure for eczema. However, since the river is now devoid of any fish or frogs, Panji says he no longer recommends the river water for drinking or bathing (70). *Enmakaje*, in this way, calls attention to questions pertaining to both human and animal rights as the toxic contamination has jeopardised the lives of human and non-human communities similarly.

The contestation of the chemical cause of the illnesses is one of the major challenges faced by the ecojustice activists featured in the novel seeking remediation measures. Lawrence Buell has noted that toxic discourse is 'a discourse of allegation' as '[d]uring two decades of ecopopulism, "almost every claim that a risk is present, almost every attribution of cause, [has been] vigorously contested" ' (659–660). The state agricultural minister in the novel whom the socio-ecoactivists meet also attempts to dismiss the allegations by saying, 'Endosulfan is not poison, it is medicine! If you are ill, go the doctor' (126). Jayarajan alleges that the Achutan Committee appointed by the Government of Kerala was composed mostly of officers of the agricultural department that promoted the use of pesticides. Addressing a gathering, he says:

> Dear friends, do you know what happened when this Achutan Committee held a hearing at the Kasaragod Collectorate? The department of agriculture brought in some two hundred workers from the PCK in its vehicles, bought them all arrack and biriyani, and made them lie before the committee. Didn't they get them to falsely testify that they had no diseases from handling endosulfan all these years? … And how many commissions have come here, since the first!

(173)

Jayarajan also asserts that the Dubey Committee appointed by the central government has given a clean chit to the use of endosulfan after manipulating the test results published by the Frederick Institute of Plant Protection and Toxicology, Chennai. According to Jayarajan, the original test results clearly indicated that there were dangerous levels of toxin content in all the collected samples. Phil Brown uses the term 'contested illnesses' to describe the scenarios where the link between illnesses and environmental exposures becomes a topic of dispute. John Blair Gamber notes how 'the cards are stacked in many ways against the victims of toxification—both by sluggishness of scientific proof and the economic and political structures that favor business interests over bodily health (especially of the communities frequently targeted for toxic exposure)' (7). The novel, therefore, attempts to raise 'toxic consciousness' (Deitering) not only by narrating the victims' experiences but also by presenting a welter of scientific information and lab test results pertaining to the toxic impact of endosulfan.[6] Jayarajan contends that repeated application of the same pesticide for more than three years in the same location is against the regulations and points out that the pests, by now, may have become endosulfan tolerant. He also cites studies that have proved that endosulfan is harmful to the crops themselves as the tree roots curl up when they come in contact with endosulfan and lose their ability to absorb fertilisers.

Enmakaje efficiently brings into focus the nefarious network involving the corporate, political, and police forces that tries to crush protests with brute force, intimidation, and intrigue. Neelakantan and Devayani are threatened multiple times by the *goondas* (thugs) of the 'pesticide lobby,' who break into their house on Jadadhari Hill. On one occasion, they come with an influential political leader who had previously promised the ecoactivists that he would work towards imposing a ban on endosulfan. He verbally abuses Neelakantan and Devayani and says in a threatening tone, 'These are my night clothes. You've seen me only in the white clothes I wear during the day … You're only going to see my real form …' (195). The leader then accuses Neelakantan of being an 'extremist' and asks his *goondas* to tie Neelakantan and Devayani to a tree and sets their house on fire (196). Before returning along with his gang, the leader warns Neelakantan and Devayani to leave Enmakaje forever as soon as his people come back in the morning and untie them. The next day, however, Neelakantan, Devayani, and Jayarajan are arrested by the police on false charges ranging from clandestine prostitution in their house to a fake currency racket conducted under the facade of environmental activism. The same politician appears at the police station and gets them released, thereby making plain the unholy alliance between him and the police. However, they are freed only after eliciting a confession from Jayarajan that they were mistaken about endosulfan and that they would leave Enmakaje for good. The novel's concluding scenes are remarkable for their allusion to the biblical story of Noah's Ark when Neelakantan and Devayani enter the 'talking cave' on Jadadhari Hill and find that all kinds of animals, reptiles, and birds have taken refuge in it 'till the [toxic] rain ends' in Enmakaje (245). The scene rightly emphasises a kind of biotic egalitarianism that appreciates the intrinsic value of every living being and their right to life on this planet.

Enmakaje skilfully draws attention to the 'corrosive communities' (Freudenburg via Picou et al.) that suffer undue psychological stress due to protracted bureaucratic processes and court deliberations while living in the scarred landscapes of Kasaragod.[7] In 2010, K. G. Balakrishnan, the chairman of the National Human Rights Commission, compared the Kasaragod endosulfan tragedy to the infamous 1984 Bhopal gas tragedy in which fifteen thousand people died after the noxious gas methyl isocyanate leaked from the Union Carbide factory that produced the pesticide Sevin (Caton and Lopez). Appropriately enough, it is asserted in *Enmakaje* that the antitoxic struggle represented in the novel is not just against the use of endosulfan, but, 'against all pesticides that lead to the earth's desertification' (177). Mangad's toxic fiction, being a genre-popularising work,[8] is a remarkable achievement for both the writer and Malayalam literature and has lent significant impetus to the anti-endosulfan campaign in Kerala.

Putrefied Waterscapes: Sarah Joseph's *Aathi* (2011) and the Disruption of a Pastoral World

Sarah Joseph (b. 1946), the critically acclaimed Malayalam writer, feminist, and environmental activist, has to her credit seven novels, five novellas, eight short story collections, and two essay collections. Her literary works give focus to the lives of the marginalised subalterns, especially women, and deal with a host of themes as diverse as female sexuality, the patriarchal oppression of women, spirituality, and environmental concerns. Some of her notable short stories and her 2009 novel *Ooru Kaval*[9] are based on the *Ramayana* and they attempt to give voice to some of the marginal characters in the epic. Joseph's debut novel *Alahayude Penmakkal* [Daughters of Alaha] (1999), which is the first instalment of the trilogy along with *Mattathi* [Bride] (2003) and *Othappu* (2005),[10] is arguably her masterpiece which fetched her multiple awards including the prestigious Sahitya Akademi and Kerala Sahitya Akademi awards. *Aathi* (2011) is her fifth novel which was published simultaneously with its English translation by Rev. Valson Thampu titled *Gift in Green*.

'Aathi' is the name of a fictional island village inhabited by the fishing and agriculture-dependent Dalit communities which, as the novel's title suggests, occupies a protagonist-like presence in the novel. Joseph describes the topography of Aathi thus:

> An island dotted with waterbodies, marshland and slush. Surrounded by backwaters, it lay secluded from the rest of the world. The [mangrove] forest on the island stood nearly submerged in water. It sloped from the east to west. During high tide, salt water rose and climbed on Aathi.
>
> (43)

The first-generation settlers of Aathi were Dalits who had fled their homes after being subjected to unbearable casteist oppression and violence. Aathi welcomed them with open hands: 'The trees here knew no taboo or untouchability. The birds parroted no religious bigotry. The trees, the birds, the fish, the earth, the water—all beckoned them: "come, come ..."' (44). This history of Aathi's early human occupants is handed down by all mothers to their children in Aathi.

Although the island is surrounded by brackish water, the water *on* the island is potable and not salty. 'Aathi' is, in fact, the corrupted form of the word *aadhi* which means 'the beginning.' Since the settlers had to literally start their lives afresh there, the land also came to be known as 'Aathi' (45). The first settlers were not traditionally fishermen, but they took to fishing to keep hunger at bay. Since the mangrove forests were the natural habitats of diverse fishes, the settlers could catch fish with their bare hands, 'like you might gather pebbles from the river bed' (45).

Kaaliappan, one of the elderly men, took it upon himself to go around to various places in search of rice that grew in salt water. One day, he returned with a handful of *Pokkali* seeds.

Pokkali is a unique variety of salt-tolerant and flood-resistant rice organically cultivated in water-logged fields. This integrated farming system benefits from the symbiotic relationship between prawns and rice where the rice residues provide food for prawns, and prawn excrements serve as fertilisers for the paddy seedlings (R. Vijayan 329–331). Kaaliappan sagely cautions the islanders that *Pokkali* cultivation demands synergism from Aathi's people since '[t]o grow rice in salt water, you must work together and help each other. You should be united just and fair. No one shall cheat anyone. If anyone does, the water will surely cheat him and everyone else as well' (46).

Aathi is presented as the quintessential pastoral idyll, a land of pristine purity and beauty which, to borrow Lawrence Buell's words, '[is] a nurturing space of clean air, clean water, and pleasant uncluttered surroundings' ('Toxic Discourse' 648). However, as Joseph rightly asserts in her afterword to *Gift in Green*, Aathi is neither a Utopia nor an escapist world of make-believe. Even today you can find Aathi-like places of primeval purity. Like the last of the trees, like the last of the residual streams, a few minds, a few slivers of the earth's surface, still hold their own.

('The Making of *Aathi*')

The images of garbage, toxin, disease, and pollution permeate the narrative space of *Aathi* only after the appearance of Kumaran, a multimillionaire and a capitalist landlord, who returns to Aathi after an absence of 36 long years. He brings with him the 'behemoth' of development and a vision to 'transform Aathi into a paradise' (41). Upon his return, Kumaran, who had despised Aathi's land and the 'water-life' of its people and was the first person in Aathi to sell his land, expresses his shock at finding 'the same drabness, the same destitution, and even the same dullness on every face [in Aathi]!' (40). The magician, who is a part of the retinue that accompanied Kumaran, shows the people 'Kumaran's dream' of Aathi through a magical performance. As the children, youth, and the elderly look on,

everything … vanished: the bank, the ferry boats, the water, the paddy fields, the canal, the pond, the wells, the palm groves and the mangroves. In the next moment, a new world appeared: huge buildings, broad roads, hotels, cinema halls, parks and glittering shopping malls. Light … noise … teeming multitudes.

(42)

In stark contrast to Kumaran's dream of Aathi is Dinakaran's dream. Dinakaran is one of the leaders of Aathi's resistance struggle. His dream is modest and one shared by most of Aathi's people:

of living in peace; farming the land, catching the fish and picking oysters, even if it was on marshland, forest and water that no one else wanted to have anything to do with, and no matter how alluring the world beyond.

(199–200)

Aathi is essentially the story of these two conflicting 'dreams.' Regrettably, it is Kumaran's dream which materialises at the end while Dinakaran's dream is shattered together with the tragic collapse of Aathi.

As the first step to actualise his 'dream,' Kumaran builds a bridge to Aathi. The bridge is built not for the benefit of the people as 'it takes more time to go around and reach the bridge than it does to take the ferry to town!' (138). It is built so that 'trucks, JCBs, drillers and tipper lorries could transport massive quantities of earth, stones, bricks, sand, cement and steel' to landfill the four hundred acres of backwaters included in the property that Kumaran has bought. The construction of the bridge ignores the fragile ecology of Aathi and disrupts the breeding sites of the fishes like prawns and *karimeen*. The farmer Thankechi points out, 'The little mangrove trees have started dying from their roots up. The prawns and karimeen have gone elsewhere, looking for safe places to breed' (142). However, even the last-ditch attempt to blast the bridge by the likes of Ponmani, Kunjoottan, Ramesh, and Shailaja—the extremists among the protesters in Aathi, as opposed to the followers of Dinakaran who believe in non-violent resistance—is foiled and the bridge is completed.

Multiple problems arise as Kumaran begins levelling the wetlands. Topographically, Aathi has a westward slope and hence, when Kumaran builds a granite embankment and begins to fill it with earth, the courtyards of those living in the low-lying places get waterlogged. The people face the threat of displacement as proceeding with the landfilling is sure to submerge the whole of Aathi. This is part of Kumaran's plan to evict the people of Aathi. The rising water gets mixed with the sewage canals and the 'black gluey water' creeps up the kitchen door of Shailaja's house located along the canal. The graphic descriptions of the putrefied waterscapes appearing in multiple chapters of the novel aptly convey the extent of 'ecosickness' (Houser) of Aathi:

An island of bloated, fetid flesh floated on it, spreading an unbearable stench. A green column of horseflies buzzed, encircling it in a perpetual drone. 'What rotting corpse is this?' mother screamed, stopping her nose. The water was stagnant. It had nowhere to go. There began a procession of the dead, the decomposing, the fly-catchers and the disease-breeding arriving one after the other. Having no egress, whatever came, stagnated and accumulated. It became impossible to open the kitchen door ... Plastic carry bags lay scattered like bloated fetuses. Over them, flies and mosquitoes droned with vengeance.

(206–207)

Her kitchen now opened into the jaws of degradation. Worms wiggled in her drinking water. The drawing bucket of her well lay rusted, its coir rope eaten by termites. Her meals were feasts for flies. Rats that came swimming, no crawling, on the thick, gluey water had colonized her bedroom. The doves had departed from her roof.

(229–230)

Contact with the grimy, stagnant water results in skin irritation and itching. Shailaja refuses food as she is 'too nauseated to swallow even [her] own saliva' and spends her day sitting on a box, refusing any contact with the floor (207).

The dichotomised realms of toxic and non-toxic environments punctuate Shailaja's life story, far more than anyone else's in Aathi. For a brief period, she works as a nurse at a hospital in the neighbouring town. At the hospital, after every delivery, Shailaja has to take the medical waste like 'placenta, severed umbilical cords, sanitary napkins, blood-soaked rags and cotton packs' (72) and flush it down the toilet. Shailaja wants to know where all the hospital waste goes. Hence, she scales the hospital's boundary wall and takes a look at the 'lake of death behind it.' She discovers that 'Placentas [are] putrefying in the water. They [are] not buried in the earth. Nor [do] they decompose to become manure for trees' (74). Shailaja also finds out that there are 'severed limbs, swabs oozing with pus, blood clots, decomposed phlegm, chemical agents, plastic bottles and bags, garbage' in the lake (75). Realising the disaster in waiting, she exclaims, 'I am doomed to live the rest of my life polluted and polluting' (75–76).

Her words take on added resonance given the fact that her married life has been marred by the toxified environment of Chakkam Kandam, the native place of her husband Chandramohan. Sewage from the numerous lodges, hotels, and wedding halls situated around the Guruvayoor Sri Krishna Temple, a famous Hindu pilgrimage centre in Kerala, is routed to the backwaters of Chakkam Kandam. According to Dana Phillips, the 'excremental ecocritic,' shit is 'a major pollutant in many locations around the globe' (178). He points out, 'Note that when I assert that ... human shit [is] *toxic*, I speak literally: [it] contains heavy metals and pharmaceuticals along with the usual array of pathogens' (181; emphasis in the original). Philips reminds us of the need to treat shit as 'a material object and vital substance' rather than 'as image, as metaphor and symbol' or '(merely) as a trope' as is employed by many fiction writers like Thomas Pynchon whose work Philip's essay pays special attention to (174–177). Drawing on Sartre and Lacan, ecocritic Timothy Morton usefully notes, 'The problem of human beingness ... is the problem of what to do with one's slime (one's shit). Ecological politics is bound up with what to do with pollution, miasma, slime: things that glisten, schlup, and decay' (*The Ecological Thought* 159).

The contamination of Chakkam Kandam depicted in the novel is based on true incidents. The novel liberally cites from the report of the Pollution Control Board to bring to light the literal 'toiletization' (Amis qtd. in Deitering 196) of the village:

The septic tank facilities in at least 90 percent of the hotels in Guruvayoor are insufficient and substandard. The actual number of people using them exceeds the norm by three to four times. It should surprise no one, then, that these septic tanks collapse. The excrement, as a result, flows through the drains and falls into Valiathodu or the big canal. This canal, which runs for another two kilometres through Guruvayoor Municipality and, thereafter, for another two kilometres through Thykkadu Panchayat, finally reaches Chakkam Kandam Kayal. All along the four-kilometre route, people live chock-a-block on the banks. Their suffering is hard to describe.

(94–95)

Shailaja realises the extent of the ecodegradation of Chakkam Kandam on her very first day of life there:

The wells, the ponds the channels, the streams and the backwaters, which spread like an ocean in front of the house, were all covered with layer upon layer of shit. 'The wind blows the stink right into our houses. We have to burn sandalwood sticks day and night to ward off the foul smell.'

(80)

Shailaja, who comes from the land of clean water and an unspoiled environment, cannot even dream of spending the rest of her life in Chakkam Kandam. 'I don't want to get used to this,' she tells the women in the neighbourhood who have come to offer her words of advice (82). Chandramohan is not ready to accept Shailaja's suggestion that they could go away and settle down in Aathi. Thus, on the fifth day after their wedding, Shailaja is back in Aathi. However, before leaving, Shailaja gives him the word that she will return 'when the waters of Chakkam Kandam clear' (85). Chandramohan, however, is not optimistic that Chakkam Kandam's waters will ever be clean again. The novel skilfully points to the 'sense of entrapment' (Buell, 'Toxic Discourse' 648) felt by the inhabitants of Chakkam Kandam and also demonstrates how the fouled oikos of Chakkam Kandam has stigmatised its people:

As a rule, people had ceased to marry their daughters to the men of Chakkam Kandam. If, by mistake, a girl was married into that lagoon of shit, she was sure to go back to her home in quick time, fleeing the horrible stench. No bride could endure Chakkam Kandam.

(81–82)

People also cannot sell their houses and leave as no one is ready to buy the land. The stigmatised toxic victims of Chakkam Kandam have, thus, become 'negatively different' (Edelstein and Wandersman 76) to the outsiders.

The degradation of the backwaters into a repulsive, foul-smelling, and disease-causing sewer calls attention to epidemiological dimensions of human excreta and raises important questions concerning the irresponsible methods of waste disposal and its larger environmental health impacts. Additionally, it also brings into focus the livelihood issues of the local fishing communities. As Chandramohan points out to a journalist named G. Nirmala:

> Water is our only source of livelihood. If we have survived, it is because of Chakkam Kandam Kayal. She used to breed as much fish as we ever needed ... In ten minutes, we could gather enough prawns with our bare hands to meet our needs Today everyone hesitates even to touch what slimes in place of that water. It is doubtful if there are any fish. Even if there are, who will eat them?
>
> (95)

Chandramohan, a retired headmaster named Parinju Chakramakkal, and the ecoactivist Dr Johnson come together and submit a petition regarding the environmental ruination of Chakkam Kandam to the District Collector. The test results collected by Dr Johnson regarding the potability of water in the wells and ponds in Guruvayoor unanimously conclude that the water is unsafe for drinking purposes. According to a medical officer's report that Chakrammakkal produces, 'the current level of coliform bacteria [in and around Guruvayoor] exceeded the permissible limit in India twofold (11,0001 per 100 ml)' (96). It also points out that an outbreak of cholera has been reported in Maruthayoor, which is a 'low-lying area where all the muck from here [i.e., Chakkam Kandam] flows and accumulates' (96). In the 2008 book *The Big Necessity*, a revealing study of the sociopolitical and environmental problems of poor sanitation and the disposal of bodily waste, the British journalist–author Rose George notes that:

> Diarrhoea—nearly 90 percent of which is caused by fecally contaminated food or water— kills a child every fifteen seconds. The number of children who have died from diarrhoea in the last decade exceeds the total number of people killed by armed conflict since the Second World War Larger than AIDS, or TB, or malaria. 2.2 million people—mostly children—die from an affliction that to most Westerners is the result of bad take-out food.
>
> (12)

She goes on to assert that '[p]ublic health professionals talk about water-related diseases, but that is a euphemism for the truth. These are shit-related diseases' (12). These diseases also drive home the point that human excreta not only has 'agency, but it also hosts a myriad agents, along with traces of our own DNA' (Phillips 180).

In Aathi, the toxic presence of Kumaran and his allies precipitates several ecocidal activities like setting fire to the 'Green Bangle,' the mangrove forest which encircles the island and is regarded as 'the pride of Aathi' (211). The Green Bangle is the rare ecological niche of green crabs, butterflies, grasshoppers, and snakes—all green in colour—that it houses. One evening, Kumaran, along with Ambu and Prakashan, sets fire to the Green Bangle and chares to death the green crabs and other insects. He then arranges to landfill the place that same night. However, when the trucks, tippers, and JCBs carrying the earth cross the bridge, a group of people led by Dinakaran and Ponmani block the way. The conflict between the two groups makes apparent the place attachment of the protestors and the indifference and profit-mindedness of Kumaran and his allies. Dinakaran cautions that burning the forest and landfilling the marsh will ultimately wipe out the population of Aathi. He also compares desecrating Aathi to betraying one's mother. In response, Kumaran suggests that Aathi's people should do away with agriculture and asks, '[W]ho says everyone should farm? It is enough if farming happens somewhere in the world' (216).

Before long, the police arrive on the scene and unleash violence on the protestors. However, they are forced to stop and withdraw when Shailaja threatens self-immolation. The lawyer Grace Chali brings in the media people who report the environmental injustice happening in Aathi. Subsequently, many ecoactivists visit Aathi and express their support for the resistance movement in Aathi. Addressing a gathering, Grace Chali explains that Kumaran's proposed plan to build an industrial township is a 'massive swindle' (224) and that his real plan is to acquire the backwaters, paddy fields, and mangrove forests at a low price and to get them landfilled. It would then be resold at exorbitant prices that will fetch him a hefty profit.

The increase in the comings and goings of the ecologically insensitive outsiders in Aathi exacerbates the degradation of the island and its waters as people leave behind 'cigarette packets, liquor bottles, leftover food, polythene bags, cola bottles, matchboxes, rotten fruits, [and] an assortment of decaying garbage' (97). A mysterious girl who first appears in the 15th chapter of the novel performs the much-needed recuperative action for the diseased ecosystem of Aathi. She scrupulously engages in removing the trash accumulated in the pathways and among the mangrove roots. The ethics of care she demonstrates offers sufficient possibilities of appreciation when looked at through the lens of ecofeminism and 'restoration ecocriticism' (Özdağ 121). It is Noor Muhammad, the storyteller who comes to Aathi, who first spots her filling her small boat with garbage. He becomes attracted to her and her work and befriends her. He finds out that the girl, who is unnamed throughout the novel, dumps the collected garbage into a deep pit on an uninhabited island adjacent to the Green Bangle. Noor Muhammad also happily notices 'new sprouts and fresh blades of grass [have] sprung up' in the places she has cleaned (98). On his last day of stay in Aathi, Noor Muhammad teams up with a group of children from Aathi to make another modest effort to dispose of the waste drained out from the city that has gathered around the concrete pillars under Kumaran's bridge. The waste, as Joseph describes, consists of 'vast quantities of stinking, decaying stuff dumped into the water from the hospital and the market: the remains of fish, fowl and animals' (259). Although when they started out, 'the children held their noses' (259) to ward off the stench, after a few hours of hard work, 'it became possible for them to look at the water without feeling nauseated' (260).

Aathi employs 'an ugly aesthetic' and 'the affect of disgust' (Houser 124) to drive home the dramatic ecological transformation of Aathi from unsullied wilderness and waters to an awful deathscape teeming with the toxic chemical, plastic, and excremental wastes and sick bodies. Heather Houser points out 'disgust's transformative role in the canon of environmental emotions' and contends, while offering a comparison between Richard Powers' award-winning novel *The Echo Maker* (2006) and David Foster Wallace's dystopian novel *The Infinite Jest* (1996), that 'Unlike the traditionally positive emotion of wonder that … creates problems of care through complex connectivity, the unpleasant emotion of disgust [can] paradoxically promote[] connection and ethical concern' (124). An important instance where *Aathi* uses 'disgust in the service of an environmental message' (Houser 122) is while describing Kumaran's new tactic of landfilling Aathi's streams. Kumaran dumps the hazardous city waste that he has bought 'on outlandishly generous terms' from the city corporation into the streams (263). Since Aathi's children reached school by walking along these streams, they were the first to witness the arrival of 'ten or fifteen' tipper lorries laden with the city's six-month waste for tipping. Reinvoking the poignant image of 'toiletization' of the oikos, the novel describes the children comparing the relentless deposition of garbage by the trucks to the act of defecation. By the evening, it has turned into a 'mountain of waste' where crows, cats, dogs, mice, bandicoots, flies, and mosquitoes forage into and vultures hovering over, 'keenly interested in this new site of death' (270). The novel significantly provides a quasi-magical realist description of the terrified children who are literally hunted down by the deadly microbes spewed out by the toxic dump that brings to the fore what Heather Sullivan calls 'the dark side of vibrant, transcorporeal exchanges in the bacterial mesh' ('Dirt Theory' 529).

Soon, Aathi confronts a medical crisis as a large number of children fall ill with typhoid—'the first epidemic in [Aathi's] history' (271). Aathi's children who have never fallen ill before begin to 'snivel and cry, rub their eyes and scratch their noses' (271). They contract fever and diarrhoea and collapse and die before they could even be carried to the hospital. The death toll reaches 19 as rumours abound that the dumping of toxic waste from the city is the cause of the killer disease. An angry mob takes to the streets and '[f]or once in his life Kumaran saw for himself what "the people" meant' (272). He finally quells the agitations by awarding compensation to the families of the victims. *Aathi* exhibits features of what Priscilla Wald terms an 'outbreak narrative' that chronicles 'epidemiological stories' where '[m]icrobes, spaces, and interactions blend together[,] animat[ing] the landscape and motivat[ing] the plot' (Wald 2). The outbreak narratives like *Aathi* offer grim reminders of the agentic powers of the 'lesser life forms' and also bring into focus 'the porosity of biosphere and semiosphere, [and] the trajectories of toxins and discourses across living bodies' (Iovino and Oppermann 5).

Another instance of environmental abuse in *Aathi* occurs when Komban Joy, who has taken Kunjimathu's paddy field on contract for prawn farming, mixes deadly pesticides in her fields. Joy was roped in by Kumaran as part of a ploy to eventually wrest the paddy fields from Kunjimathu. The five acres of *Pokkali* field owned by Kunjimathu was the only obstacle for Kumaran to start his construction work in the stretch of land that includes the government land and Ganesha Subramaniyam's land. Joy uses DDT on the first day of the month of Thulam (October–November in the Gregorian calendar) to 'eradicate' the prawn field. The aftermath of the DDT use involved the death of yellow butterflies which is evocatively described by Joseph:

> That was the day the yellow butterflies perished in their thousands. On the ridges of the paddy fields, in courtyards, and in front of Thampuran's shrine, they fell dead and lay like withered laburnum flowers. It was the children who noticed them first, and it saddened them greatly. Sitting by the dead butterflies, they stroked with their index fingers the delicate wings of the tiny yellow creatures that had always eluded their hands. They tried to revive them by blowing on them. Then they dug little pits and buried them. They were unaware at that time of the tragedy that had befallen the green frogs that were their pets. Dead, they lay in Kunjimathu's Pokkali paddy field, their white underbellies exposed like mute metaphors of helplessness.
>
> (177–178)

Additionally, two days before ending his contract, Joy mixes endosulfan in Kunjimathu's fields 'in order to grab the whole of the fish harvest.' The whole of Aathi is shocked to hear about this 'infernal treachery' (167).

A boy named Baaji, who first notices the tragedy, initially assumes that there are some hunters around the place as he saw numerous dead water birds lying around. When Markose cautions the people that 'it [is] fatal to eat fish exposed to endosulfan' Baaji wonders, 'If so, of what use was the fish that Komban Joy had caught using this deadly thing?... . All of Kunjimathu's five-acre Pokkali paddy field lay poisoned to death. How could it be farmed ever again?' (169–170). When beaten up by the people, Joy reveals his unholy connections with Kumaran as well as the shocking fact that Kumaran has usurped several people's land in Aathi by forging counterfeit title deeds. Thus, almost overnight, Aathi's people become, in Markose's words, 'aliens ... in our own land and paddy fields' (183). It is evident that Kumaran and his aides treat Aathi's people and the environment as 'expendables' and that they problematically endorse an instrumental rationality that 'try[] to make everything dollarable' (Muir qtd. in Buell, 'Toxic Discourse' 651). The various characters in *Aathi* demonstrate a diverse set of connections—cooperative, symbiotic, or confrontational/predatory—between themselves and their environment (Gamber 3). Ultimately, it drives home the point that whatever the nature of these connections is, there is no escaping the reality of the interrelationality between human life and 'other' life (Gamber 3), which is the primary principle of ecology.

Aathi also competently wields a powerful ecofeminist language and ethics and deploys a number of strong woman characters like the mysterious waste-disposing girl, Shailaja, and Kunjimathu who all speak for and take care of the environment. The narrator and the characters in the novel consistently use feminine pronouns and maternal metaphors to refer to Aathi's land, water, and other natural elements. While for the storyteller Noor Muhammad, water is 'a mother's lap' (34), for Ayyappan, Shailaja's father, it resembles a 'playful' young girl and, during high tide, 'a wanton woman' (157–158). According to Ayyappan, it was as if the water were saying 'I am free; let me be' (157). Ayyappan also talks about the respect and sensitivity with which their generation managed water while farming and how they took 'care not to affront her' (157).

Relatedly, during Kunjimathu's conversation with her female friends, as they wait to watch the tide rising, she construes the rising tides as the water's sensual awakening:

'Kunjimatho?' 'Hmm?'
'The sea: is it male or female?' 'Female.'
'How do you know?'
'Women experience this sort of arousal under the moonrise of men, don't they?'
...

Every woman is an ocean for whom the moon stays beyond reach forever! For that reason, the arousal within her would never cease. Mother
knew this. Grandmother did too, as also *her* mother and grandmother
…

(191–193)

While sharing with Dinakaran his fears of losing their environmental
justice battle, Ponmani draws explicit parallels between respect for his
mother and respect for Aathi. He also invokes the practice of touching
the mother's feet for forgiveness if the children accidentally step across the
body of their mother when she lies on the floor and wonders at Kumaran's
impudence in working towards establishing a mega city by 'disembowel-
ling the entrails of Aathi' (278). The attitude of respect for Mother Nature
apparent in Dinakaran's words resonates with the Indian tradition of reverence for *Prakriti*, which the Indian ecofeminist Vandana Shiva describes
as the 'inherently active, a powerful, productive force in the dialectic of the
creation, renewal and sustenance of all life' (*Staying Alive* 37). According
to Shiva, *Prakriti* embodies 'the feminine principle,' and it is the 'death of
Prakriti' that is the reason for the ecological crisis (39–40).

The environmental justice struggle in Aathi is given significant
momentum by Kunjimathu by her act of refusing to get up from the
waist-deep water after she understands that Aathi's rhythmic tides have
been disrupted. She boldly declares, 'I shall live working on my land
and water. I'd rather die here, right now, than accept anything less. If
all these water beds are landfilled and erased, how can we work on the
land and survive?' (204). As the news spread, every one of Aathi's people
come to Kunjimathu and stay on expressing their solidarity with her.
Shailaja is able to stem the police brutalities against the protestors by
threatening to commit suicide. The lawyer Grace Chali, who conscien-
tiously works to uncover Kumaran's unlawful activities, gives legal and
strategic advice to the protestors and even procures a stay order from
the court on Kumaran's real estate projects, is another strong female
presence in the novel.

The various ecological problems depicted in *Aathi* are inspired by the
real incidents of environmental injustice happened in Valanthakkadu in
south Kerala. In an interview with Valson Thampu, Sarah Joseph describes
memories of her visit to Valanthakkadu:

I recall my experiences while visiting an exceptionally beautiful island
called Valanthakkaddu in Ernakulam district of Kerala. About fifty families that subsist on fishing, picking mussels and farming Pokkali rice
comprise the inhabitants of Valanthakkadu. They told me they earn as
much as Rs 300 a day from picking mussels. I asked them if they could

earn more. They replied, 'Why should we?' They could count on the fish and mussels—and their fixed deposits—to meet their needs every day without fail. Given that, they had no need to gather more! I doubt if those who are caught in the rat race of development can understand the sanity and spirituality of this outlook.

In her afterword to *Gift in Green,* Joseph acknowledges that

While *Gift in Green* was on the anvil, several of its characters kept visiting me, providing invaluable help with research and documentation in the form of records, newspaper clippings and real-life events. They sustained me by sharing frequent and prolonged sessions and through marathon phone calls.

The first public reading of Aathi was also held in Valanthakkadu (L. Menon).

A report by Haritha John published in *The News Minute* provides important details of the mass environmental justice movement in Valanthakkadu against a proposed hi-tech city on the island by levelling its wetlands:

In 2009, the natives successfully stalled the proposed Hi-Tech city from being set up on the island. But not before a 600-acre mangrove forest that surrounded the isle was ravaged, as part of the said pro-ject. In a series of blatant violations of Coastal Regulation Zone Laws, Kerala Conservation of Paddy Land and Wetland Act (2008), National Environment Policy (2006), Kerala Forest Policy (2008) and the National Wetland Conservation Programme, Shobha Developers–real estate moghul [sic]—had signed a Memorandum of Understanding (MoU) with the Kerala government in August 2007 to set up the Rs 5000–crore Hi-Tech city.

The ambitious project envisaged the establishment of a township with commercial complexes, multiplexes, star hotels, an IT research centre, an 'oceanarium' and a ropeway—all this at the cost of mangroves, paddy fields, and water bodies that lend the island its lush green cover.

The report also cites Gopi, one of the local activists, who describes their unsuccessful protests against the dumping of medical waste 'through large pipes' by an Ernakulam-based hospital into the water bodies of Valanthakkadu. Reminiscent of Shailaja's experiences in the novel, Gopi points out, 'Even now, you get to see blood-clotted cotton swabs, surgical waste, syringes, even septic waste floating on the water' (John).

Although the people's struggle against the proposed hi-tech city in Valanthakkadu was a success, *Aathi* concludes ambivalently suggesting, at best, fewer chances of an eventual success for the islanders' environmental justice battle. The death of Dinakaran who is washed ashore wrapped in a mat that is described in the last few pages of the novel simulates the death of Thampuran, Aathi's god who is displaced from his shrine by Kumaran, narrated in the novel's prologue. The novel's prologue, which employs a mix of prose and verse, delineates the story of the nearly dead man who is washed ashore bundled in a mat. One of the ancestors of the people of Aathi pulled out the man whom they refer to as 'Thampuran.' He also gave Thampuran a palm full of water to drink after which Thampuran died. Even the forests, birds, and fishes wished to die with him. The ancestors, then, reasoned that the incident of Thampuran washing ashore on the day of *patthamudayam* must have some significance. Thereafter, *patthamudayam* became a day of festival for Aathi. The prologue ends with the line, 'Man created God' (2).

Likewise, when Dinakaran is washed ashore in a mat, the people of Aathi fish him out and give him water to drink. When he dies, the forests, fishes, and the birds 'long[] and yearn[]' to die with him (347). As is his wont at the end of every storytelling event in Aathi, the Introducer is heard asking the question, 'Dinakara, how are we to apply this story gainfully to our lives?' (348) which is important as it relates to the power of storytelling and also to the yoking of the present time with the mythic time. More importantly, the novel's final question also alerts the readers to the fact that the ecological message of a toxic fiction like *Aathi* should not be missed.

Resisting the Diesel Power Plant: Environmental Pollution and Dipping Ground Water Levels in Balakrishnan Mangad's *Bhoomiyude Kannu* (2004)

Balakrishnan Mangad (1946–2005) was a journalist and the author of five Malayalam novels and two short story collections. Mangad also penned the script for the film *Sammohanam* (1994), directed by C. P. Padmakumar, which was based on Mangad's short story 'Rithubhedangal' and for two television serials, 'Kazhchakal' and 'Uchcha Veyil.' His novels and short stories are noted for their faithful portrayals of the rural north Malabar settings and culture which are rare in Malayalam literature, especially during the period when his important works came out. His characters typically speak in the local Kasaragod slang while local beliefs and cultural traditions like *Theyyam* make a prominent presence in his works.

Mangad's *Bhoomiyude Kannu* [The Eye of the Earth] (2004) offers a compelling narrative of environmental despoliation following the commissioning of a diesel power plant managed by the Kolkata-based

R. V. G. Company, a multinational corporate, in an anonymous village in north Malabar. The diesel power plant is brought to the village through the doublespeak of 'development.' The novel prominently carries the elements of fantasy as the human, non-human (chiefly, trees), and superhuman—that is, the spirits of dead people who lived in the village—share prominent narrative spaces and enact important roles in the environmental justice struggle against the hazardous power plant. In fact, the first note of caution in the novel against the establishment of the diesel power plant is sounded by Janu, the spirit persona of a 17-year-old girl who lived in the village four or five generations ago and died from a snakebite. Janu tells Chekkan to whom she takes fancy, 'Don't be overjoyed about the proposed project. It had better not come. Its coming will ruin this place. It will rain fire on the earth. The earth will crack open. Water will dry up' (9).

The Company heralds its operation in the village by committing multiple acts of violence. One fine morning, the people are surprised to find out that the company has opened its office in Kammaran's house after evacuating him and his son overnight. The superintendent of the company claims to have paid ten lakh rupees to Kammaran and informs the gathered crowd that both Kammaran and his son have been provided accommodation in a palace-like house in the city. According to the superintendent's version, Kammaran could be termed the first 'developmental refugee' of the village. 'Developmental refugee' is a concept put forward by the American social anthropologist Thayer Scudder 'to convey the calamitous fallout of megadams (largely World Bank funded) that he had charted for decades in the global South' (Nixon, *Slow Violence* 152). Rob Nixon further notes,

> The 'developmental refugee' is a poignantly paradoxical figure. Development implies positive growth, ascent toward a desirable end; refugee implies flight from a grave threat—in this case, the threat of development inflicted destitution or even, when it comes to megadams, of drowning.
>
> (*Slow Violence* 152)

The story of the silent migration of Kammaran, expectedly, is met with incredulity by the congregated villagers as they recall Kammaran's deep affiliation with the village. The company's superintendent makes an appearance when the crowd refuses to disperse and insists on knowing what actually happened to Kammaran. He flies into a rage and threatens everyone that R. V. G. Company is a powerful multinational company that has enough clout in the government and that if the crowd needles him anymore, he will arrange for their eviction.

The superintendent who first appears in the novel holding a mobile phone in his hand is a figure of modernity and is also a symbolic doppelganger of the thermal power plant installed in the village. His arrogant words spell out the company's instrumental approach to people and the environment, in addition to reminding the natives of their disposability. In *Slow Violence and the Environmentalism of the Poor* (2011), Rob Nixon adapts Kevin Bale's famous expression of 'disposable people' to environmental contexts in the Global South and argues that 'ecological and human disposability' is one of the conditions that sparks environmental justice struggles (4).

He usefully notes:

> What does it mean for people declared disposable by some 'new' economy to find themselves existing out of place in place as, against the odds, they seek to slow the ecological assaults on inhabitable possibility? What does it mean for subsistence communities to discover they are goners with nowhere to go, that their once-sustaining landscapes have been gutted of their capacity to sustain by an externalizing, instrumental logic? The desperate entrapments, the claustral options that result have galvanized environmental justice insurrections, in the global South and beyond.
>
> (19)

The company also threatens the spiritual tradition of *Theyyams* in the village as the company constructs walls enclosing the land where *Theyyams* are annually performed. Popular ritualistic dance and a form of worship, *Theyyam* is performed in north Malabar regions mainly by the members of Dalit communities although it is also respected and worshipped by those in the higher strata of the caste system like the Brahmins. When Malinguman repeatedly entreats the supervisor not to occupy the *Theyyakkavu*, the latter reminds indifferently that '*Theyyam* is not important to us, but the diesel plant is' (14). Malinguman and other villagers are visibly shocked to discover that their sacred space is threatened. They wonder,

> The beliefs of so many generations are crumbling. Such a hazard was unexpected. What is the use of living if the *Theyyams* of the kavu are lost? What will be the fate of this land? How will the rains come? And the sunlight?
>
> (14)

It is the rituals like *Theyyams*, which are versions of 'embedded ecologies' (Nagarajan), that have truly anchored the lives of the community in a matrix of interrelations for aeons. 'Embedded ecologies' is a critical framework proposed by Vijaya Nagarajan who uses it to refer to 'the multiple ways in which culture frames and reveals the complex relationships between nature and culture' (452). The insensitive actions of the company personnel deal a death blow to the presence of this delicate harmony in the village.

The company builds giant walls through the village which seek to divide 50 acres of land. Chekkan describes the wall construction as a 'laceration' of the land (16). Without consulting Chanthu, the company also fences in his land including his newly built well. The wall stands pressed against the front door of Chanthu's hut, thereby obstructing access to the house. When Ambadi, Chekkan, and Choman demolish the wall, the superintendent calls up the police. The police inspector Nareekkutty arrives at the spot and beats Ambadi with his *lathi*. His collusion with the company becomes amply clear when he says: 'Company will fortify the place and murder people. Nobody should utter a single word against it. If you do, you'll be arrested and put in lock up. There, you'll be beaten to death!' (18).

Things get worse as someone sets Chanthu's house on fire that night, and the next morning, he is found hanging from a cashew tree some distance away. The company's hand in Chanthu's death is widely suspected as everyone notices the expression of fear on Chanthu's face. This incident leads to the first collective protest against the company when people stage a demonstration by carrying Chanthu's corpse to Kammaran's house, now occupied by the superintendent, and squat down in front of the house. 'The corpse that lay in front of them,' the narrator describes, 'gave them strength. The corpse seemed to grow in significance for them' (23).

The novel also deals with the significant issue of appropriation of agricultural land. The protesting village farmers' claims to the land are sharply refuted with the counter allegation that the farmers' forefathers had illegally occupied the public land in the first place. Throughout the novel, the Company and its pawns, like the police inspector Narikkutti, speak to the local community in the language of brute violence. For instance, when the villagers demand to see the Company's ownership documents, Narikkutti retorts: 'The company doesn't need any document. If you come to me asking for any document, I'll kill you and then hang you' (29). There is also no hope for employment opportunities for the villagers in the company whose farmland appropriations effectively debilitate the village's agrarian economy. The environmental justice activist Kunjishnan explains to the villagers:

> You might be thinking that when the power plant comes, our village will get better and go places [economically]. But, the fact is that the company will prosper by ruining the land. They need only technicians in the company. So, the villagers have no chance of getting employed there. Two or four people might get the position of an attender or a guard. What is the benefit of that?
>
> (37)

The relationship between the Company and the local community closely mirrors that of the coloniser and the colonised and the villagers feel 'estranged from the land on which they walked, loved and embraced' (35). Before long, the villagers, triggered by the anxiety of toxification of their village oikos, come together to launch a steadfast resistance against the diesel power plant that amply bears out Buell's observation regarding 'pollution's power as a social unifier' (Buell, 'Toxic Discourse' 651). Kunjishnan, the leader of the ecojustice movement, validly calls for the prioritisation of the consent of the affected community over legal sanctions. He tells the Company's superintendent, 'You should first get the licence from the local people. Aren't we who have to live here? Aren't we who have to put up with the waste? You didn't ask our permission! ... Let the Company shut down!' (45). Kunjishnan also denounces the government for attempting to establish the diesel power plant willy-nilly, with no regard for the local ecology and by accepting hefty bribes from the Company.

The village-oikos depicted in the novel perfectly illustrates the interconnectedness of beings, which Timothy Morton calls 'the mesh' (*The Ecological Thought* 94) where the web of relations extends from the human to the non-human and to the superhuman (i.e., the spirits of people who lived in the village). In the novel, the non-human elements of nature like the trees, wind, and the river as well as the spirits of the dead are endowed with agentic qualities and are capable of conversing with a host of human characters in the novel like Chekkan, Kunjishnan, Kunjishnan's mother Parvathy, and Gurukkal. Moreover, the character named Pavithran who leads the rather extremist faction of the socio-environmental justice against the company is presented as having superhuman powers like the ability to read minds, appear and vanish at will, recall past lives, and ride the bicycle through the sky. The non-human and superhuman elements in the novel play multiple roles—they offer counsel and confidence to the protestors, averting dangers, and drawing attention to the nefarious activities of the company. The spirits are presented as hybrid beings endowed with corporeal possibilities and a still extant affinity towards the land. For instance, in the agricultural field, Janu joins other women in planting paddy seedlings. It is the same field in which she had worked when she was alive. The novel also dramatically presents the scene in which legions of spirits swarm the protest tent on the day it was erected, 'as though they had taken charge of the struggle' (69). The attachment exhibited by these spirits to the place they once lived is evocative of the American environmental writer Gary Snyder's memorable line: 'Our place is part of what we are.' The spirits appearing in the novel are tethered for good to the land on which they had worked and lived. The novel's protagonist Chekkan's dead father who frequently appears to him relevantly tells him, 'The relationship to the soil is that strong. Even if the body is lost, the spirit hovers above the land. This is my land' (10). Similarly, another spirit named Rudran Nainar elaborates to Kunjishnan, 'When the Company starts functioning, things will get worse. Poison will spread. The earth will rot. The grass and trees will rot. So will the sky and the humans. Even the spirits will be miserable' (70). Thus, the novel puts forward a non-anthropocentric world view where 'human agency is only a part of the [broad] picture' (Iovino and Oppermann 3).

Kunjishnan, the ecoactivist in the novel, uses a blend of scientific facts and sentimental rhetoric to drive home to the villagers the environmental tragedy in waiting. He explains to the villagers how the Company will use cheap, crude diesel to run the diesel plant which will release toxic gases like carbon monoxide and sulphur oxide into the air along with half-burnt carbon powder. The carbon powder will settle on people, courtyards, and also wells if the power plant's chimneys are not tall enough. The half-burned carbon monoxide is highly toxic and will affect haemoglobin in the blood; the burned sulphur oxide will cause acid rains which will destroy agricultural crops and vegetation; lung diseases will spread across the village. Additionally, Kunjishnan points out that the traces of diesel will sink to the earth, turning the well water black, and making it undrinkable (37–38).

A significant article titled, 'Environmental Impact of Power Plants' by Robert E. Donovan corroborates the different ecological problems of the diesel power plant highlighted by Kunjishnan in the novel. Donovon points out:

> The second largest class of pollutants is sulfur oxides. Sulfur dioxide is considered to be one of the most dangerous large-scale pollutants in the atmosphere. It is a highly corrosive compound, is injurious to vegetation in concentrations commonly found in large cities, and has been linked to increased mortality rates among people suffering from respiratory disorders. By far the greatest fraction of fossil plant discharge is in the form of sulfur oxide.

He also notes how 'fine particles of ash and other materials settle on window sills, on laundry hung out to dry, and in people's lungs' and can cause 'somatic damage' (Donovan 5). An informative brochure titled 'Environmental Impacts of Power Plants' published by the Public Service Commission (PSC) of Wisconsin, likewise, asserts that the use of large quantities of ground water by power plants creates a 'cone of depression' around the well leading to the lowering of water levels in the nearby water sources.

There are 19 diesel power plants in India, two of which are in Kerala—in Brahmapuram and Kozhikode. Diesel power plants fall under the category of thermal power plants in which electrical energy is generated by using fuels like coal and gas, in addition to diesel.

Thermal power comprises about 65% of the total power generation in India (Kasturi 10). The operation of thermal power plants poses the double threat of draining the earth's finite fossil fuel reserves and contributing to the global warming by way of large-scale emission of greenhouse gases into the atmosphere. Alarmingly, India is seeking to expand its thermal power generation to 1.3 times of its existing capacity with the Ministry of Environment and Forests having given clearance to 'nearly 200 projects for generating close to 2, 20, 000 mw of power' (Kasturi 10). Another act of ecological harm that the company does is the chopping down of the Kanjiram (Strychnos nux-vomica) tree which Kunjishnan describes as the 'tree of truth.' Kunjishnan says, 'The chopping of the Kanjiram tree will erode the land's virtues' (132). Raman Chankaran, a spirit who witnessed the incident describes the incident thus:

> The villains came carrying ropes and axe in the dead of night when the village lamps closed their eyes. The superintendent had understood somehow that the Kanjiram tree was becoming a threat to his people. That was the reason he bought the piece of land—to destroy the tree. Kanjiram knew about it. It tried to scare and make the villains withdraw by taking on different hues. It turned golden in the moonlight. Then it switched to green, blue, reddish blue, and red. Red, as in the shade of congealed blood! But the villains did not turn back. They dealt a heavy blow to the tree. It tried to shield itself and hit them hard with its branches. But it was of no avail. They continued with their blows. The tree went into death throes and was smashed into smithereens. It fell down with a heavy noise. Then, it became silent. They cut down the tree into small pieces and carried them away. Only a stub oozing water remained.
>
> (132)

Evidently, the Kanjiram tree is presented as endowed with magical faculties, and its felling notably generates an outpouring of grief from the human and non-human inhabitants of the village. After listening to Raman Chankaran, Kunjishnan looks up to find countless spirits, with their faces lowered in sympathy, hovering around the place. In the morning, villagers arrive in droves to the spot of violence and stand there in visible shock. Parvathy wails aloud, covering her face with both hands. The novel presents the general reactions to the cutting of the Kanjiram tree as strikingly much the same as the murder of a fellow human being, which essentially point to the unique environmental ethos of the village community.

The novel, significantly, also calls attention to the protracted nature of the environmental justice struggles. Many years pass between the beginning of the antitoxic struggle and the final order from the central government stopping the operation of the power plant in the village. Thus, towards the end of the novel, Kunjishnan and Chekkan, who entered the struggle as young men, appear as aged men with grey hair, with the former also having become a hunchback.

Moreover, Kunjishnan's and Chekkan's entire lives were so immersed in the ecojustice movement that they had forgotten to get married. In parallel to these individual tragedies is the sharp dip in the health of the village oikos following the expansion of the diesel power plant by the Company. Over the years, the Company has increased the number of its generators and chimneys that have ensured the constant presence of thick black smoke covering the sky over the village, concealing clouds and stars. Other ecological problems that have manifested in the village include the black grime covering the agricultural fields, hills, and wells; acid rain; stunted growth in plants and trees; cracking up of the rice fields; crop failure; and the contamination of well water as diesel residues reach the water sources of wells. Many people are bedridden or have died due to lung diseases.

Bhoomiyude Kannu, in marked contrast to *Enmakaje*, however, ends with a successful resolution of the environmental justice fight. The novel's concluding chapter mentions the central government's decision to send a team of experts to detoxify the village and a team of doctors to give expert medical care to the ailing patients. The novel's climax, in this manner, is also an articulation of the power of optimism and faith in the eventual deliverance of justice.

The village-oikos gripped with an 'ecosickness' (Houser) caused by air and water pollution depicted in this novel functions as a synecdoche for the Gaian systems. Mangad's novel—perhaps all toxic fictions, for that matter—belongs to the genre of 'Anthropocene Fictions' proposed by Adam Trexler. In his 2015 book, Trexler prefers the term 'Anthropocene' to other related terms like 'climate change' and 'global warming' because, as he notes, '[b]oth *climate change* and *global warming* are easily bracketed as prognostications that might yet be deferred, but *Anthropocene* names a world-historical phenomenon that has arrived.' *Bhoomiyude Kannu* successfully paints the Anthropocenic world by deploying a series of significant images including fog, acid rain, fly ash, diesel-tinged water, and the diesel power plant with chimneys spewing smoke.

The three novels studied in this chapter demonstrate how 'citizen action can make a difference' (Brown xiv) in resisting environmental damage. Though the toxic fictions analysed in this chapter narrate stories of localised contamination, they have universal appeal and significance. The characters in these novels incessantly 'oscillat[e] between implacable outrage and miserable uncertainty' (Buell, 'Toxic Discourse' 661) as they engage in unequal battles to defend their land and water from pollution. Disaster researchers have usefully differentiated between 'natural disasters' and 'technological disasters' where the former refer to 'the acts of God'[11] while the latter are 'human-caused' and are regarded as creating 'a far more severe and long-lasting pattern of social, economic, cultural and psychological impacts than do natural [disasters]' (qtd. in Picou et al. 1495). The human-induced environmental afflictions depicted in these toxic fictions need to be categorised under 'technological disasters.' Anthony Giddens prefers to call technological disasters, including global warming, 'manufactured risks' while he puts natural disasters under the head of 'external risks.' Giddens expatiates on the differentiation in the following manner:

> In all traditional cultures, one could say, and in industrial society right up to the threshold of the present day, human beings worried about the risks coming from external nature—from bad harvests, floods, plagues or famines. At a certain point, however—very recently in historical terms—we started worrying less about what nature can do to us, and more about what we have done to nature. This marks the transition from the predominance of external risk to that of manufactured risk.
>
> (44)

The three toxic fictions studied in this chapter identify anthropocentrism and an instrumental view of nature as the root causes of ecological problems. As T. V. Reed sagely observes,

> What [is being] left out ... [is the understanding that] human beings [are] connected to nature, not only as appreciators but also as destroyers. To privilege the first without dealing seriously with the second is a recipe for continued ecological disaster.
>
> (150)

These toxic narratives endorse, as a possible remedy, 'responsibility,' both of the corporate industry and the lay people, in caring for the earth, promoting sustainable development and keeping the planet habitable for future generations. Being 'affective ecological writings,' these toxic fictions maintain an anxious tone and principally seek to inspire ethical actions by eliciting 'emotive responses to environmental conditions[.] ... [That is,] if we *feel*, we will act in a productive way' (Potter 2; emphasis added). They also seem to endeavour to provoke 'anticipatory fear' in the readers by equipping them to 'imagine worse-case scenarios' (Edelstein and Wandersman 97) when confronted with maldevelopmental projects that may ruin their familiar ecosystems. Sanchar Sarkar and Swarnalatha Rangarajan call this 'anticipatory fear' 'ecopremonition' which they argue is a productive impulse that can motivate people facing environmental damage to engage in acts of care, healing, and 'symbiotic coexistence' (62).

The discourse on toxicity that these selected novels engage in furthers the counters of contemporary ecocriticism in that 'it underscores the point that environmentalism must make concerns for human and social health more central and salient than it traditionally has if it is to thrive, perhaps even to survive' (Buell, 'Toxic Discourse' 639–640).

Notes

1 Two major setbacks were the withdrawal of the United States and Canada from the Kyoto Protocol in 2001 and 2012, respectively.
2 Reverend Ben Chavis, former executive director of the United Church of Christ Commission for Racial Justice, is credited with coining this term (see Sze 175).
3 J. Devika's English translation of *Enmakaje*, titled *Swarga*, was published in 2017. The excerpts used in this study are taken from this translation.
4 Rev. Valson Thampu's English translation of *Aathi* titled *Gift in Green* was published in 2011. The direct quotations from the novel used in this section are excerpted from Thampu's English translation.
5 *Theyyam* is an age-old ritualistic dance form performed in north Kerala.
6 Most of these scientific facts have been discussed earlier in Chapter 2 while analysing Leelakumariamma's oiko-autobiography *Jeevadayini* (2011).
7 Picou et al. argue,

> The litigation process itself can be a source of stress for litigants (Cohen & Vesper 2001; Lees-Haley 1988; Strasburger 1999) ... Lawsuits filed in the aftermath of large-scale technological disasters are typically complex because of the scientific nature of factual information and, in most cases, the involvement of multiple parties. In such cases, litigation is stressful due to the adversarial nature of the process itself and legal and scientific uncertainties regarding key aspects of the case.
>
> (1497)

8 Ambikasuthan Mangad's *Enmakaje* has attained both critical and popular success. *Enmakaje Padanangal* [Critical Essays on *Enmakaje*], edited by Santhosh Echikkanam and first published in 2010, is an anthology of critical essays devoted to the study of *Enmakaje*.
9 *Ooru Kaval* is the retelling of the *Ramayana* story from the perspective of Angada, the son of the monkey king Vali. The novel's English translation by Vasanthi Sankaranarayanan titled *The Vigil* was published in 2014. Five of Joseph's short stories based on *The Ramayana* are available in English translation in *Retelling the Ramayana: Voices from Kerala* (2005).
10 *Othappu*'s English translation by Rev. Valson Thampu titled *Othappu: The Scent of the Other Side* was published in 2009.
11 In the Anthropocene age, however, as Timothy Morton argues, '*acts of God* turn out to be acts of humans as a geophysical force' (Morton, *Dark Ecology* 14).

4 Extractivist Fictions

Anti-mining Struggles in Three Malayalam Novels

Cornucopian arguments regarding the abundance and inexhaustibility of nature's gifts are often used to justify resource extractivism and other ecologically destructive practices. Extractivist cultures typically involve massive, technology-driven resource exploitation activities managed by private interests in concert with the nation-states that render both the environment and the local inhabitants disposable (see Nixon 71). According to the Uruguayan social science researcher Eduardo Gudynas, the term 'extractivism' is being used since the 1970s in the context of the mining and oil export industries. 'Extractivism' should be understood as different from 'extraction.' Anna J. Willow argues that 'Unlike extraction, extractivism is both principle and practice' (2). Extractivism is profit-motivated and insensitive to the harm wrought upon people and the environment. By widening the chasm between the rich and the poor, it aggravates social inequities. Willow asserts,

> More than just a way of using the land, extractivism is also a way of thinking. It is a way of being in the world [. . .] Extractivism is ... a political as well as an environmental project, both a social and an ecological problem.
>
> (2)

Junka-Aikio and Cortes–Severino distinguish 'extractivism' from 'extraction' by calling the former 'a paradigm of severe exploitation' that characterises contemporary capitalism and neoliberalism (177). Jingzhong Ye et al. underscore the twin features of extractivism thus:

> it implies (if not requires) monopoly control over specific natural resources (minerals, oil, gas, fertile land, aquifers, woodlands, etc.) and it results in their ruthless exploitation. After the resource in question

DOI: 10.4324/9781003301318-4

has been extracted, only 'negative externalities' remain: pollution, impoverished populations, exhausted resources, etc.

(1)

This chapter examines three novels from the south Indian state of Kerala that narrate resource extractivism. The first novel, *Manal Jeevikal* [Sand Creatures] by G. R. Indugopan chronicles exploitative black sand mining activities in the Appadam village of Kerala while *Manalazham* addresses the menace of sand mining in Mannida and relates a resistance movement led by the schoolteacher Satchidanandan against the mining activities. *Kalpramanam* [Proof Etched in Stone] by Rajeev Sivasankar focuses on the environmental impact of stone quarrying in Pazhukka.[1] I propose the term 'extractivist fiction' to refer to novels like *Manal Jeevikal*, *Manalazham*, and *Kalpramanam* that evince a sustained engagement with the theme of resource extractivism.[2]

Resource extractivism has a long and embattled history. The large-scale resource plunder of the South Asian and African nations began when these countries were colonised by various European powers. Human resources, especially in the form of slaves, and natural resources like minerals, ivory, diamond, and gold as well as raw materials such as timber were transferred from resource-rich colonies to home countries to meet the growing demands of the Industrial Revolution. According to Rob White, the very history of the modern world is founded on resource extraction and disputes regarding natural resources (55). Frantz Fanon, in *The Wretched of the Earth* (1961), famously noted:

> Capitalism, in its expansionist phase, regarded the colonies as a source of raw materials which once possessed could be unloaded on the European market … Europe is literally the creation of the Third World. The wealth which smothers her is that which was stolen from the under-developed peoples.
>
> (26–58)

The extractivist projects located in many parts of the world betray, even in present times, a grammar of 'resource colonisation' (White 55). The watershed Chipko movement that happened in the 1970s that first gave global visibility to Indian environmental justice issues was an anti-extractivist struggle as it sought to prevent the commercial extractivism of forest resources such as timber and resin (Gadgil and Guha 101–102; Shiva and Bandyopadhyay 137). In the context of the Indian mining industry, resource colonisation may also take the form of, what Joan Martinez-Alier et al. call, an 'ecological internal colonialism,' where 'the Indian economy exploits some states as providers of raw materials' ('Changing' 467).

The availability of fast-depleting natural resources across the globe is remarkably unequal. For instance, 63.3% of the earth's oil reserves are in the Middle East (Simmons 6), and more than half of the global stock of gas reserves is located in just three countries, namely, Iran, Qatar, and Russia (60% in 2008) (Hafezi; Macalister). It is estimated that we will run out of oil in 40 years, natural gas in 60 years, coal in 197 years, and lignite in 293 years (Klimiuk and Pawloski 5). A slow but sure awakening to this fact has triggered several military conflicts since the late twentieth century to seize control of these resource assets, which Michael Klare has famously referred to as 'Resource Wars' in his 2001 book. Examples of resource wars include the infamous invasion of Iraq (2003–2011) by the United States and the UK, the Iran–Iraq War (1980–1988), the Gulf War (1990–1991), and the Sudanese Civil War (1983–2005) (Gökay; Klare, 'Twenty-first century').

The 'resource-cursed'[3] countries are typically animated by environmental justice debates and they witness a slew of anti-extractivist movements. Environmental degradation, community health hazards, loss of livelihoods, and insufficient share of the benefits of resource extractivist industries (like fewer job opportunities as a result of more mechanised mining practices) are some of the reasons that push the local population around the mining sites to environmental justice struggles (Starke). The environmental justice narratives emerging from the many mining regions of India tell familiar tales of environmental racism in which the native tribal populations are pitted in long-drawn struggles against resource-extracting corporations acting in cahoots with the government. Poorvi Kulkarni notes that

Half of India's top mining areas are in tribal lands ... Between 2011 and 2014, 48 mining leases were approved in tribal areas across the country by the union ministry of mines. The average proportion of forests in India's mineral producing districts is 28%, more than the national average of 20.9%, and mining invariably leads to their depletion and displacement.

The predominantly tribal regions in the central Indian state of Maharashtra to the eastern state of West Bengal house rich mineral reserves including coal, bauxite, and iron ore and have witnessed a slew of environmental justice movements led by grassroots leaders. A recent notable example is the anti-mining environmental justice struggle in the Indian state of Odisha spearheaded by Prafulla Samantara. Samantara, the winner of the 2017 Goldman Prize, successfully led a 12-year-long legal battle against the destruction of the Niyamgiri Hills regarded as sacred by the local Dongariya Kondh tribals for the proposed open-pit bauxite mining by the UK-based Vedanta Resources and state-owned Orissa Mining Corporation (OMC).

The resource wealth of Kerala is composed of a variety of heavy mineral sands (ilmenite, rutile, zircon, monazite, sillimanite), gold, iron ore, bauxite, graphite, china clay, gemstones, magnetite, steatite, and so on. The mining activities are, however, undertaken to extract only the heavy mineral sands, china clay, limestone/lime shell, silicate sand, and granite ('Mineral Resources of Kerala') besides sand from rivers and paddy fields.

The three novels[4] taken up for analysis, namely, *Manal Jeevikal*, *Manalazham*, and *Kalpramanam* belong to the 'second wave' of environmental writings in Malayalam as they emphasise environmental justice concerns arising out of resource grab by industrial forces. The principal intent of writing novels anchored in ecojustice issues like extractivism seems to be to disseminate 'conservation education,' the lack of which was famously lamented by the American environmental writer Aldo Leopold in his *Sand County Almanac* (1989). Literary representations of extractivism play another significant role as well, namely, transposing the issue from the level of 'knowing' about it to the level of 'feeling.' Perhaps, the use of affect to unobtrusively instil the environmental ethics of conservation and frugality in readers is also the unique service that any environmentally oriented literary writing aims to offer. Speaking in the context of ecopoetry, Jorie Graham, in an interview, usefully points out: '[The skeptical readers] feel they "know this information already, so why do they need it in a poem." That is precisely the point. They "know" it. They are not "feeling it"' (qtd. in Shoptaw). *Manal Jeevikal*, *Manalazham*, and *Kalpramanam* achieve this feat of evoking emotive responses to destructive extractivist activities by anchoring their narratives in a careful combination of environmental facts, details about the psychological impact of extractivist activities on local communities as well as local myths associated with the threatened local ecologies of Kerala villages. Literary treatments of extractivist activities can have a surprisingly powerful on-the-ground impact as well. For instance, in 2015, the media reported that all residents of the Vallicode-Kottayam village who were threatened by extensive stone quarrying activities carried out in Thadiyurulippara had decided to read *Kalpramanam* to gain awareness about the ecological problems caused by the quarrying activities and the need to stand up against environmental injustice ('Quarrykku'). Instances like this when a work of fiction energises an environmental justice movement have the potential to radically transform the standing of creative ecowritings in society.[5]

In this chapter, I employ the term 'extractivist fiction' as opposed to 'extractive fiction,' a recent coinage of Matthew S. Henry in his article titled, 'Extractive Fictions and Postextraction Futurisms: Energy and

Environmental Injustice in Appalachia' (2019), both to reflect the subtle difference between 'extractivism' and 'extraction' as well as to highlight the over-exploitative nature of the resource-mining activities depicted in *Manal Jeevikal, Manalazham,* and *Kalpramanam.* Another useful term to study literary works that narrate extractive activities is 'resource conflict literature' (2018) proposed by Alok Amatya. I decided against using this term in this essay as the term's accent is on the impacted community's struggle against resource grab rather than the ecocidal activity of exploitative mining. *Manal Jeevikal, Manalazham,* and *Kalpramanam* are representative samples of a rapidly expanding corpus of eco-fictions emerging from India and could be read in conversation with works like the (Indian) English novel 12*Oxygen Manifesto: A Battle for the Environment* (2019) by Atulya Misra that narrates how its protagonists come together to launch an environmental movement to save the planet; Indra Sinha's *Animal's People* (2007) that is based on the 1984 Bhopal tragedy; Na. D'Souza's Kannada novella *Dweepa* [Island] (1978) that foregrounds the displacement of the natives of an island village following the rise in the river water level caused by the construction of a dam; and the Bengali writer Mahasweta Devi's works like *Aranyer Adhikar* [Right to the Forest] (1977), *Chotti Munda and His Arrow* (1980), 'Pterodactyl, Puran Sahay, and Pritha' (1995), and *The Book of the Hunter* (2002) that famously thematise tribal landlessness and resource conflicts.

In the following sections, I show how G. R. Indugopan's *Manal Jeevikal,* Hari Kurisseri's *Manalazham,* and Rajeev Sivasankar's *Kalpramanam* engage in 'resource talk' by launching a powerful critique of the maldevelopmental aspects of extractivist projects in the context of Kerala. I use the term 'resource talk' to refer to the articulation of the discourse on resource (ab)use in works of literature. Typically, a part of non-fiction works, resource talk appears in transformed ways in novels like *Manal Jeevikal, Manalazham,* and *Kalpramanam,* as I have stated earlier, as a medley of ecofacts, myths, and persuasive stories. The impact of it is more powerful, as it is subliminal, upon readers. Given that all three novelists are comparatively new voices in Malayalam literature that have, as yet, received limited critical attention, the present chapter also seeks to perform the significant function of (re)presenting these novels to the Malayalam *and* the wider Anglophone audiences.

Rising Sea Levels and Disappearing Villages: The Black Sand Mining in *Manal Jeevikal* (2013) by G. R. Indugopan

Indugopan states in his preface to the novel that *Manal Jeevikal* is directly based on the real-life incident of black sand mining in Alappad Panchayat in the Kollam district of Kerala (7). The village's name, however, is tweaked to Aappadam in the novel while most of the other details like the name of the mining company (Rare Earths) appear unchanged. The protagonist of the novel is Neelakandan, an ex-Communist, freedom fighter, and a previous Member of Parliament who has retired to an isolated rented house located in a narrow strip of land between the Kayamkulam lagoon and the sea. The region is the locus of severe black sand mining and consequently, all the other houses in the neighbourhood have been washed away by the encroaching sea. According to Neelakandan, the sea has encroached on the land by at least 2 km in the past 80 years. The biggest coastal inundation in Kerala occurs in Aappadam Panchayat which is under the threat of being engulfed by the sea.

The mineral sand deposit on the beaches of Kollam is worth US$640 billion. As a doctoral researcher named Sreedharan Karthavu points out in the novel, 'The industrial eyes from across the world will not withdraw from the black sand shores until the sand remains here. They will hover around here' (72). Karthavu's words that suggest the neocolonial character of the extractivist activities resonate with the legacy of black sand extractivism in the Kollam district in the early twentieth century that involved colonial actors. The novel presents the history of black sand mining in Kollam via a description of Neelakandan's dream in which the German chemist Hershamberg appears to narrate the tale. The story is largely faithful to the historical account of how the German chemist C. W. Schomberg[6] happened to know about the black sand deposits in Kerala (Chatterjee 51). In Neelakandan's dream, Hershamberg narrates how he landed at the Indian port of Kanyakumari (now a part of Tamil Nadu) in 1908 and successfully traced the black sand deposit to the shores of Manavalakkurichi near Kanyakumari and also from the stretch of land from Neendakara to Azheekkal in the Kollam district. Neelakandan's dream informs the readers how Hershamberg, in 1910, founded the first black sand mining plant in Travancore (the present-day Thiruvananthapuram, the capital of Kerala), which was later taken over by the London Cosmopolitan Mineral Company that renamed it as Travancore Minerals Ltd. and also how the British subsequently came in large numbers with their eyes set on the black sand deposits in Kollam. The novel further notes that black sand is still being mined for ilmenite used in aircraft construction and is being exported to different foreign countries since 1922 (46–47). In the novel, Sreedharan Karthavu also significantly warns the eco-activist named de Souza not to be tricked by the company's public status:

> You think Rare Earth Company is a public company. But that is just a label. In [today's]world, any difference between public and private companies is just an illusion. You are being deceived by the security of the term 'government-owned.' … Do something to avoid being bulldozed.
>
> (72)

Karthavu's words resonate with the concept of 'neo-extractivism' proposed in 2009 by Eduardo Gudynas. Neo-extractivism, used primarily to ana-lyse exploitative mining activities in Latin America, is different from the traditional form of extractivism in that while the latter is principally practised by global corporate companies and other private establishments, the former involves (i) state governments engaging in resource mining via nationalising companies and (ii) the profit from resource extracitivism which is used for social welfare measures like poverty reduction schemes (Burchardt and Dietz 470). This neo-extractivist policy may be seen as a part of 'new developmentalism,'[7] albeit it still seems to be inspired by the 'old colonial formula for generating wealth, namely the expansion of pri-mary export production' (North and Grinspun 2).

One of the significant ways extractivist fictions engage in resource talk and put their anti-extractivist message across is by narrating the emo-tional impact of extractivism on local communities. *Manal Jeevikal* tell-ingly foregrounds how receding shorelines precipitate trauma in Appadam residents. The college student and local eco-activist de Souza is 'terrified' of the sea that is acting wayward due to indiscriminate sand mining activities. The old fishermen appear restless and develop memory lapses. Recurrent nightmares mar their sleep. The 'extractivist trauma' that these local people experience mirrors the stress on the environment caused by exploitative mining. Their extractivist trauma is a variety of 'solastalgia' that signifies, as Glenn Albrecht et al. put it, '[the] place-based distress in the face of the lived experience of profound environmental change' (S96). The psychological suffering of the members of the impacted communities derives from their deep topophilic connection to their local ecology. By presenting trauma as one of the significant ramifications of extractivism, *Manal Jeevikal* broadcasts the extractivist problem as an insidious threat.

The voice of environmental justice activism in the novel is that of de Souza who organises an 'Environmental Water March' in 50 boats from Cheriyazheekkal to Neendakara to spread awareness about the ecological problems of illegal black sand mining. When he comes to know about the plan of the Rare Earths Company (REC) to start mining in Chalithura, the only region that still has extractable black sand, he spearheads a people's resistance movement to protect the 60 houses that face the threat of coastal flooding because of mining. He also mediates the meetings between the members of the affected community and REC to negotiate monetary com-pensation for the former. Only 18 families manage to receive the compen-sation of Rs. 10,000 for each cent of land from the company. The others, forced to leave their ancestral houses behind and move to houses located further away from the coast, are unable to lay claim to *patta* titles and, therefore, have become ineligible for monetary compensation from the company. The company dispossesses the local community by capitalising on legal loopholes and engaging in sophistry. During a negotiation meeting, REC's representative shockingly blames the sea for encroaching on people's property and refutes the charge of indiscriminate mining. He says, 'It is the sea that has to address [your concerns]. The company can't be held accountable' (134).[8] The company's myopic environmental perception and scientific ignorance become immensely apparent when the REC's representative declares, 'If the sand is mined, more sand will emerge from the bottom of the sea!' (134). The words of REC's representative betray the dangerously instrumental approach to nature that guides extractivist industries and aptly demonstrate what Yvette Jackson calls, 'the established anthropocentric perception of the environment as an infinite resource for human exploitation' (119).

Manal Jeevikal ominously concludes with a tragic scene in which Neelakandan's house is washed away in the middle of the night, drowning him as well in the process, which portends the eventual destruction of the coastal village. The twin tragedies of de Souza's suicide and Neelakandan's death by drowning in the lone house that had stood as a veritable symbol of anti-extractivist resistance[9] signal the local community's total victimization under the predatory mining project. That Alappad Panchayat, the prototype of the Aappadam village in the novel, was Kerala's worst-hit village in the disastrous 2004 tsunami, killing 132 persons, accentuates the place's precarious ecology. In addition to the submergence of coastal villages, the encroaching briny water is also debilitating the paddy cultivation in the region. The three famous agricultural fields, namely, Panakkada, Mukkumbuzha, and Ponmana, that were once harvested thrice a year without fail have reportedly become a part of history ('Kerala'). In his candid testimony titled 'Ningal Kuzhikkunnu, Njangale Kadaledukkunnu' [When You Dig, the Sea Washes Us Away] that precedes the novel, Sreekumar, who was Indugopan's local informant, calls attention to the important issue of the loss of livelihood of the fishing community of Alappad and the predicament of living in constant fear of being washed away by the expanding sea. He poignantly notes, 'Our bellies are mostly empty. The coast too is being wasted [through mining]. Driving us away, [the miners] have impoverished what remains of this land' (15).

The socio-environmental costs of exploitative sand mining, which is the primary focus of *Manal Jeevikal*, is a theme less explored in contemporary literary and cultural texts in Malayalam.[10] *Manal Jeevikal* raises a raft of significant questions related to land abuse, human rights and survival, homelessness, resource ownership, ecological health, and environmental injustice that victimises the local, subalternised fishing community. *Manal Jeevikal*, as an extractivist narrative, is remarkable for its lucid style and fast-paced narration marked by a deeply empathetic tone while describing the hardships of the local community. The novel emphasises that the vulnerabilities of local communities and ecologies of the Global South are intricately imbricated when they encounter the ruthless forces of globalisation and liberalisation.

Degrading Land and Lowering Water Table: Land Sand Extractivism in *Manalazham* (2015) by Hari Kurisseri

Hari Kurisseri (b. 1970) is a renowned journalist, cartoonist, and painter. *Manalazham*, Kurisseri's first novel, deals with a number of ecological problems like rampant illegal sand extraction, the levelling of hills by soil mining, and the air pollution from open brick kilns in the fictional village named Mannida situated on the banks of Kallada River and the resistance movement led by the novel's protagonist Satchidanandan. Satchidanandan, a physically challenged person with a limb disability, comes to Mannida as a guest teacher of Sanskrit at the Nelppura Higher Secondary School. Satchidanandan has a history of environmental justice activism and has previously participated in the successful anti-stone quarrying agitation in Vanamkolli. Once he discovers the environmental problems that the village faces due to extensive sand mining, he decides to move the court to obtain a ban on sand mining. He is helped by the local villagers like Radhakrishnan, Santhosh, Prasobhan, and Krishna Pillai who together form *Mannida Samrakshana Samithy* [Mannida Protection Committee] to carry forward the case.

In her reading of the novel, Seema Jerome notes that the name 'Mannida' is an anagram of the real village called 'Mannadi' in the Pathanamthitta district while 'Kalarimukku,' also mentioned in the novel, is 'Karalimukku' in West Kallada Panchayat in Kollam district. Both Mannadi and Karalimukku, and West Kallada in general, are facing rampant sand mining. The *Paristhithi Samrakshana Ekopana Samithy* [The Environmental Protection Coordination Committee] chairman Odanavattam Vijaykumar attests that 'a good portion of the West Kallada Panchayat will soon vanish' if the mining is not stopped ('Eco group'). A study usefully shows that

> [S]and gravel are mined world-wide and account for the largest volume of solid material extracted globally and the highest volume of raw material used on earth after water (about 70%–80% of the 50 billion tons material mined/year). Formed by erosive processes over thousands of years, they are now being extracted at a rate far greater than their renewal.
>
> ('The Mining')

Kiran Pereira elaborates on the significance of sand to the construction industry:

Very few people would place 'precious' metals and diamonds in the same category as sand or gravel. In the public consciousness, the former are definitely deemed more valuable than the latter. Yet, one would be surprised at how fundamental sand or gravel is to our very existence. Without sand/gravel, there can be no buildings, no glass, no electronic chips, and no ceramics and taken to its extreme, without sand there can be no sandy beaches, no rivers and perhaps no oceans as well. Sand mining also called sand dredging or simply dredging is an activity that underpins the 'development' engine. Without sand, one of the largest industries in the world, the construction industry would come to a grinding halt.

(2)

Interestingly, the focus of *Manalazham* is not river sand mining which is, in fact, one of the serious environmental problems in present-day Kerala that has pushed many rivers like Bharathapuzha, Pampa, Manimala, and Achankovil to near death (G. K. Nair, 'Sand Mining Spells Doom'). The novel, instead, draws attention to the practice of sand mining from paddy fields. Kerala's paddy fields are 'typical wetlands' that lie waterlogged (Dayana 105) and are ecologically important because:

[p]addy lands perform a number of ecological functions. They function as feeders of water aquifers and retain the ground water level of the area. They are the water reservoirs of the state. Destruction and permanent conversion of this ecosystem will threaten the water security. Another function of paddy field is from offering food security and biodiversity conservation ... They maintain fertility and productivity. They undertake hydrological function. They provide habitat to plants, predators and microorganisms. Numerous economic services are also done by these paddy lands. Even though privately owned, this open access property is used for collecting grass, fodder, catching fish, gathering medicinal plants and collecting wild vegetables, materials for housing and handicrafts.

(Dayana 198–199)

G. K. Nair, in a news report titled 'Sand mining shifts from rivers to paddy fields in Kerala,' published in *The Hindu Business Line*, sheds light on this new trend of sand extraction from paddy fields. He points out that the sand miners have turned to the sand deposits in low-lying areas in the Pathanamthitta and Alappuzha districts following a government ban on river sand mining. The authorities are helpless regarding the exploitative sand mining happening in low-lying embankments in Nedumbram, Thalayar, and Venmani.

In the opening chapter of the novel, Satchidanandan gets off the bus at Kalarimukku on his first visit to join the school and immediately observes how 'the direction to Mannida is clear thanks to the chain of water on the road' formed by the countless trucks plying in the region carrying the sand load (7). He learns about the presence of child labour when a few students in his class tell him that they are part-time labourers engaged in sand mining activities. When Satchidanandan asks a student what he aspires to become in life, the latter gives a shocking reply that he wants to be a part of the sand mining business. The flawed priority of money over the oikos revealed by the student's statement is, sadly, something shared by the majority of the villagers of Mannida which is pushing the village towards an ecologically destructive, downward spiral.

The pervasive presence of sand lorries marks the village space of Mannida. The roads in Mannida are dominated by tipper lorries carrying extracted sand. These speeding lorries breed terror in the minds of the villagers of Mannida. Satchidanandan observes that 'the villagers step aside if they hear the buzz of the lorries' (23). He also notices how buses make way for the rushing sand lorries. The novel also addresses the issue of deaths by accidental exposure to the deep holes left by sand mining. The novel describes multiple such deaths involving both people and animals, mostly cows. Radhakrishnan informs Satchidanandan how the sand mining activities have created big pond-size pits across the Panchayat. These pits do not serve any ostensible purpose other than stopping burglars and thieves from venturing into the Panchayat for the fear of accidentally falling into them. The sinkholes that act as death traps also deter people from distant places to come to the *mundaka* paddy fields in Mannadi for fishing, thus adversely affecting their daily earnings. Only those who reside on the banks of the paddy fields know the location of the new sinkholes in the paddy fields. People also try to avoid walking across the fields as 'the places that were [plain] land yesterday might be deep pits today' (59). On seeing Satchidanandan taking bath in the Kallada River, the temporary ferryman Lonappan is quick to warn him, 'You will find the sea less deep! Sir, you be careful while taking bath here!' (41) These words aptly foreground the extent to which unbridled mining activities have tampered with the natural depth of the river. According to the Public Relations Officer who visits the village to assess its environmental problems, 'The wounds left in the river by mining may be healed because of the river's current. However, these sinkholes [in the paddy fields] will remain here forever' (72). The unknown sinkholes on the way to school worry the parents of school-going children. The death of the *Anganwadi* student Chithira, the fisherman named Divakaran, and the unknown *Ammankoda thullal* dancer are some of the sinkhole disasters described in the novel.

The severe environmental cost of the exploitative mining of sand becomes apparent when the groundwater level drops in Mannida and the people begin to face water shortage. The father of one of Satchidanandan's students complains that, for the first time in his memory, water in his well has gone dry. The perennially water-rich Akathukavu temple pond also dries up. Water collected from different parts of the village proves undrinkable as it is either stinky or salty. Satchidanandan explains that the problem occurs because the groundwater is being absorbed into the deep holes left by sand mining. The loss of the natural filter of sand and dirt has turned the well water saline.

The indiscriminate mining of sand has also caused the decimation of much of the medicinal plant population. For instance, a local Ayurvedic physician observes that the practice of growing rubber trees in the agricultural fields, from which sand has been extracted, has resulted in the loss of the natural biodiversity of the region. Satchidanandan makes a concerted effort to sensitise his students to the environmental problems of the village. He also gets both Malayalam and English newspapers to publish reports on the illegal sand mining in Mannida. Additionally, he sends multiple complaints, enclosed with newspaper clippings, to the Chief Minister and the District Collector and strives to uncover the nexus involving the sand mafia and the people in power. When he meets the District Collector to submit his complaint regarding the indiscriminate sand extraction in Mannida, Satchidanandan tells him how the police raids are becoming a mockery. He points out that the sand mafia directly hands over to the police the sand loads to be confiscated which, when auctioned, are bought back by the contractors. These contractors, then, get the permission ticket to transfer that load but end up transferring ten times more sand. The novel graphically describes the corruption in bureaucracy that enables the sand mafia to engage in illegal mining and go scot-free. For each motor without a licence, the miners pay bribes to the officials ranging from the village officer to the *tehsildar* besides giving shares of mining to the police officers starting from the constables to the Deputy Superintendent. As Satchidanandan rightly observes, the miners become the mafia because the concerned officers do not act in strict adherence to the existing rules and regulations.

The narrator memorably presents the Mannida economy, which is based on resource extraction and the culture of greed that it has engendered, and contrasts it with the agriculture-dependent lifestyle of the earlier generations. The local man named Radhakrishnan tells Satchidanandan how the price of the plots of land has risen by 10 to 20 times per cent. While the forefathers of Mannida stepped into their compounds and agricultural fields carrying spades and reaped good harvests, the youth of the current generation used the spades only to look for extractable sand. The story of Renjith, the nephew of the sand contractor Chandran Pillai, perfectly epitomises the promises of the resource-based economy of Mannida. Renjith, who is an MBA graduate and has previously worked in a couple of companies, returns to Mannida eyeing 'the economics of sand' offered by the village (128). He has 15 acres of land which contain sand deposits worth crores of rupees. In his estimation, these sand deposits could fetch him about five times more than what he might earn if he worked in multinational companies like Wipro or Infosys. Ultimately, Renjith wishes to launch the Mannida brand sand in the market. When the District Collector points out the environmental risks associated with the illegal sand mining activities, the district-level political leader draws a far-fetched parallel between the sand mining in Mannida and the oil extraction practices in the Middle East. The politician asserts:

> Don't people extract oil from the earth in Saudi Arabia? So, what is wrong with earning some cash by mining sand that is most important for the development of the village? Isn't it self-reliance? Didn't Mahatma Gandhi also say the same? … Isn't this very much like the petrodollar? Have you heard about any environmental problems anywhere in the Middle East? … How will the village get any better if you sit hugging all the sand after disrupting the job and livelihoods of thousands of people?
> (64)

The politician's argument is important as it appropriately brings to the fore the skewed land–people relationship maintained by most of the residents of Mannida. The fact that the people in Mannida who do not have land to sell out for sand mining are living in grinding poverty reveals the other, grim side of this story.

Some people in Mannida engage in sand mining under the ruse of practising commercial brackish water fish farming. The likes of Ramesan, Chandran Pillai, Bennichan, and Raghavan have opened their fish farms for this purpose. The court order which decreed that permissions should be granted to dig ponds to encourage fish farming has rendered the officials at the Geology Office helpless in this matter. Those who got permission to dig ponds, however, extract five times more sand than allowed, and when a pond is ready, they change the plot. Satchidanandan investigates this matter and meets the geologist who reminds Satchidanandan of the fact that their office has the power to grant permissions to only dig ponds—that they do not issue clearances for sand transportation. This means the police, the revenue department officers, and even the geologists could raid and seize any transported sand load. Satchidanandan alerts three newspapers about this malpractice and gets reports published in the papers the next day.

Manalazham also focuses on the menace of the levelling of hills by the contractors to build/widen the highways. Radhakrishnan points out that, in the last five years, the contractors made four hills of Mannida disappear by wielding JCBs and tipper lorries. P. R. of the District Environment Coordination Committee draws attention to the important role played by the hills in storing water. In line with this, eminent scientist D. Padmalal asserts that '[the levelling of hills] has become a common phenomenon in Kerala in the past few years and even now many educated people continue to believe that hills and wetlands are wastelands' (qtd. in G. K. Nair, 'Kerala's'). G. K. Nair further explains:

> Hills and wetlands are … two important water storing systems that play an important role in maintaining the hydrological cycle of the tropical and subtropical regions. In hills, water will be usually preserved in higher elevations either in the soil/ weathered horizons or sedimentary layers. The gradient helps in groundwater flow. During summer, rivers and lakes will be fed by the stored water in the hills and hillocks. Hence, hills are called 'Thannir kudangal (water pots)' and wetlands as 'Thannir thadangal (water reservoirs).'
>
> ('Kerala's')

The experience of the residents in the neighbourhood attests to these findings as they complain that their wells have run dry early in the summer in the past five years. One young man also narrates the case of a nearby well that has permanently dried up. A well that is left intact by the quarrymen in the near-levelled Thevarkunnu too stands waterless.

The destruction of hills is a rampant environmental problem in present-day Kerala. Shiekha E. John et al. point out that quarrying of soil from hills transforms the topographical features of the basin area which causes the instability of the adjoining land and buildings, besides other environmental problems like the dwindling of biodiversity and vegetation and increased soil erosion. The soil extraction from the hills also causes atmospheric pollution due to the destruction of vegetation and the presence of soil particles in the air. The soil particles present in the air can pose health risks like respiratory ailments (Shiekha E. John et al. 518).

The novel's omniscient narrator compares the strip of land from where the Kanathar hillock is gouged out to a beautiful woman whose breasts have been removed. In a similar vein, Satchidanandan, throughout the novel, refers to the extensive sand mining in the paddy fields of Mannida as 'land abuse' and calls the illegal sand mining a 'daily rape' (52). The novelist, here, clearly borrows from the ecofeminist vocabulary that routinely finds connections between the exploitation of women and nature/earth. Mary Hamer argues,

> Humans are raping the Earth. Rape is about Power, control & domination of another entity. Homo Sapiens [sic] are, drilling, mining, blasting, damming, extracting & bombing the Earth's outer land mass— As a Penetrating sexual predator rapes it's [sic] victim & then leaves the victim for dead. & The Earth is hurting.

In the context of Marlowe's *Dr. Faustus*, Heather Sullivan, similarly, demonstrates how 'mining ... is as much about spreading illusions of power as it is about extracting and displacing matter at whim' ('Dirty Nature' 117). The rampant illegal mining practices in Mannida seem to exemplify the pervasive presence of the 'ecological rape culture' (Wilson, 'Rape of the Land'), where the feminised earth body is repeatedly abused by the machine-wielding alpha males.

Satchidanandan regards land sand mining as an open violation of the Kerala Land Utilisation (KLU) order of 1967. The objectives of the order, which pertains to the whole of Kerala, are twofold:

> (1) to bring occupied waste or arable lands likely to be left fallow during a cultivation season under cultivation with paddy or other food crops
> (2) to prevent the conversion of any land cultivated with food crops for other purpose, except with the written permission of the District Collector (or Revenue Divisional Officers).
>
> (Government of Kerala)

In fact, considering the petition of Chellamma seeking protection for her one-and-a-half acre of paddy field and a family shrine from the dangers of the mining activities in the adjacent plots of land, the High Court had ruled that the sand miners should be charged under the KLU order. As the miners did stop the extraction activities following the Court ruling from the strips of land next to Chellamma's, no case was levelled against anyone.

Another severe environmental problem in Mannida concerns the operation of brick kilns in the paddy fields of the village. These kilns do not have chimneys, and hence, the noxious fumes released from the kilns spread out to the neighbouring houses causing distress, especially to asthma patients. When the workers do not get enough wet soil, they burn the *vandal* which is garbage dirt containing a mixture of decomposed leaves and other materials. This process of combustion exudes toxic gases. One night, Satchidanandan wakes up from sleep choking as his house is filled with the polluted air from the kiln fire. He starts perspiring and also coughs hard. The magnitude of the problem becomes clearer to him when, at school, one of Satchidanandan's students narrates how his asthmatic grandfather shifted to a house on the opposite bank of the river for the first few days of *vandal* burning in the kilns. Calling the police is of no use as they do not entertain complaints against the rich kiln owner. This incident brings to the fore the disposability of the victimised villagers as the entire system is favoured towards the environmental polluters (see Nixon, *Slow Violence* 4).

The environmental problems of the rampant brick and clay mining from the paddy fields in the state are appropriately foregrounded in an important study by V. Santhosh et al. They note:

> The increasing demand for building materials has led to indiscriminate exploitation of clay–rich topsoil from wetlands including the paddy lands of Central Kerala in the southwestern coast of India. Loss of fertile topsoil, shrinkage of agricultural lands and consequent food security issues, erosion of naturally evolved nutrients, lowering of water table in wells adjacent to the mining sites, etc., are some of the major environmental issues arising from indiscriminate brick and tile clay mining.
>
> (2111)

Certain brick kilns have installed decoy 'show chimneys' which, obviously, do not serve the purpose and the smoke escapes through all four sides of the kilns. The major pollutants from the brick kilns are:

1 Carbon dioxide (CO_2);
2 Carbon monoxide (CO);
3 Sulphur dioxide (SO_2);
4 Nitrogen oxides (NO_x); and
5 Suspended Particulate Matter (SPM)

besides the 'high volume of bottom ash as residue' (*Guidelines* 2).

The Central Pollution Control Board, Delhi (CPCB) considers the brick making industry as 'a highly resource-intensive and energy-intensive as well as polluting industry' because of the 'obsolete traditional production technologies employed in India' ('Guidelines' 1). A report titled 'Brick Kilns: Major Source of Air Pollution in South Asia' published in *Down to Earth* cites Ellan Baum, the executive director of US-based Climate and Health Research Network, who, in a similar vein, points out that 'brick kilns in South Asia are based on obsolete technologies and release huge amounts of pollutants' and suggests improving the technology to reduce the air pollution from the kilns (Jitendra). Asserting that 'emissions would be reduced by 70 per cent if the brick kilns were modernised,' Baum goes on to explain, 'Traditional brick kiln technologies like FCBTK (fixed chimney bull trench kiln) emit high amounts of black carbon. There is need to transition from traditional kiln technologies to modern ones such as VSBK (vertical shaft brick kilns) or tunnel kilns' (Jitendra). A smattering of protests, like the residents of the north colony coming together to douse the fire in the kiln with water, against the burning of open brick kilns have happened in Mannida. The *Mannida Samrakshana Samithy* [The Mannida Protection Council] is founded to marshal such scattered resistances against the various environmental problems in Mannida. The main objectives that the Council seeks to meet are stopping sand mining from agricultural fields, taking legal action against those who mine their fields and compounds, and also installing chimneys in the clay brick factories in Mannida. Various issues like the threats of the sand mining mafia, physical assault, overspeeding of the sand lorries, domination of the roads by the sand miners, the parents' anxiety about sending children to school in paths ridden with sinkholes left by sand extraction, and the illnesses caused by the brick kiln smoke are raised in the council's first meeting. Although Radhakrishnan invited over one hundred people, only 15 show up at the first meeting. Satchidanandan, nevertheless, considers the meeting a success calling it 'a small wave formed upon dropping a pebble into a pond' (46). The council passes a resolution that land sand extraction should be stopped.

Satchidanandan pursues the legal route to stop illegal sand mining in Mannida with the support of a few villagers. He hires a lawyer and files a lawsuit in the Kerala High Court. He also collects newspaper clippings and pieces of evidence to prove that illegal sand extraction is rampantly practised in Mannida. The High Court bans land sand mining in Mannida and directs the police to place pickets to avoid sand transportation. The Court instructs that no mining permission can be granted in the name of fish farming or house building. Additionally, the High Court also orders that the monitoring committee should meet every month at the Panchayat Office to review the work undertaken in the previous month.

Acting on the Court order, the police and RDO raid the sand mining sites and confiscate the motors and hoses that are kept hidden. The sand loads are also seized from ten different locations. However, after a few days of calm, sand mining resumes in Mannida under the cover of night. The motors are brought to the paddy fields at midnight, and the lorries roll in by three in the morning. They wrap up the sand extraction by eight o'clock in the morning. In an attempt to prevent sand mining activities, Santhosh and Prasobhan, who are Satchidanandan's allies, hold up the sand lorries. Subsequently, the lorry drivers pick a fight with them and manage to get away with the lorries. Four or five bike riders who trail these lorries brandish weapons at the duo and also hurl invectives at them.

The efforts of Santhosh and Prasobhan to stop illegal sand mining appropriately assume the dimension of 'ecotage' which refers to sabotage perpetrated for ecological reasons. One early morning, the duo place metal spikes on the road through which sand lorries ply, in an attempt to get back at the sand mafia. After running over the metal spikes, one of the sand lorries loses control and crashes into the river, killing the lorry cleaner. Following the incident, the police arrest Satchidanandan, in addition to Santhosh and Prasobhan, alleging his involvement in 'terrorist activities.' The magistrate remands them to prison. Upon release on bail, Satchidanandan, as a last-ditch effort, launches an indefinite hunger strike demanding an immediate cessation of sand mining in Mannida.

On the sixth day of his hunger strike, a weak Satchidanandan is forcibly arrested and shifted to the hospital. He, however, protests against being treated and continues his hunger strike in the hospital as well. Objecting to Satchidanandan's arrest, the *Mannida Samrakshana Samity* declares a *hartal* in the village. That day, the District Collector, the local MLA, and other officials visit Satchidanandan in the hospital to listen to his grievances. After the meeting, the District Collector significantly announces a 'mini emergency' in Mannida. According to the order,

'The sand mining is banned for two months. Severe actions will be charged against sand transporters. The ban will return to force at the end of the stipulated two months. The state government will pass a law about banning land sand mining afterwards.

(187)

Satisfied with the promises, Satchidanandan ends his fast. The novel concludes with Satchidanandan leaving the hospital, and Mannida as well, for his girlfriend Maya's house in Alappuzha since his tenure at the school has also come to an end.

The novel has a brief epilogue titled 'Phala sruti'[11] which refers to the traditional trope of stating, at the end of Hindu religious books, the benefits of reading those books. The novel's 'Phala sruti' delineates the life in Mannida after Satchidanandan has left. Sand mining continues unchecked in Mannida. The policemen now unabashedly vie with each other to get the picketing duty so that they can collect bribes from the mining mafia. Radhakrishnan concentrates on his dairy business, careful not to embroil himself in anything that might affect his public image as he has received assurances of being named as the party candidate in the next Panchayat election. Chellamma leaves Mannida and migrates to the city. While Santhosh obtains a job in a bus body manufacturing unit, Prasobhan works as a private bus cleaner. In this way, the epilogue demonstrates how things are as usual, if not worse, in the village after

Satchidanandan's epic struggle and return. If the original 'Phala srutis' of Sanskrit hymns are meant to illustrate the benefits of chanting the respective hymns, the novel's 'Phala sruti' evinces, ironically, that no good result has come out of Satchidanandan's labour. As the novel's blurb rightly puts it, Satchidanandan 'leaves [Mannida] defeated, although he believed he has won the battle!' Mannida's tragedy essentially shows how the entrenched corruption of society can stifle the voices of ecological wisdom. The novel offers a cautionary warning to the many real-life Mannidas in Kerala and the world over that are following similar paths. As the critic P. K. Anil Kumar observes, 'It is for the first time in Malayalam novel tradition that a physically challenged person has become the protagonist.' The parallels between Satchidanandan's disabled body and the maimed earth body of Mannida cannot be missed. Anil Kumar points out that

> We may read the disability of Satchidanandan as symbolising the wounded nature. We need to realise the fact that when Satchidanandan was valiantly fighting to protect the environment of Mannida, those who had no physical disabilities were sleeping under the covers of indifference and cowardice.

Sara J. Grossman, who describes herself as 'an environmental humanities scholar and a disabled woman,' argues that disabled people resonate with and finds echoes in damaged environments: 'I found comfort in environments whose burdens were as heavy as my own and utilized these environments as partners for mourning as well as spaces of alternative strategy for practicing nonnormativity' (243). Ecocritic Sarah Jaquette Ray uses the term 'ecological other' to refer to disabled bodies. In her 2013 book titled *The Ecological Other: Environmental Exclusion in American Culture*, she revealingly argues that the Western 'environmental literature and adventure culture' presuppose a 'complete, whole, preferably fit body' and asserts that 'the disabled body is the other against which modern environmentalist identity has been formed' (37). In her essay titled 'Risking Bodies in the Wild: The "Corporeal Unconscious" of American Adventure Culture' included in the collection *Disability Studies and the Environmental Humanities: Toward an Eco-Crip Theory* (2017) which she co-edited, Ray also points out how disability has become 'an overdetermined metaphor for bodily *dis*connection to the physical environment' in much of the mainstream environmental literature. This book and the emergence of 'eco-crip' theory attempt to remedy this non-engagement of the environmental humanities with the concerns of disability studies. Scholars like Eli Clare significantly question the binaries of the 'normal and abnormal' and 'natural' and 'unnatural' and call them the 'human illogic' (Clare 264). In *Manalazham*, Satchidanandan appropriately draws attention to the oppression of the disabled in an ableist society. He says, 'The state of affairs is such that even claiming the rights of the disabled is subject to the kindness of the abled people. The disabled are indeed marginalised in society' (16). Satchidanandan's words call for 'eco-ability,' which is a philosophical position that 'combines the concepts of interdependency, inclusion, and respect for difference within a community' and includes '*all* life, sentient and nonsentient' (Nocella II). Satchidanandan's struggle for environmental justice could also be understood as a variant of the 'subaltern environmentalism' which I have discussed in Chapter 1 of this book.

Threatened Oikic and Sacred Spaces: Stone Quarrying in *Kalpramanam* (2014) by Rajeev Sivasankar

Rajeev Sivasanker (b. 1967), one of the promising new writers in Malayalam, has to his credit two short story collections and 14 novels. Themes in his works include the cult of Satan worship in Kerala and the 'underbelly of faiths and beliefs' (Jacob 'Thathwamasi') (*Thamovedam*), black magic, astrology and *vastu* (*Pranasancharam*), the life of the Hindu saint Adi Shankara (*Maraporul*), and the myth of Kali depicted in the Indian epic *Mahabharata* (*Kalipakam*). Rajeev Sivasankar's extractivist fiction *Kalpramanam* narrates the issue of extensive quarrying of stone by private companies and the myriad environmental and health problems it causes. The incidents of the novel unfurl between the years 2001 and 2014. Pazhukka, the fictional village in southern Kerala in which the novel is set, houses several ancient hills and caves where mythical sages are believed to have meditated. The village's ecological problems begin with the arrival of the Mumbai-returned local man named Sasankan who personifies anthropocentric greed and environmental insensitivity in the novel. Sasankan ushers in a horde of moneybags who buy Pazhukka's rocky plots of land by offering mind-boggling prices. Soon, they launch extensive stone quarrying using powerful modern technology in these lands by flouting several existing rules and regulations.

The novel clearly distinguishes between the small-scale stone mining by Nanu, a local villager, and the exploitative quarrying by big industries. Being driven by an ecological ethic of reverence for the hills, Nanu always asks the hill's permission, before applying gunpowder to a new rock or hill for a blast, by performing the ritual of smashing a coconut. After the blast, he places the first splinter broken off from the rock on a stool and throws flowers at it, as though performing a *puja*. Nanu's ecological vision gets clear expression in his words to a few school-going children who stop by his workplace:

My children, this wide world belongs to God. Even if to take a pinch of soil, we have to ask His permission. Do you know how long it takes for a rock to become a rock? Hills are older than our great-great-great grandfathers. So, we too should give them that respect. If we do disrespectful things and play with the hill, we will surely get its reward.

(46)

By contrast, the ecocidal proportions of the blasts carried out on the hills by quarrying companies using heavy machinery are highlighted by invoking the image of the atom bomb explosion in Hiroshima. The omniscient narrator describes the impact of witnessing the first blast on the hills on the local poet named Mathew Poongavil:

A murder of crows flew above the trails of smoke that looked like mushrooms in the northern sky. As the hood of the smoke trail rose, reminding one of the bomb explosion in Hiroshima, it was the image of the thousand-headed Anantha[12] that appeared in his poetic mind.

(66)

Sivaraman Nair, who was near the quarry when the first blast happened, also invokes the analogy of a bomb to convey the force of the blast. He says:

It is a sight that one should not miss. They put the gun–powder in not just one or two, but a hundred holes! Then they pass electricity through them and blast the rocks in one go. Half of Chelappara is gone! The rocks fly up to the sky like rubber balls If this goes on, the entire Chelappara will be loaded into trucks and be gone in a month's time! What a difference between the firecracker that the poor Nanu used and the bomb that these people use now!

(67)

Nanu's reverential relationship with nature is underpinned by his awareness of the spiritual significance of the Pazhukka hills that the quarrying mafia is neither cognisant of nor cares about. The hills of Pazhukka are steeped in a number of fascinating mythico-spiritual tales. The *paras*[13] found in Pazhukka are part of the Agastya Hill that belongs to the Western Ghats, a UNESCO World Heritage site. The mythico-spiritual relevance of the place is evident from the very name of the hill that is known after Agastya, the ancient Hindu sage and scholar who is considered the father of Siddha medicine and the first practitioner of Nadi astrology. The Pazhukka villagers often refer to him as 'Kuru Muni' [The Short Sage] because of the short physical stature of the sage. He is believed to be still present in the form of his *sukshma sarira* [subtle body] in the Agastya Hill. According to Gangadharan, the name 'Sooryappara,'[14] the enduring belief in the presence of Agastya who offered Sri Rama the mantra dedicated to the Sun God, the perennially water-rich pond in the middle of a rock that is believed to be the place where Kala Purusha (time personified as a man) sleeps, all point to the possibility of a now-lost Sun Temple in Pazhukka. The animistic reverence towards the Sun and the multiple spiritual associations with the natural elements also become, for the villagers, a means of re-enchanting nature which involves becoming 'emotionally engaged with nature' (Mathews, 'On Desiring Nature' 3). Balakrishnan, an eco-activist in the novel, validly reasons that this spiritual assignment to the hills must have emerged from a deep nature conservation ethic of their ancestors and states that it could have had a deterrent effect on acts of ecological depredation. He says,

> Hill is the basic source of life. River, forest, swamp, wetland, and bio-diversity all originate from the hill. That is the reason our ancestors worshipped the hill as God. They associated hills with the tales of Sri Rama, Sita and the Pandavas to pre–vent people from ravaging them.
>
> (54)

Due to the close entanglement of eco-cultural spaces in Pazhukka, the invasive presence of extractivist forces in the village commits double violence.

Kalpramanam's resource talk is principally animated by a string of valid connections it makes between the phenomenon of the drying up of wells and other water resources in the village and the operation of quarries, stone crushers, and the sand handling plant. The novel expresses pronounced anxiety about the slow desertification of the village. 'Each rock is a water reservoir,' points out Balakrishnan, 'The water that percolates during the rainy season through the small cracks of the rocks will be stored there. Rocks ensure that the groundwater levels don't decline' (157). The operation of the sand handling plant installed in Rakshasappara precipitates serious groundwater depletion as it draws water from four bore wells from a depth of 2000 feet, forcing people in the neighbourhood to dig deeper to find water in their home wells. Besides causing water scarcity, excessive stone quarrying engenders a number of other environmental problems in Pazhukka as well. Pazhukka witnesses a slew of disasters like cyclones, well collapses, and landslides. In a major earthquake, a large piece of rock rips out of Sooryappara and falls down. Sixteen wells in Pazhukka cave in, throwing the villagers into a state of panic. At the Panchayat office, Balakrishnan makes a well-argued case implicating the mining activities in the well collapses:

Isn't it clear that the wells collapse because the crushers and the sand handling plants mine water? ... In a study conducted by the State Remote Sensing and Environment Centre, it is clearly stated that wells cave in because of the pressure variations of the underground water. I have a copy of the report with me.

(212)

Balakrishnan's daughter Devi asserts that Pazhukka's landslides are due to the filling up of rainwater in gaping giant holes left by incessant quarrying from the hills. Speaking to the Panchayat President, Balakrishnan again argues:

These stone quarries are operated using a highly powerful nitrate mixture, safety fuse, electric detonator and other machinery. According to the Indian Bureau [of] Mines Act, there should be two-and-a-half acres of available land to give clearance to mining activities in any zones. The stone quarries in Pazhukka operate without following these stipulations. Even to extract soil for house construction, the house owner has to get his neighbour's permission if the distance between the houses is less than twenty meters. But here, the quarry workers carry out blasts very close to our houses and the broken stone pieces dangerously fall into our front yards. The walls of our houses develop cracks. If the Panchayat President says that this is all a part of 'developmental activities,' it is hard for us to believe blindly.

(88)

Another ecological problem of Pazhukka after the large-scale extractivist activities started is the sharp dip in the village's non-human population as various species of birds, butterflies, and snakes disappear en masse. The village also experiences erratic monsoons that adversely affect the agricultural yield. Chemicals, metal powder, and gunpowder accumulate in wells and ponds and make the water undrinkable. Ratnakaran who runs a shop complains of having to wipe clean the coating of rock powder from the glasses of cupboards every hour. The airborne rock powder also mixes with food and contaminates it. Pazhukka becomes a cancer cluster with a large number of children developing lung cancer. Doctors observe that multiple kilos of rock powder are being accumulated in the lungs of adults in Pazhukka, posing dangerous health problems. Pazhukka gradually transmogrifies into 'a trans-corporeal landscape' (Alaimo 45) marked by an incessant circulation of rock dust and chemicals between the environment and human bodies. According to Stacy Alaimo, trans-corporeality is an especially useful framework to study environmental justice narratives. Trans-corporeality prompts us to think of the environment not as an 'inert, empty space or as a resource for human use' but as 'a world of fleshy beings with their own needs, claims, and actions' (2). Through trans-corporeality, Alaimo calls for an acknowledgement of the immediacy of the environment and thinking beyond the traditional dichotomies defined by 'bodily natures' to reach a web of material interconnections among all organisms. The expansive conception of corporeality that this term suggests has interesting implications for the study of extractivist fictions. While trans-corporeality acknowledges the environment as an 'embodied' sphere and individual bodies as deeply embedded in ecosytemic bodies, it also posits that the environmental harm that the extractivist activity brings about is tantamount to self-harm. The anti-extractivist struggle, like that spearheaded by people like Udayabanu, Ratnakaran, and Balakrishnan in *Kalpramanam*, becomes, by the same token, a unique struggle to save the activists' own immersive, trans-corporeal selves from harm.

Udayabhanu, Ratnakaran, and Balakrishnan launch the environmental justice movement to oppose the 'distorted and myopic [versions of] development' (251). Balakrishnan invokes the Gandhian term 'Satyagraha' to refer to their peaceful protest strategy that involves forming human chains, marching to the Panchayat Office, meeting with the elected representatives and rallying support from other major environmental justice activists. Eventually, the Court passes the significant judgement of temporarily stopping the operation of the quarry functioning on a private *patta* land. The order, however, does not carry any immediate positive consequences for the village oikos because the quarry owners, as is typical of extractivist industries, had already mined out loads of crushed stone required for the next ten or 15 years from each quarry.

The concluding chapters of the novel take part in the debate about the Madhav Gadgil Commission Report (2011)[15] and the Kasturirangan Panel Report (2013)[16] which deal with the protection of the Western Ghats. While the activists associated with the Pazhukka Protection Council welcome the Madhav Gadgil Commission Report, the Christian farmers of Pazhukka oppose both the Madhav Gadgil Commission and the Kasturirangan Panel reports. Many people describe them as inimical to the farmers and take major exception to the non-inclusion of Pazhukka in the human settlement area. At the height of the protests, Madhav Gadgil himself arrives in Pazhukka to visit Chelappara and Palppara, which also dissolves the thin line between fiction and reality in the novel. Making an influential ecologist such as Gadgil deliver anti-extractivist rhetoric in Pazhukka's Satyagraha tent is as much an attempt at convincing the readers of the dangers of extractivism as it is just another realistic trope employed in the novel. It also demonstrates how disaster narratives are, as Mark D. Anderson has shown, loaded with political discourses. He notes, 'Simply choosing disaster as the narrative thread that ties together different elements that come into play in any narrative constitutes a political posture: disaster narratives serve to legitimize or delegitimize political discourse, always in competition with rival versions' (7). *Kalpramanam*, as a 'literary mediation' (Anderson 2) of a disaster, 'delegitimize[s] the political discourse' by mounting strident criticism of the opportunist interventions of politicians in Pazhukka's extractivist issue. In the novel, Devi asserts:

> With reports, discussions and controversies, the politicians dragged the issue for three or four years. It will continue like this for many more years ... To politicians, it is not the environment, but their [political] survival is the issue ... The political ingenuity is in engaging with the issues and dragging them out without ever solving them.
>
> (292)

The quasi-documentary tone of narration and the inclusion of paratextual materials like the excerpts from newspaper articles and television news reports in *Kalpramanam* are the author's attempt at 'factualizing [his] version of events' (Anderson 7) associated with Pazhukka's ecodisaster to put his anti-extractivism message across. The pronounced resource talk in this novel that gives visibility to the environmentally debilitating dimensions of stone quarrying also rescues the issue from slipping into the 'resource unconscious' (Amatya and Dawson 9) of the contemporary Malayalam novel. Sivasankar's aesthetic choice of a direct, no-frills style and starkly realist mode of narration to render Pazhukka's extractivist problem mirrors Indugopan's narrative strategy in *Manal Jeevikal*.

The anti-extractivist struggle led by Pazhukka Protection Council becomes seriously crippled by the internal divisions created by the debates surrounding various Commission Reports. Even when his daughter calls their environmental justice struggle 'a meaningless fight' and 'a failure' (293), Balakrishnan finds comfort in having strived to serve the larger cause of their fight, namely 'the protection of this earth; not just for the benefit for a few of us, but for all people' (291). The novel's climactic scenes are tragic and involve a dream-like event pointing to an imminent ecoapocalypse that will annihilate Pazhukka. *Kalpramanam* raises significant questions about the politics of mining and developmentalism in the contexts of Kerala and the Global South. It highlights a number of issues like the misuse of agricultural land, careless handling of explosives in quarries, air and water pollution, displacement of people as well as the hypocrisy of the political parties that thrive on opportunism, and the use of misinformation while dealing with environmental causes. The environmental justice concerns expressed by the activists in the novel demonstrate their deep topophilic connection to the land bolstered by an earth-centred spirituality. The fictional village of Pazhukka in which the novel is set is representative of several real-life Kerala villages like Muthalamada and Ambittan Tharissu in Palakkad, Natyanchira in Thrissur, Malayattoor in Ernakulam, Chathalloor and Thekkanmala in Malappuram (Das 65; Nabeel) that are ravaged by the operations of the stone quarries/crusher units and are waging environmental justice battles. The key strength of *Kalpramanam* (and also *Manal Jeevikal* and *Manalazham*) perhaps lies in this fierce immediacy of the extractivist problem in Kerala that it masterfully dramatises.

G. R. Indugopan, Hari Kurisseri, and Rajeev Sivasankar, the authors of *Manal Jeevikal*, *Manalazham*, and *Kalpramanam*, respectively, belong to the new crop of writers who have, as yet, received limited critical attention in Malayalam. This chapter, therefore, is probably the first attempt in English to comparatively read the three novels using the ecocritical framework and to locate them in the tradition of extractivist narratives from Kerala. *Manal Jeevikal*, *Manalazham*, and *Kalpramanam* analysed in this chapter essentially deal with 'material flows' (Martinez-Alier et al., 'Changing') or 'the movement of matter' as the extracted resources are transferred from the mining sites to locations far and wide. The despoiled worlds of these extractivist fictions demonstrate what Alejandra Espinosa Andrade aptly calls an 'extractive-uncanny space' that 'generate[s] a non–specific feeling, a sense of abandonment, real or imaginary, nostalgia, fear, among others' (321).

The three novels foreground how the resource grab by the external forces significantly obliterate the land-based self-determination of the affected local communities (see Willow 4). They are also important narratives of ecological disasters that present convincing tragedies, by employing apocalyptic images, about profit-mongering humans hubristically altering the earth and the climate. The 'unhappy endings' of all three extractivist fictions are poignant reminders of the fact that the chances of the environmental justice struggles ending in failures are high as the political and bureaucratic authorities repeatedly fail to execute the environmental rules and regulations and often operate hand in glove with the profit-seeking environmental exploiters.

Notes

1   All three novels are published by two of the leading publishing houses in Kerala, viz. Chintha Books (*Manal Jeevikal*) and Sahitya Pravarthaka Sahakarana Sangham (SPCS) (*Manalazham* and *Kalpramanam*). SPCS is the writers' cooperative society that has a chain of bookstores called National Book Stall across Kerala.

2 While *Manal Jeevikal* identifies the global transaction of black sand mined from Kerala, *Kalpramanam* does not specify the locations to which the quarried stone from Kerala is being sent.

3 'Resource curse' is a concept proposed by Richard M. Auty in his 1993 book titled *Sustaining Development in Mineral Economies: The Resource Curse Thesis*. Resource curse reveals a 'paradox of plenty' where the '"natural asset" can distort the economy to such a degree that the benefit actually becomes a curse' (Auty i). This happens, Auty argues, because of 'Dutch disease' which is caused by the strengthening of local currency due to huge revenues gained from mining activities. This unequal emphasis on mineral mining for revenue generation debilitates non-mining activities and the mineral economies go through incessant boom-and-bust cycles wherein gains of booms are not appropriately offset by the losses during the periods of economic slowdown. Mineral-mining countries, according to Auty, are vitiated by corrupt governments, poor economic growth, as well as damaged environments.

4 As Alok Amatya and Ashley Dawson have argued, resource extraction has been a thematic point of interest in many novels since *Robinson Crusoe* (1719). An important lacuna in this regard is in the nineteenth century, as they usefully point out,

> All too often, however, resource extraction and the colonial location of such extractions are rendered invisible in novels written during Britain's Age of Empire. Indeed, it might be said that, in the nineteenth century, the novel comes to be characterized by a constitutive absence that centers on empire and resource extraction. We might call this the novel's resource unconscious.
>
> (9)

Many twentieth- and twenty-first-century novels like Abdelrahman Munif's 'petrofiction' (Ghosh) classic titled *Cities of Salt* (1987), Helon Habila's *Oil on Water* (2010), Jennifer Haigh's *Heat and Light* (2016), and Chandrahas Choudhury's most recent Indian English novel *Clouds* (2019) have, however, turned the spotlight back on the issue of resource grab by giving prominent narrative spaces to discuss extractivist activities carried out by the predatory corporate forces.

5 The most famous example of an environmental book engendering sweeping changes in environmental attitudes is the ban on the use of DDT introduced in the United States and other parts of the world following the publication of Rachel Carson's *Silent Spring* (1962).

6 S. Mohammed Irshad, however, cites the German native's name as Chombarg.

7 Lisa L. North and Ricardo Grinspun also study 'neo-extractivism' in the context of Latin American countries. I refer to this framework as Kerala is comparable to most Latin American countries in multiple ways, including the common political tradition of communism in both places.

8 All translations from *Manal Jeevikal*, *Manalazham*, and *Kalpramanam* used in this chapter are mine.

9 The owner of the house in which Neelakandan lived had resisted Company's forceful eviction by approaching the court.

10 *Passenger* (2009), a popular Malayalam thriller movie, narrates the black sand mining activities and the anti-mining resistance movement in a coastal village of Kerala.

11 *Sabdatharavali*, the Malayalam dictionary, defines 'Phala sruti' as 'the sentence given at the end of a book describing the benefit of reading or listening to the recital of a book' (1316).

12 In *Puranas*, Anantha is a thousand-headed serpent on which the Hindu god Vishnu sleeps.

13 *Para* means simply a 'rock' or a 'boulder.' It can, however, refer to a hillock by extension.

14 'Soorya(n)' is the Malayalam term for the Sun.

15 In the novel, the Western Ghats Ecology Expert Panel Report is referred to as 'Madhav Gadgil Commission Report,' after its chairman, the renowned environmentalist Dr Madhav Gadgil. The Panel submitted its report to the Government of India on 30 August 2011. The Madhav Gadgil Commission Report termed the entire Western Ghats an 'Ecologically Sensitive Area' and demarcated the region into three Ecologically Sensitive Zones (ESZ). The report opposed the building of dams in the ESZ1 which crushed the hopes for the Athirappally Dam Project in Kerala and further recommended regulations on mining activities in ESZ 1 and 2 (Bose).

16 In August 2012, the Union Ministry of Environment and Forests (MoEF) appointed a ten-member High-Level Working Group, also known as the Kasturirangan Panel chaired by the space scientist Dr Krishnaswamy Kasturirangan. It was formed to review the Madhav Gadgil Commission Report. The Kasturirangan Panel rejected the Madhav Gadgil Commission Report and diluted the stringent regulations recommended by its predecessor. In contrast to the Madhav Gadgil Commission Report, which included 64% of the Western Ghats under the ESZ, the Kasturirangan Panel Report termed only 37% of the region as ESZ. Thus, according to this report, about 60,000 sq. km of Western Ghats belonging to six states would be 'a no-go area for commercial activities like mining, thermal power plants, polluting industries and large housing plans' ('37% of Western Ghats'). Significantly, the Kasturirangan Panel also demarcated a 'cultural land- scape,' consisting of human settlements and a 'natural landscape,' comprising most of the ecologically sensitive areas.

5 Conclusion

The 11 contemporary Malayalam environmental writings studied in this book tell compelling stories of the material embeddedness of the human and the non-human agents in the subalternised landscapes. Dealing with either real or fictionalised socio-environmental justice activism in Kerala, these narratives inspiringly offer scenarios where ecosensitive humans plunge into action to save abused environments. The studied narratives call for what the environmental philosopher Freya Mathews refers to as 'fitting into nature,' which involves 'more than merely not harming [the nature] … [but] actively replenishing it, actively reconstituting the biosphere in everything we do' ('On Desiring Nature' 2). Such an ethic of Earthcare stems from an understanding that the health of humans is predicated on the health of the environment and that humans and non-humans are engaged in a constant dialogue whose disruption will tip the ecological balance. The conception of 'nature' in these texts, it must be noted, is not a homogenised or romanticised entity as is often the case in first-wave environmental writings. Environmental justice enframes the selected ecotexts which anchors them in the 'second wave' of environmental literature. I have shown in this book how the selected ecotexts participate in the environmental justice discourse which identifies that factors like caste, class, gender, and socio-economic position affect an individual's chances of exposure to environmental degradation as the environmentally polluting industries and activities are disproportionately concentrated in locations where such socially disempowered communities live. Increasing inequality in today's hypercapitalised world has sparked increasing environmental justice struggles which, as Laura Pulido points out, share 'counterhegemonic, or subaltern, location—[as] they exist in opposition to prevailing powers' (4). Pulido considers grassroots environmental justice struggles as the drivers of environmental and social change as sustainable development has transmogrified into the meaningless form of 'controlled capitalism' (xvi). The ecotexts studied in this book evince a subversive

DOI: 10.4324/9781003301318-5

tendency that Pulido gestures at as they use the written word to resist the state's forces of dominance which incessantly act in cahoots with private vested interests engaged in ecocidal activities.

This book, which covers both fiction and nonfiction titles, is thematically divided into three main chapters. Although some of the novels, like *Enmakaje, Aathi, Manal Jeevikal*, and *Manalazham*, studied in this book take up environmental abuses of real-life places in Kerala, the narratives do not slip into a monotonous journalistic style as they convey the urgency of the issues. A majority of the selected texts including *Mother Forest, Mayilamma, Enmakaje, Aathi, Bhoomiyude Kannu, Manal Jeevikal*, and *Kalpramanam* evocatively depict local myths, customs, and beliefs of the local communities which serve to assert the 'rootedness in place' (Reed 148) of the speakers/characters in the texts. All the studied texts present some of the key topical socio-environmental issues of Kerala that reveal strong interconnections between the ecological and social. The interpenetration of the ecosocial realms happens, as I have reiterated elsewhere in this book, typically in the environmentalism of the Global South. As eminent ecocritic Timoth Morton points out, 'Thinking ecologically isn't simply about nonhuman things. Ecology has to do with you and me' (*The Ecological Thought* 4). Following the theories of ecoglobalism and eco-cosmopolitanism which suggest that the local and the global are interdependent, the rest of the world is bound to find relevance in and inspiration from the localised environmental justice struggles and pollution problems dealt with in these texts. Being first published between the years 2002 and 2015, these narratives emerge from the era when India adopted the LPG (Liberalisation, Privatisation, and Globalisation) policy which has serious environmental ramifications as the nature of human–nature interactions transformed for the worse during this period. The studied writings, hence, cohere with familiar globalisation narratives of land appropriations, livelihood loss, damages to local ecosystems, and the unbridled interventions of government-sanctioned predatory global corporates in Kerala's resources leading to higher levels of environmental pollution and enormous depletion of environmental assets. As a whole, these narratives pose pointed questions like, '[W]ho has the power to impose decisions on resource extraction, land use, pollution levels, biodiversity loss, and more importantly, who has the power to determine the procedures to impose such decisions?' (Martinez-Alier et al., 'Social Metabolism' 2).

The three thematic points upon which this book hinges are subaltern environmentalism, toxicity, and resource extractivism. The lens of subaltern environmentalism is employed to analyse the oiko-autobiographies of the four ecoactivists in Chapter 2. The five subaltern oiko-autobiographies analysed in this chapter are significant socio-environmental writings that effectively highlight how 'exploitation of nature always occur[s] through the exploitation of the subalterns' (Armerio 178). They, at the same time, are also important personal testimonies which constitute 'the lifeblood of the environmental justice movement[s]' (Evans 29). Some of the thematic questions like pesticide poisoning and water mining that come up in this chapter closely resonate with the tropes of toxicity and resource extractivism discussed in detail in Chapters 3 and 4.

The pollution stories told by the three 'toxic fictions' studied in Chapter 3 are primarily analysed by employing the framework of 'toxic discourse' proposed by Lawrence Buell. These narratives deploy apocalyptic imageries and present 'dark ecologies' (Morton) filled up with slush, garbage, faeces, pus, chemical toxins, plastic, stink, and mosquitoes. Timothy Morton explains that dark ecology contains 'the disgusting, inert and meaningless' (*Ecology* 195) and significantly declares, 'Ecological art is duty bound to hold the slimy in view' (*Ecology* 159). These toxic fictions are important 'material narratives' which demonstrate how 'material forms—bodies, things, elements, toxic substances, chemicals, organic and inorganic matter, landscapes, and biological entities – intra-act with each other and with the human dimension' (Iovino and Oppermann 6–7). The parallels between the diseased bodies and the sickened oikos offered by these toxic fictions are hard to miss. The novel *Bhoomiyude Kannu*, additionally, also draws attention to the problem of delayed justice in the matter of anti-toxic struggles. In the novel, the polluting diesel power plant is shut down following years of protests, after doing much harm to the environment and wasting the lives of the protestors. The symbolism of water in *Aathi* befits the frame of reference of 'postcolonial blue' which Sharae Deckard contrasts with 'postcolonial green' that addresses the land. The environmental justice vision that these novels endorse acts interspecially as toxins pose health risks to both human and non-human beings. A disanthropocentric practice of cooperation and an 'entangled empathetic engagement with each other and other animals' (Gruen, *Entangled Empathy*) could, as these pollution narratives seem to recommend, help us survive on this toxified planet.

The three extractivist fictions examined in Chapter 4 share the common theme of anti-mining activism. The large-scale extraction of black sand from the beaches, sand from paddy fields, and stone from hills and rocks, without any concern for the damage to the environment, depicted in *Manal Jeevikal*, *Manalazham*, and *Kalpramanam*, respectively, points to the lack of 'ecological conscience' in the extractors (Leopold, *Sand County Almanac* 221). These novels crucially object to the commodification of nature which promotes exploitative mining that not just depletes the resources but also irreparably ravages the land. The resistance efforts by the members of the affected communities depicted in these novels are 'ecological distribution conflicts,' a term coined by Martinez-Alier and O'Connor in 1996 (Conde and Martinez-Alier), which signifies 'struggles over the burdens of pollution or over the sacrifices made to extract resources' (Martinez-Alier et al., 'Social Metabolism' 2). While the severe ecological problems of mining depicted in these novels certainly urge us to think of alternative methods to meet the demands for energy and construction materials, as Rob White rightly notes, 'The point is not necessarily to stop mining (although this may be warranted in some instances) but to ensure the least harm when doing it' (53).

This book holds up the 11 contemporary Malayalam environmental justice narratives as offering a substantial contribution to the burgeoning body of environmental literature from India. The environmental justice texts analysed in this book could be read in conversation with other significant ecotexts from India like *Animal's People* (2007) by Indra Sinha which is based on the harrowing realities of the 1984 Bhopal gas tragedy; *The Hungry Tide* (2004) by Amitav Ghosh, a remarkable novel set in the Sundarbans that brings into focus important Southern environmentalist issues like the state's problematic preference for the welfare of endangered species like the Bengal tiger to that of the poor, local people resulting in the eviction of the latter to make way for a nature reserve; *The Last Jet-Engine Laugh* (2000) by Ruchir Joshi which presents a dystopian future characterised by acute water crisis; and the Tamil novella *Thanneer* [Water] (1973) by Ashokamitran which is set in the late 1960s Madras City and also depicts the issue of severe water shortage faced by the city-dwellers. This, of course, is only a representative list as any socially committed writer from India cannot refrain from writing about environmental issues owing to the close intermingling of the eco-social realms in India.

There is now a fast-growing body of environmental justice writings in Malayalam and it is not possible within the scope of this book to take up all those texts for analysis. Some of the notable contemporary environmental justice writings from Kerala that I had to leave out include, among others, the oiko-autobiographies, *Chengara Samaravum Ente Jeevithavum* (2013) by Seleena Prakkanam, *Vishamazhayil Polliya Manassu* (2010) by Sri Padre, *Chorinte Manamulla Cheru* (2010) by Pallikkal Bhavani, and the toxic fictions, *Bhopal* (2009) by K. Aravindakshan and *Kanyadhaivangal* (2013) by Annie Andrews. Another issue concerns the problems of translation as the primary texts used in this book are written originally in Malayalam which I had to render in English for citation purposes as the majority of these writings have not been hitherto translated into English. It is almost a critical platitude to state that the translation of texts invariably entails the transference of cultures also. While doing translations, I, therefore, had to negotiate with two contrasting cultures and with the unique workings of the two languages to come up with equivalents in English that do justice not only to the sense of the original sentences but also to their tone and essence. Often, I had to italicise and keep the original words like *para*, which contextually carries the dual meanings of a rock and the hill, and add a footnote. The book also calls for translations ranging from the titles of essays, books, and other texts originally written in Malayalam to excerpts from the primary and secondary texts that I have cited during my analyses. It is the act of translation, however problem-ridden the task is, that fulfils the primary function of this book, namely, to render the presence of contemporary environmental justice narratives in Malayalam visible to the Anglophone readership.

Works Cited

Abbey, Edward. *Desert Solitaire*. 1968. U of Arizona P, 1988.

Abraham, Sheeba. 'Impact of Paddy Land Conversion in Kerala: A Case Study.' *Summary of Minor Research Project*, www.macollege.in/uploads/research_wo rks/doc_75.pdf. Accessed 14 Oct. 2017.

Abram, David. *Becoming Animal: An Earthly Cosmology*. Pantheon, 2010.

Abrams, M. H. *A Glossary of Literary Terms*. Thomson, 2006.

Adamson, Joni, Mei Mei Evans, and Rachel Stein. 'Introduction.' *The Environmental Justice Reader: Politics, Poetics and Pedagogy*, edited by Joni Adamson, Mei Mei Evans, and Rachel Stein, U of Arizona P, 2002, pp. 3–14.

Adamson, Joni and Scott Slovic. 'The Shoulders We Stand On: An Introduction to Ethnicity and Ecocriticism.' *MELUS*, vol. 34, no. 2, Summer 2009, pp. 5–24. *JSTOR*, www.jstor.org/stable/pdf/20532676.pdf?refreqid=search:ea959635d 5d999b6aa74ed6e98808822. Accessed 19 Feb. 2018.

Agarwal, Ravi. 'India's Pollution Challenges.' *Toxic Links*, toxicslink.org/?q=art- icle/indias-pollution-challenges. Accessed 13 Oct. 2017.

Agrawal, Pragyan. 'Shocking Secrets of Brahmastra.' *Speaking Tree*, www.speak ingtree.in/allslides/1a-416777. Accessed 18 Feb. 2017.

Aiyer, Ananthakrishnan. 'The Allure of the Transnational: Notes on Some Aspects of the Political Economy of Water in India.' *Cultural Anthropology*, vol. 22, no. 4, 2007, pp. 640–658, doi: 10.1525/can.2007.22.4.640. Accessed 19 Feb. 2018.

Ajeesh, T. *Jeevadayini*. DC Books, 2011.

Ajitha, K. *Kerala's Naxalbari: Ajitha, Memoirs of a Young Revolutionary*. Translated by Sanju Ramachandran, Srishti, 2008.

———. *Ormakkurippukal*. NBS, 1994.

Alaimo, Stacy. *Bodily Natures: Science, Environment, and the Material Self*. Indiana UP, 2010.

Albrecht, Glenn et al. 'Solastalgia: The Distress Caused by Environmental Change.' *Australasian Psychiatry*, vol. 15, no. 1, 2007, pp. S95–S98.

Allister, Mark. 'Introduction.' *Eco-man: New Perspectives on Masculinity and Nature*, edited by Mark Allister, U of Virginia P, 2004, pp. 1–13.

———. *Refiguring the Map of Sorrow: Nature Writing and Autobiography*. U of Virginia P, 2001.

Amatya, Alok. *Resource Conflict Literature: Reading Indigenous Struggles.* 2018. U of Miami, PhD dissertation.

Amatya, Alok and Ashley Dawson. 'Literature in an Age of Extraction: An Introduction.' *MFS Modern Fiction Studies*, vol. 66, no. 1, 2020, p. 119.

Ammons, Elizabeth and Madhumita Roy, editors. *Sharing the Earth: An International Environmental Justice Reader.* U of Georgia P, 2015.

Anand. *Jaiva Manushyan.* 1991. DC Books, 2012.

Anderson, Linda. *Autobiography.* Routledge, 2001.

Andrews, Anni. *Kanyadhaivangal.* Current Books, 2013.

Aravindakshan, K. *Bhopal.* DC Books, 2009.

Armbuster, Karla. ' "Buffalo Gals, Won't You Come Out Tonight": A Call for Boundary-Crossing in Ecofeminist Literary Criticism.' *Ecofeminist Literary Criticism: Theory, Interpretation, Pedagogy*, edited by Greta Claire Gaard and Patrick D. Murphy, U of Illinois P, 1998, pp. 97–122.

Armerio, Marco. 'Garbage Under the Volcano: The Waste Crisis in Campania and the Struggles of Environmental Justice.' *A History of Environmentalism: Local Struggles, Global Histories*, edited by Marco Armiero and Lise Sedrez, Bloomsbury Academic, 2014, pp. 16–184.

Asher, R. E. and T. C. Kumari. *Malayalam.* Routledge, 1997.

Ashokamitran. *Water.* Translated by Lakshmi Holmström, Katha, 2001.

'Asian Tsunami: Lessons from the Survivors.' Compiled by B. S. Kakkilaya. *Back 2 Cradle*, www.back2cradle.org/tsunami3.htm. Accessed 30 Oct. 2017.

Asokan, Anu T. 2014. 'Environmentalism of the Poor: An Ecocritical Reading of the Selected Fictional Works of Mahasweta Devi.' Diss. Indian Institute of Technology Madras, 2014.

Athmaraman. 'Harithavabhodham: Aadyangurangal.' *Harithaniroopanam Malayalathil*, edited by G. Madhusoodanan, Current Books, 2015, pp. 30–38.

Auty, Richard M. *Sustaining Development in Mineral Economies: The Resource Curse Thesis.* Routledge, 1993.

Bahinipati, Chandra Sekhar and Nirmal Chandra Sahu. 'Mangrove Conservation as Sustainable Adaptation to Cyclonic Risk in Kendrapada District of Odisha, India.' *Asian Journal of Environment and Disaster Management*, vol. 4, no. 2, 2012, pp. 183–202, papers.ssrn.com/sol3/Delivery.cfm/SSRN_ID2400011_code1736285.pdf?abstractid=2400011&mirid=1

Balakrishnan, V. V. 'Tradition and Modernity: An Analysis of Some Indian Responses with Particular Reference to the Creative and Discursive Writings of O. V. Vijayan.' Diss. Mangalore, U, 1996. *Shodhganga*, shodhganga.inflibnet.ac.in/handle/10603/131317. Accessed 15 Oct. 2017.

Barad, Karan. *Meeting the Universe Halfway: Quantum Physics and the Entanglement of Matter and Meaning.* Duke UP, 2007.

Barry, Glen. 'After Disaster, Drive to Restore Mangroves in India.' *EcoInternet*, 3 Jan. 2005, ecointernet.org/2005/01/03/after_disaster_drive_to_restor. Accessed 30 Oct. 2017.

Barry, Peter. 'Ecocriticism.' *Beginning Theory: An Introduction to Literary and Cultural Theory.* Viva Books, 2011, pp. 240–261.

Basheer, Vaikom Muhammad. 'Bhoomiyude Avakashikal.' *Bhoomiyude Avakashikal*. DC Books, 2014, pp. 7–21.

———.'The Rightful Inheritors of the Earth.' Translated by Vanajam Ravindran, *Basheer Fictions*, edited by Vanajam Ravindran, Katha, 1996, pp. 81–84.

Bate, Jonathan. *Romantic Ecology: Wordsworth and the Environmental Tradition*. Routledge, 1991.

Beck, Ulrich. *Risk Society: Towards a New Modernity*. Sage, 1992.

Bennett, Jane. *Vibrant Matter: A Political Ecology of Things*. Duke UP, 2009.

Bhaduri, Amita. 'Undisposed Toxic Waste Still Haunts Bhopal's Groundwater.' *Your Story*, 07 Aug. 2017, yourstory.com/2017/08/undisposed-toxic-groundwater/. Accessed 14 Oct. 2017.

Bhaskaran. *Janu: C. K. Januvinte Jeevitha Katha*. DC Books, 2002.

———. *Mother Forest: The Unfinished Story of C. K. Janu*. Translated by N. Ravi Shanker, Kali for Women & Women Unlimited, 2004.

Bhatt, S. C. and Gopal K. Bhargava, editors. *Land and People of Indian States and Union Territories*. Vol. 14. Kalpaz, 2006.

Bijoy, C. R. 'Kerala's Plachimada Struggle: A Narrative on Water and Governance Rights.' *Economic and Political Weekly*, vol. 41, no. 41, 2006, pp. 4332–4339. *JSTOR*, www.jstor.org/stable/pdf/4418807.pdf. Accessed 19 Feb. 2018.

Bijoy, C. R. and K. Ravi Raman. 'Muthanga: The Real Story: Adivasi Movement to Recover Land.' *Economic and Political Weekly*, vol. 38, no. 20, 2003, pp. 1975–1982. *JSTOR*, www.jstor.org/stable/pdf/4413574.pdf?refreqid=excels ior%3Ad343645df2a31e1c877f52c7a575ca8a. Accessed 19 Feb. 2018.

Borlik, Todd A. *Ecocriticism and Early Modern English Literature: Green Pastures*. Routledge, 2011.

Bose, Rajanya. '6 Points Made by Madhav Gadgil Report That Centre Ignored.' *DNA*, 28 Aug. 2014, www.dnaindia.com/india/report-6-points-made-by-mad hav-gadgil-report-that-centre-ignored-2014329. Accessed 06 Aug. 2017.

Brown, Phil. *Toxic Exposures: Contested Illnesses and the Environmental Health Movement*. Columbia UP, 2007.

Buell, Lawrence. *The Environmental Imagination: Thoreau, Nature Writing, and the Formation of American Culture*. Harvard UP, 1995.

———. *The Future of Environmental Criticism: Environmental Crisis and Literary Imagination*. Blackwell, 2005.

———. 'Toxic Discourse.' *Critical Inquiry*, vol. 24, no. 3, Spring 1998, pp. 639–665. *JSTOR*, www.jstor.org/stable/pdf/1344085.pdf?refreqid=search%3A0c810 b895fc739caa4af80cfccac574b

———. *Writing for an Endangered World: Literature, Culture, and Environment in the U.S. and Beyond*. The Belknap P of Harvard UP, 2001.

Bunsha, Dionne. 'The Rise of Print.' *Frontline*, vol. 19, no. 14, 2002, www.frontl ine.in/static/html/fl1914/19140810.htm. Accessed 23 Oct. 2017.

Bunyan, John. *Grace Abounding to the Chief of Sinners*. Google Books, books.google.co.in/books?id=FZAEAAAAQAAJ&printsec=frontcover#v= onepage&q&f=false. Accessed 29 Oct. 2017.

Burchardt, Hans-Jürgen and Kristina Dietz. '(Neo-)extractivism – a new challenge for development theory from Latin America.' *Third World Quarterly*, vol. 35, no. 3, 2014, pp. 468–486.

Butler, Octavia E. *Parable of the Sower*. Warner Books, 1993.

Carson, Rachel. *Silent Spring*. Mariner Books, 1962.

Castillo, Ana. *So Far From God*. W. W. Norton, 1993.

Caton, Peter and Beatriz Lopez. 'Revealed: the child victims of pesticide poisoning in India.' *Ecologist*, 04 Jan. 2012, www.theecologist.org/News/news_analysis/1189820/revealed_the_child_victims_of_pesticide_poisoning_in_india.html. Accessed 02 Apr. 2017.

Chakkuvally, Saif. *Chorinte Manamulla Cheru*. DC Books, 2010.

Chakrabarty, Dipesh. 'Postcolonial Studies and the Challenge of Climate Change.' *New Literary History*, vol. 43, no. 1, Winter 2012, pp. 1–18. www.jstor.org/stable/23259358

Chapple, Christopher Key. 'Toward an Indigenous Indian Environmentalism.' *Purifying the Earthly Body of God: Religion and Ecology in Hindu India*, edited by Lance E. Nelson, State U of New York P, 1998, pp. 13–38.

Chatterjee, K. K. *Uses of Metals and Metallic Minerals*. New Age International, 2007.

'Chief Seattle's 1854 Oration.' *Halcyon*, 13 Nov. 2017, www.halcyon.com/arbor hts/chiefsea.html. Accessed 21 Feb. 2018.

Choudhury, Chandrahas. *Clouds*. Atria, 2019.

Ciafone, Amanda. 'If 'Thanda Matlab Coca-Cola' Then 'Cold Drink Means Toilet Cleaner': Environmentalism of the Dispossessed in Liberalizing India.' *International Labor and Working-Class History*, vol. 81, Spring 2012, pp. 114–135, doi: doi.org/10.1017/S0147547912000075. Accessed 20 Sept. 2015.

Clare, Eli. 'Meditations on Natural Worlds, Disabled Bodies, and a Politics of Cure.' *Material Ecocriticism*, edited by Serenella Iovino and Serpil Oppermann, Indiana UP, 2014, pp. 204–218.

Cohen, Jeffrey Jerome. 'Storied Matter.' Foreword. *Material Ecocriticism*, edited by Sernella Iovino and Serpil Oppermann, Indiana UP, 2014, pp. ix–xii.

Coleman, Patrick. Introduction. *Confessions* by Jean-Jacques Rousseau. Translated by Angela Scholar, Oxford UP, 2000, pp. vii–xxix.

Comfort, Susan. 'Struggle in Ogoniland: Ken Saro-Wiwa and the Cultural Politics of Environmental Justice.' *The Environmental Justice Reader: Politics, Poetics and Pedagogy*, edited by Joni Adamson, Mei Mei Evans, and Rachel Stein, U of Arizona P, 2002, pp. 229–246.

Conde, Marta and Joan Martinez-Alier. 'Ecological Distribution Conflicts.' *EJOLT*, www.ejolt.org/2016/04/ecological-distribution-conflicts/. Accessed 03 Dec. 2017.

'Converting Forest to Agriculture.' *Orang Utan Republik*, www.orangutanrepub lik.org/become-aware/issues/environmental-challenges-a-solutions/converting-forest-to-agriculture. Accessed 17 Dec. 2017.

Coole, Diana and Samantha Frost, editors. *New Materialisms: Ontology, Agency, and Politics*. Duke UP, 2010.

Coupe, Laurence, editor. *The Green Studies Reader: From Romanticism to Ecocriticism*. Routledge, 2000.

Crosby, Alfred W. *Ecological Imperialism: The Biological Expansion of Europe, 900–1900*. Cambridge UP, 1986.

Crutzen, Paul J. 'Geology of Mankind.' *Nature*, vol. 415, no. 23, 2002, www.nat ure.com/articles/415023a. Accessed 03 Dec. 2017.

Daly, Mary. *Gyn/Ecology: The Metaethics of Radical Feminism*. Beacon, 1978.

Das, Neethu. 'Quarry mafiakkethere Chathallooril Samaram Sakthamakunnu.' *Keraleeyam*, Jan. 2015, www.keraleeyammasika.com/media/2015/02/quarry-mafiyakkethire-chathalloor.pdf. Accessed 08 Aug. 2017.

Das, Saudamini and Jeffrey R. Vincent. 'Mangroves Protected Villages and Reduced Death Toll during Indian Super Cyclone.' *Proceedings of the National Academy of Sciences of the United States of America*, vol. 106, no.18, 2009, pp. 7357–7360, www.ncbi.nlm.nih.gov/pmc/articles/PMC2678660/pdf/zpq7357.pdf. Accessed 30 Oct. 2017.

David Vincent Meconi, S. J. 'Introduction.' *The Confessions: With an Introduction and Contemporary Criticism*. By Saint Augustine of Hippo, edited by David Vincent Meconi S. J., Ignatius, 1997.

Dayana, M. K. 'Land Use Controls with Special Reference to Wetlands.' Diss. Cochin U of Science and Technology, 2015. *Shodhganga*, shodhganga.inflibnet.ac.in/handle/10603/102586. Accessed 09 Aug. 2017.

d'Eaubonne, Françoise. *Le Féminisme ou la Mort*. Pierre Horay, 1974.

Deckard, Sharae. 'Water, Waste, Land: Environment and Extractivism in South Asian Fiction.' *Academia*, www.academia.edu/33262854/Water_Waste_Land_Environment_and_Extractivism_in_South_Asian_Fiction. Accessed 22 Oct. 2017.

Deitering, Cynthia. 'The Postnatural Novel: Toxic Consciousness in Fiction of the 1980s.' *The Ecocriticism Reader: Landmarks in Literary Ecology*, edited by Cheryll Glotfelty and Harold Fromm, U of Georgia P, 1996, pp. 196–203.

Deleuze, Gilles and Felix Guattari. *A Thousand Plateaus: Capitalism and Schizophrenia*. Translated by Brian Massumi, The Athlone P, 1992.

DeLoughrey, Elizabeth and George B. Handley, editors. *Postcolonial Ecologies: Literatures of the Environment*. Oxford University Press, 2011.

DeLoughrey, Elizabeth, Renée K. Gosson, and George B. Handley. *Caribbean Literature and the Environment: Between Nature and Culture*. UP of Virginia, 2005.

Devi, Mahasweta. *Aranyer Adhikar*. Kaaruna Prakashni, 1977.

———. *Chotti Munda and His Arrow*. Translated by Gayatri Chakravorty Spivak, Blackwell, 2002.

———. 'Pterodactyl, Puran Sahay and Pirtha.' *Imaginary Maps*. Translated by Gayatri Chakravorty Spivak, Routledge, 1995, pp. 106–200.

———. *The Book of the Hunter*. Translated by Sagaree Sengupta, Seagull Books, 2002, pp.1–138.

Devika, J. 'Caregivervs.Citizen? Reflections on Ecofeminism from Kerala State, India.' *Man in India*, vol. 89, no. 4, 2010, pp. 751–769.

Diamond, Stuart. 'The Bhopal Disaster: How It Happened.' *The New York Times*, 28 Jan. 1985, www.nytimes.com/1985/01/28/world/the-bhopal-disaster-how-it-happened.html?pagewanted=all. Accessed 14 Oct. 2017.

Di Chiro, Giovanna. 'Environmental Justice.' *Key Words for Environmental Studies*, edited by Joni Adamson, William A. Gleason, and David N. Pellow, New York UP, 2016, pp. 100–105.

Dilipkumar, Lakshmi Chithra and Swarnalatha Rangarajan. 'Eco-ability and the Corporeal Grotesque: Environmental Toxicity in Cherrie Moraga's Heroes and Saints and Ambikasutan Mangad's Swarga.' *Studies in the Humanities*, vol. 46, no. 1–2, 2020.

Donovan, Josephine. 'Animal Rights and Feminist Theory.' *Ecofeminism: Women, Animals, Nature*, edited by Greta Gaard, Temple UP, 1993, pp. 167–194.

Donovan, Robert E. 'Environmental Impact of Power Plants.' *The Military Engineer*, vol. 63, no. 411, January–February 1971, pp. 5–8. *JSTOR*, www.jstor.org/stable/44565753. Accessed 11 March 2023.

D'Souza, Na. *Dweepa*. Translated by Susheela Punitha, Oxford UP, 2013.

Echikanam, Santhosh, editor. *Enmakaje Padanangal*. DC Books, 2010.

'Eco Group to Hold Convention.' *The Hindu*, 27 May 2009, www.thehindu.com/todays-paper/tp-national/tp-kerala/Eco-group-to-hold-convention/article16603886.ece. Accessed 04 July 2017.

Edelstein, Michael R. and Abraham Wandersman. 'Community Dynamics in Coping with Toxic Contaminants.' *Neighborhood and Community Environments: Human Behavior and Environment Volume 9*, edited by Irwin Altman and Abraham Wandersman, Springer Science + Business Media, 1987, pp. 69–109.

Ehrlich, Paul. *The Population Bomb*. 1968. Ballantine, 1988.

Emery, Chris. 'Mangroves Reduced Storm Death Toll.' *Frontiers in Ecology and Environment*, vol. 7, no. 5, 2009, p. 237. www.jstor.org/stable/pdf/25595135.pdf?refreqid=search:2feecbb0dd652cb38c5e412f8b93127b. Accessed 19 Feb. 2018.

'Environmental Impacts of Power Plants.' Public Service Commission of Wisconsin, pp. 1–20, psc.wi.gov/thelibrary/publications/electric/electric15.pdf. Accessed 06. Apr. 2017.

'Environmental Racism.' *Food Empowerment Project*, www.foodispower.org/environmental-racism/. Accessed 16 Feb. 2018.

Evans, Mei Mei. 'Testimonies.' *The Environmental Justice Reader: Politics, Poetics and Pedagogy*, edited by Joni Adamson, Mei Mei Evans, and Rachel Stein, U of Arizona P, 2002, pp. 29–43.

'Facts about Water and Sanitation.' *Water*, water.org/water-crisis/water-sanitation-facts/. Accessed 21 Sept. 2015.

Fanon, Frantz. *The Wretched of the Earth*. Trans. Richard Philcox. Grove Press, 2004.

Farr, Cecilia Konchar. 'American Ecobiography.' *Literature of Nature: An International Sourcebook*, edited by Patrick D. Murphy, Terry Gifford, and Katsunori Yamazato, Fitzroy Dearborn, 1998, pp. 94–97.

Gaard, Greta. 'Living Interconnections with Animals and Nature.' *Ecofeminism: Women, Animals, Nature*, edited by Greta Gaard, Temple UP, 1993, pp. 1–12.

Gadgil, Madhav and Ramachandra Guha. *Ecology and Equity: The Use and Abuse of Nature in Contemporary India*. Routledge, 1995.

Gamber, John Blair. *Positive Pollutions and Cultural Toxins: Waste and Contamination in Contemporary U.S. Ethnic Literatures*. U of Nebraska P, 2012.

Gandhi, Indira. 'Man and Environment.' *Safeguarding Environment*. New Age International, 1992, pp. 13–22.

Garrard, Greg. *Ecocriticism*. Routledge, 2004.

'Gender and Water.' *United Nations Department of Economic and Social Affairs*, 23 Oct. 2014, www.un.org/waterforlifedecade/gender.shtml. Accessed 30 Oct. 2017.

George, K. M., editor. *Best of Thakazhi S Pillai*. Roli Books, 1999. *Google Books*, books.google.co.in/books?id=l6tyBAAAQBAJ&printsec=frontcover&dq=george+thakazhi&hl=en&sa=X&ved=0ahUKEwjPwpqHtPTWAhVFvY8KHWObAtUQuwUIKDAA#v=onepage&q=rice%20bowl&f=false. Accessed 16 Oct. 2017.

George, P. T. 'The Promised Land: Adivasi Land Struggles in Kerala.' *Ritimo.org*. Ritimo, 18 Dec. 2014, www.ritimo.org/The-Promised-Land-Adivasi-Land-Struggles-in-Kerala. Accessed 14 Oct. 2017.

George, Rose. *The Big Necessity: The Unmentionable World of Human Waste and Why It Matters*. Metropolitan Books, 2008.

George, Tessy K. 'Ecosensibility in Narrative Fiction: A Reading of the Novels of Mulk Raj Anand and M T Vasudevan Nair.' Diss. Kannur U, 2007. *Shodhganga*, shodhganga.inflibnet.ac.in/handle/10603/2583. Accessed 17 Dec. 2017.

Ghosh, Amitav. *The Glass Palace*. Random House, 2002.

———. *The Hungry Tide*. HarperCollins, 2004.

———.'Petrofiction: The Oil Encounter and the Novel.' *The Imam and the Indian: Prose Pieces*. Ravi Dayal, 2002, pp. 75–89.

Giddens, Anthony. *Runaway World: How Globalization Is Reshaping our Lives*. Routledge, 2000.

Glotfelty, Cheryll. 'Literary Studies in an Age of Environmental Crisis.' Introduction. *The Ecocriticism Reader: Landmarks in Literary Ecology*, edited by Cheryll Glotfelty and Harold Fromm, U of Georgia P, 1996, pp. xv–xxxvii.

Gökay, Bluent. 'Why Oil Was a Prime Motivator for the Iraq War.' *Newsweek*, 07 Oct. 2016, www.newsweek.com/why-oil-was-prime-motivator-iraq-war-478764. Accessed 09 Aug. 2017.

Gore, Al. *Earth in the Balance: Forging a New Common Purpose*. Earthscan, 2007. *Google Books*, books.google.co.in/books?id=VurZAAAAQBAJ&printsec=frontcover#v=onepage&q&f=false. Accessed 31 Oct. 2017.

Government of Kerala, Agricultural (NCA) Department. *Kerala Land Utilisation Order, 1967–Disposal of Applications for Conversion of Land for Non-food Crop Users by District Collectors and Revenue Divisional Officers*. Institute of Land and Disaster Management, ildm.kerala.gov.in/wp-content/uploads/2017/01/GO-Rt-No.157.2002.AD-Dt-05.02.2002.pdf. Accessed 10 Aug. 2017.

Grey, William. 'Gaia Theory Well Aired.' Review of *Gaia: A New Look at Life on Earth*, by James Lovelock. *Academia*, www.academia.edu/7688749/Review_of_James_Lovelock_Gaia_A_New_Look_at_Life_on_Earth. Accessed 15 Oct. 2017.

Griffin, Susan. *Woman and Nature: The Roaring Inside Her*. Harper and Row, 1978.

Grossman, Sara J. 'Disabilities.' *Environmental Humanities*, vol. 11, no. 1, May 2019, pp. 242–246.

Gruen, Lori. *Entangled Empathy: An Alternative Ethic for Our Relationships with Animals*. Lantern Books, 2015. *Google Books*, books.google.co.in/books?id=IUOuDAAAQBAJ&printsec=frontcover#v=onepage&q&f=false. Accessed 23 Oct. 2017.

Guha, Ramachandra. 'Radical American Environmentalism and Wilderness Preservation A Third World Critique.' *Environmental Ethics*, vol. 11, no. 1, 1989, pp. 71–83.

Guha, Ramachandra and J. Martinez-Alier. *Varieties of Environmentalism: Essays North and South*. Earth Scan Publications, 1997.

Guha, Ranajit. 'Preface.' *Selected Subaltern Studies*, edited by Ranajit Guha and Gayatri Chakravorty Spivak, Oxford UP, 1988, pp. 35–36.

'Guidelines on Brick Manufacturing Unit.' Pollution Control Board Assam, pcbassam.org/Notice/brick/Guidelines%20of%20Brick%20Kiln%20in%20 Assam.pdf. Accessed 10 Aug. 2017.

Habila, Helon. *Oil on Water*. W. W. Norton & Company, 2010.

Hafezi, Parisa. 'Russia, Iran, Qatar agree to form 'big gas troika.'' *Reuters*, 21 Oct. 2008, www.reuters.com/article/us-iran-gas-opec-idUSTRE49K36H20081021. Accessed 10 Aug. 2017.

Haigh, Jennifer. *Heat and Light*. Ecco, 2016.

Hamer, Mary. 'The Rape of the Earth and the Human Ego.' *Counter Currents*, 14 May 2010, www.countercurrents.org/hamer140510.htm. Accessed 09 Aug. 2017.

Heering, Alexandra de. 'Dalits Writing, Dalits Speaking: On the Encounters between Dalit Autobiographies and Oral Histories.' *Dalit Literatures in India*, edited by Joshil K. Abraham and Judith Misrahi-Barak, Routledge, 2016, pp. 206–223.

Heise, Ursula. *Sense of Place and Sense of Planet: The Environmental Imagination of the Global*. Oxford UP, 2008.

Hogan, Linda. *Solar Storms*. Scribner, 1995.

Houser, Heather. *Ecosickness in Contemporary U.S. Fiction: Environment and Affect*. Columbia UP, 2014.

Howarth, William. 'Imagined Territory: Writing of Wetlands.' *New Literary History*, vol. 30, no. 3, Summer 1999, pp. 509–539. *JSTOR*, www.jstor.org/ stable/pdf/20057553.pdf?refreqid=excelsior:a5816ceed7a72f5a4e37f320d9577 2af. Accessed 19 Feb. 2018.

Hubbell, Sue. *A Country Year: Living the Questions*. Mariner Books, 1999.

Huggan, Graham and Helen Tiffin. *Postcolonial Ecocriticism: Literature, Animals, Environment*. Routledge, 2006.

Hultman, Martin. 'Green Men? Exploring Industrial-, Ecological-, and Ecomodern Masculinity,' www.genanet.de/fileadmin/user_upload/dokumente/Gender-Klima-Energie/Hultman_Green_Men._Exploring_Industrial-Ecological-and_Ec omodern_Masculinity.pdf. Accessed 04 Dec. 2016.

Indugopan, G. R. *Manal Jeevikal*. Chintha, 2013.

Iovino, Serenella. 'Pollution.' *Keywords for Environmental Studies*, edited by Joni Adamson, William A. Gleason, and David N. Pellow, New York UP, 2016, pp. 167–168.

Iovino, Serenella and Serpil Oppermann. 'Introduction: Stories Come to Matter.' *Material Ecocriticism*, edited by Serenella Iovino and Serpil Oppermann, Indiana UP, 2014, pp. 1–17.

Iovino, Serenella and Serpil Oppermann. *Material Ecocriticism*. Indiana UP, 2014.

Irshad, Mohammed S. 'Governing Disaster Risk and 'Survivability': The Case of Two Villages in Kerala, India.' *International Journal of Emergency Management*, vol. 10, no. 3–4, 2014, pp. 276–287. *Research Gate*, doi: doi.org/10.1504/IJEM.2014.066486 Accessed 25 Oct. 2017.

Jackson, Yvette. 'Evolutionary Spiral in the Development of Environmental Ethics.' *Macquarie Journal of International and Comparative Environmental Law*, vol. 3, no. 2, 2006, www.austlii.edu.au/au/journals/MqJlICEnvLaw/2006/11.html. Accessed 08 Aug. 2017.

Jacob, Shaji. 'Novelile Haritha Adhyamikata.' *Haritha Niroopanam Malayalathil*, edited by G. Madhusoodanan, Current Books, 2015, pp. 471–479.

———. 'Thathwamasi.' *Marunadan Malayali*, 13 Aug. 2016, www.marunadanm alayali.com/column/pusthaka-vich-ram/maraporul-by-rajeev-sivasankar-51653. Accessed 30 July 2017.

Jameela, Nalini. *Oru Laingikathozhilaliyude Atmakatha*. DC Books, 2005.

———. *The Autobiography of a Sex Worker*. Translated by J. Devika, Westland Books, 2007.

Jayasree, G. S. 'Adivasi Rachana: Life, Land, and Language.' Introduction. *Kocharethi: The Araya Woman*. By Narayan. Translated by Catherine Thankamma, Oxford UP, 2011, pp. xv–xxx.

Jeffrey, David Lyle. *People of the Book: Christian Identity and Literary Culture*. Wm. B. Eerdmans, 1996.

Jesme, Sister. *Amen: Oru Kanyasthreeyude Atmakatha*. DC Books, 2009.

———. *Amen: The Autobiography of a Nun*. Penguin, 2009.

Jitendra. 'Brick Kilns Major Source of Air Pollution in South Asia.' *Down to Earth*, 12 Mar. 2015, www.downtoearth.org.in/news/brick-kilns-major-source-of-air-pollution-in-south-asia-48956. Accessed 18 July 2017.

John, Babu. 'Endosulfan DurithabadithareSahayikkuka.' *Endosulfan Bheekaratha*, edited by Babu John, Chintha, 2011, pp. 9–14.

John, Haritha. 'An Island in the Outskirts of Kochi Isolated by State Government Apathy.' 19 Nov. 2016, www.thenewsminute.com/article/island-outskirts-kochi-isolated-state-government-apathy-53136. Accessed 15 Mar. 2017.

John, Shiekha E., Maya, K., and Padmalal, D. 'Environmental Impact Assessment of Soil Quarrying from the Hills of Central Kerala, Southwest Coast of India.' *International Journal of Scientific and Research Publication*, vol. 6, no. 8, 2016, pp. 514–521, www.ijsrp.org/research-paper-0816/ijsrp-p5670.pdf. Accessed 10 Aug. 2017.

Joseph, Sarah. *Aalahayude Penmakkal*. Current Books, 1999.

———. *Aathi*. Current Books, 2011.

———. *Gift in Green*. Translated by Valson Thampu, Harper Perennial, 2011.

———. *Mattathi*. Current Books, 2003.

———. *Ooru Kaval*. Current Books, 2009.

———. *Othappu*. Current Books, 2005.

———. *Othappu: The Scent of the Other Side*. Translated by Valson Thampu, Oxford UP, 2009.

———. 'Speaking of Aathi.' Interview by Valson Thampu. *Gift in Green* by Sarah Joseph. Translated by Valson Thampu, Harper Perennial, 2011.

———. 'The Making of *Aathi*.' *Gift in Green* by Sarah Joseph. Translated by Valson Thampu, Harper Perennial, 2011.

———. *The Vigil*. Translated by Vasanthi Sankaranarayanan, Harper Perennial, 2014.

Joshi, Ruchir. *The Last Jet-Engine Laugh*. HarperCollins, 2000.

Junka-Aikio, Laura and Catalina Cortes-Severino. 'Cultural Studies of Extraction.' *Cultural Studies*, vol. 31, no. 2, 2017, pp. 175–184.

Kakkanadan, G. V. *Orotha*. Sankeerthanam, 2002.

Kapoor, Dip. 'Indigenous Struggles for Forests, Land, and Cultural Identity in India: Environmental Popular Education and the Democratization of Power.' *Counterpoints*, vol. 230, 2004, pp. 41–55. *JSTOR*, www.jstor.org/stable/pdf/42978360.pdf?refreqid=excelsior%3A90e97b809791355899f566a245ba8011. Accessed 19 Feb. 2018.

Karan, P. P. 'Environmental Movements in India.' *American Geographical Society*, vol. 84, no. 1, 1994, pp. 32–41. *JSTOR*, www.jstor.org/stable/pdf/215779. pdf?refreqid=search%3Aff65b6bbb71149ae8cbebcb0690feb9f. Accessed 19 Feb. 2018.

Kasturi, Kannan. 'New Thermal Power Clusters.' *Economic and Political Weekly*, vol. 46, no. 40, 2011, pp. 10–13. *JSTOR*, www.jstor.org/stable/pdf/23047413. pdf?refreqid=excelsior%3Aa6831e705af125cd4e913c3e69c3c230. Accessed 19 Feb. 2018.

'Ken Saro-Wiwa.' *Encyclopædia Britannica*, www.britannica.com/biography/Ken-Saro-Wiwa. Accessed 30 May 2017.

'Kerala Theerathe Aprathyakshamakunna Karimanal Khananam.' *Siraj*, 29 Dec. 2013, www.sirajlive.com/2013/12/29/76714.html. Accessed 08 Aug. 2017.

Keraleeyam, Robin. 'Makkalkku Kodukkan Nammakku E Bhoomiyallellu.' *Kallen Pokkduan: Karuppu, Chuvappu, Pachcha*, edited by K. P. Ravi and Anandan P, Green Books, 2013, pp. 223–224.

Khan, Maria and Md. Tarique. 'Industrial Pollution in Indian Industries: A Post Reform Scenario.' *Journal of Energy Research and Environmental Technology*, vol. 2, no. 2, 2015, pp. 182–187, www.krishisanskriti.org/vol_image/08Jul20151 1074486%20%20%20%20%20%20%20%20%20%20%20Maria%20K han%20%20%20%20Energy%20%20%20%20%20%20%20%20%20%20 %20%20%20%20%20182-187.pdf. Accessed 13 Oct. 2017.

Kinver, Mark. 'Tsunami: Mangroves "saved lives." ' *BBC*, 25 Dec. 2005, news.bbc. co.uk/2/hi/science/nature/4547032.stm. Accessed 30 Oct. 2017.

Klare, Michael T. *Resource Wars: The New Landscape of Global Conflict*. Metropolitan Books. 2001.

———. 'Twenty-First Century Energy Wars: How Oil and Gas Are Fuelling Global Conflicts.' Energypost.edu. *Energypost*, 15 July 2014, energypost.eu/twenty-first-century-energy-wars-oil-gas-fuelling-global-conflicts/. Accessed 09 Aug. 2017.

Klimiuk, Ewa and Artur Pawloski. 'Biofuels and Sustainable Development.' *Biomass for Biofuels*, edited by Katarzyna Bulkowska et al., CRC, 2016, pp. 3–12.

'Kozhikode: Mangrove Messiah Gets a School, Posthumously.' *Deccan Chronicle*, 28 Sept. 2017, www.deccanchronicle.com/lifestyle/pets-and-environment/280 917/kozhikode-mangrove-messiah-gets-a-school-posthumously.html. Accessed 16 Feb. 2018.

Kreps, David. 'Introducing Eco-Masculinities: How a Masculine Discursive Subject Approach to the Individual Differences Theory of Gender and IT Impacts an

Environmental Informatics Project.' *Americas Conference on Information Systems 2010 Proceedings*, pp. 1–8, usir.salford.ac.uk/10308/1/Introducing_Eco-Masculinities How_a_masculine_discursive_subject.pdf. Accessed 04 Dec. 2016.

Krishna Pillai, Changampuzha. *Ramanan*. 1936. SPCS, 1987.

Kulkarni, Poorvi. 'As Maharashtra Makes Big Mining Push, Tribals Push Back.' *Business Standard*, 22 Jan. 2017, www.business-standard.com/article/current-affairs/as-maharashtra-makes-big-mining-push-tribals-push-back-117012200539_1.html. Accessed 09 Aug. 2017.

Kumar, Anil P. K. 'Manalazhathil Nirayunna Bhoomiyude Nilavilikkunna Raktham.' *Left Click News*, 23 Nov. 2016. leftclicknews.com/single_news.php?nid=8722. Accessed 22 July 2017.

Kumar, Mohan Y. S. 'Oru Doctorude Sankadangal.' *Endosulfan Bheekaratha*, edited by Babu John, Chintha, 2011, pp. 59–67.

Kumaranasan, N. *Veenapoovu*. 1907. SPCS, 1976.

Kurisseri, Hari. *Manalazham*. SPCS, 2015.

Kurup, G. Sankara. *Odakkuzhal*. 1950. SPCS, 1987.

———. *Sooryakanthi*. SPCS, 1981.

Kurup, O. N. V. "Bhoomikkoru Charamageetham." *ONVyute Kavithakal*. DC Books, 2008, pp. 377–379.

'Kyoto Protocol.' *Encyclopædia Britannica*, www.britannica.com/event/Kyoto-Protocol Accessed 14 Feb. 2017.

Leelakrishnan, Alamkod. *Nilayude Theerangaliloode*. DC Books, 2011.

Leopold, Aldo. *Desert Solitaire*. U of Arizona P, 1968.

———. *Sand County Almanac, and Sketches Here and There*. 1949. Oxford UP, 1989.

Limbale, Sharankumar. *The Outcaste: Akkarmashi*. Translated by Santosh Bhoomkar, Oxford UP, 2003.

Lipman, Zada. 'Trade in Hazardous Waste: Environmental Justice Versus Economic Growth Environmental Justice and Legal Process.' *Basel Action Network*. Basel Action Network, archive.ban.org/library/lipman.html. Accessed 02 Apr. 2017.

Lovelock, James. *Gaia: A New Look at Life on Earth*. Oxford UP, 2000.

Lyotard, Jean-François. 'Ecology as Discourse of the Secluded.' *The Green Studies Reader: From Romanticism to Ecocriticism*, edited by Laurence Coupe, Routledge, 2000, pp. 135–138.

Maathai, Wangari. *Unbowed: A Memoir*. 2006. Anchor Books, 2007.

Macalister, Terry. 'Russia, Iran and Qatar Announce Cartel That Will Control 60% of World's Gas Supplies.' *The Guardian*, 22 Oct. 2008, www.theguardian.com/business/2008/oct/22/gas-russia-gazprom-iran-qatar. Accessed 09 Aug. 2017.

Madhusoodanan, G. *Kathayum Paristhithiyum*. 2000. DC Books, 2011.

———. 'Vimarshanathile Haritha Vaividhyam.' Introduction. *Harithaniroopanam Malayalathil*, edited by G. Madhusoodanan, 2002. Current Books, 2015, pp. 9–29.

'The Man of Mangrove Forests.' *La Paz Group*, 5 Oct. 2015, lapazgroup.net/2015/10/05/the-man-of-mangrove-forests/. Accessed 21 Nov. 2016.

Manes, Christopher. 'Nature and Silence.' *The Ecocriticism Reader: Landmarks in Literary Ecology*, edited by Cheryll Glotfelty and Harold Fromm, U of Georgia P, 1996, pp. 15–29.

Mangad, Ambikasuthan. *Enmakaje.* 2009. DC Books, 2012.

———. *Kunnukal Puzhakal.* Green Books, 2009.

———. *Marakkappile Theyyangal.* DC Books, 2014.

———. 'Sheevothi Purathu; Potti Akathu.' *Harithaniroopanam Malayalathil,* edited by G. Madhusoodanan, Current Books, 2015, pp. 192–201.

———. *Swarga.* Translated by J. Devika, Juggernaut Books, 2017.

Mangad, Balakrishnan. 2004. *Bhoomiyute Kannu.* DC Books, 2009.

Markose, Ambili Anna. 'Endangering Minority: Malabar and Migrant Christian in Discourse.' *Alternative Voices: (Re)searching Language, Culture, Identity,* edited by S. Imtiaz Hasnain, Sangeeta Bagga-Gupta, and Shailendra Mohan, Cambridge Scholars Publishing, 2013, pp. 186–197.

Martinez-Alier, Joan. 'Environmentalism(s).' *Key Words for Environmental Studies,* edited by Joni Adamson, William A. Gleason, and David N. Pellow, New York UP, 2016, pp. 97–100.

———. 'The Environmentalism of the Poor.' *Geoforum,* vol. 54, 2014, pp. 239–241, ac.els-cdn.com/S0016718513000912/1-s2.0-S0016718513000912-main.pdf?_tid=1903a76c-b1a3-11e7-a599-00000aab0f6b&acdnat=1508070151_a6371c63a03409176a4fb6c9dc6f0eec. Accessed 15 Oct. 2017.

———. *The Environmentalism of the Poor: A Study of Ecological Conflicts and Valuation.* Edward Elgar Publishing, 2002.

Martinez-Alier, et al. 'Social Metabolism, Ecological Distribution Conflicts, and Valuation Languages.' *Ecological Economics,* vol. 70, no. 2, 2010, pp. 1–6, icta.uab.cat/99_recursos/1289813089221.pdf. Accessed 22 Oct. 2017.

Martinez-Alier, Joan, Federico Demaria, Leah Temper, and Mariana Walter. 'Changing Social Metabolism and Environmental Conflicts in India and South America.' *Journal of Political Ecology,* vol. 23, no.1, 2016, pp. 467–491, journals.uair.arizona.edu/index.php/JPE/article/view/20252/19868. Accessed 24 Oct. 2017.

Martinez-Alier, Joan and Mariana Walter. 'Social Metabolism and Conflicts over Extractivism.' *Environmental Governance in Latin America,* edited by Fabio De Castro, Barbara Hogenboom, and Michiel Baud, Palgrave Macmillan, 2016, pp. 58–85, link.springer.com/content/pdf/10.1007%2F978-1-137-50572-9_3.pdf. Accessed 24 Oct. 2017.

Mathew, Roy. 'Endosulfan Destroyed Biodiversity of Kasaragod Villages.' *The Hindu,* 22 April 2011, www.thehindu.com/news/national/kerala/endosulfan-destroyed-biodiversity-of-kasaragod-villages/article1717767.ece. Accessed 21 Sept. 2015.

Mathews, Freya. 'Community and the Ecological Self.' *Ecology and Democracy,* edited by Freya Mathews, Frank Cass, 1996, pp. 65–98.

———. 'On Desiring Nature.' *Indian Journal of Ecocriticism,* vol. 3, 2010, pp. 1–8.

———. 'Relating to Nature: Deep Ecology or Ecofeminism?'. *Feminist Ecologies: Changing Environments in the Anthropocene,* edited by Lara Stevens, Peta Tait, and Denise Varney, Palgrave Macmillan, 2018, pp. 35–56.

———.*The Ecological Self.* Routledge, 1991.

Mavelikkara, Francis T. *Swapnangal Vilkkanundu.* SPCS, 2013.

McCarthy, Cormac. *The Road*. Vintage, 2006.

McKibben, Bill. *Eaarth: Making a Life on a Tough New Planet*. Times Books, 2010.

———. *The End of Nature*. Random House, 1989.

Mda, Zakes. *The Heart of Redness*. Oxford UP, 2000.

Meher, Rajkishor. 'Globalization, Displacement and the Livelihood Issues of Tribal and Agriculture Dependent Poor People: The Case of Mineral-based Industries in India.' *Journal of Developing Societies*, vol. 25, 2009, pp. 457–480, doi: 10.1177/0169796X0902500403. Accessed 13 Oct. 2017.

Menon, Leela. 'Aathiyil Kathanamundayirunnu.' *Janmabhumi*, 19 July 2011, www.janmabhumidaily.com/news7912. Accessed 15 Mar. 2017.

Merchant, Carolyn. *Earthcare: Women and the Environment*. Routledge, 1996.

———. *Radical Ecology: The Search for a Livable World*. Routledge, 2005.

———. *The Death of Nature: Women, Ecology and the Scientific Revolution*. Harper & Row, 1980.

Mies, Maria and Vandana Shiva. *Ecofeminism*. Zed Books, 1993.

'Mineral Resources of Kerala.' *Envis Centre: Kerala*, www.kerenvis.nic.in/Database/Mineral%20Resources%20of%20Kerala_1365.aspx. Accessed 10 Aug. 2017.

'The Mining of Sand, a Non-renewable Resource.' *Green Facts*, www.greenfacts.org/en/sand-extraction/l-2/index.htm. Accessed 19 July 2017.

Misra, Atulya. *Oxygen Manifesto: A Battle for the Environment*. Rupa, 2019.

Mohan, Sana. 'Land Struggles in Contemporary Kerala.' *The Hindu Business Line*, 19 Dec. 2011, www.thehindubusinessline.com/opinion/land-struggles-in-contemporary-kerala/article27290300.ece. Accessed 14 Oct. 2017.

Moraga, Cherríe. 'Heroes and Saints.' *Heroes and Saints & Other Plays*. West End Press, 1994, pp. 85–149.

Morton, Timothy. *Dark Ecology: For a Logic of Future Coexistence*. Columbia UP, 2016.

———. *Ecocriticism on the Edge: The Anthropocene as a Threshold Concept*. Bloomsbury. 2015.

———. *Ecology without Nature: Rethinking Environmental Aesthetics*. Harvard UP, 2007.

———. *Hyperobjects: Philosophy and Ecology after the End of the World*. U of Minnesota P, 2013.

———. *The Ecological Thought*. Harvard UP, 2010.

Mukherjee, Upamanyu Pablo. *Postcolonial Environments: Nature, Culture and the Contemporary Indian Novel*. Palgrave Macmillan, 2010.

Mukundan, M. *Daivathinte Vikruthikal*. 1989. DC Books, 1996.

———. *Delhi*. Current Books, 1969.

———. *Delhi Gadhakal*. DC Books, 2011.

———. *God's Mischief*. Translated by Prema Jayakumar, Penguin, 2002.

———. *Mayyazhippuzhayude Theerangalil*. 1974. DC Books, 2013.

———. *On the Banks of the Mayyazhi*. Translated by Gita Krishnankutty, DC Books, 2014.

Munif, Abdelrahman. *Cities of Salt*. Translated by Peter Theroux, Vintage International, 1987.

Muraleedharan, et al. 'The Conservation of Mangroves in Kerala: Economic and Ecological Linkages.' *Kerala Forest Research Institute*, 2009, www.docs.kfri.res. in/KFRI-RR/KFRI-RR353.pdf. Accessed 30 Oct. 2017.

Nabeel, C. K. M. 'Khanikalil Ninnu Malakalkku Oru Charama Geetham.' *Keraleeyam*, July 2014, www.keraleeyammasika.com/media/2014/08/khanika lil-ninnum-malakalkku-oru-charamageetham.pdf. Accessed 08 Aug. 2017.

Næss, Arne. 'Self-Realization: An Ecological Approach to Being in the World.' *The Ecology of Wisdom: Writings by Arne Naess*, edited by Alan Drengson and Bill Devall, Counterpoint, 2008, pp. 81–96.

———. 'The Shallow and the Deep, Long Range Ecology Movements: A Summary.' *The Selected Works of Arne*, edited by Alan Drengson, Springer, 2005, pp. 7–12.

Næss, Arne and George Sessions. 'The Deep Ecology Platform.' *Deep Ecology*, www.deepecology.org/platform.htm. Accessed 16 Oct. 2017.

Nagarajan, Vijaya Rettakudi. 'Rituals of Embedded Ecologies.' *Hinduism and Ecology: The Intersection of Earth, Sky, and Water*, edited by Christopher Key Chapple and Mary Evelyn Tucker, Harvard UP, 2000, pp. 453–468.

Nair, Edassery Govindan. 'Kuttippuram Palam.' *Edasserikkavithakal*. Mathrubhumi Books, 2012, pp. 388–390.

Nair. G. K., 'Kerala's Wetlands and Hills under Threat: Expert.' *The Hindu Business Line*, 03 Jan. 2013, www.thehindubusinessline.com/news/national/keralas-wetla nds-and-hills-under-threat-expert/article4269321.ece. Accessed 18 July 2017.

———. 'Sand Mining Shifts from Rivers to Paddy Fields in Kerala.' *The Hindu Business Line*, 04 July 2002, www.thehindubusinessline.com/2002/07/04/stor ies/2002070401621900.htm. Accessed 04 July 2017.

———. 'Sand Mining Spells Doom for South Kerala Rivers.' *The Hindu*, 20 Dec. 2012, www.thehindubusinessline.com/news/national/sand-mining-spells-doom-for-south-kerala-rivers/article4222003.ece. Accessed 04 July 2017.

Nair, S. Jayachandran. 'Jeevikkunna E Lokathe Ariyanulla Sramam.' *Silent Valley: Oru Paristhithi Samarathinte Charithram* By Saji James, DC Books, 2010, pp. 9–10.

Nair, Sindhu. 'Janu and Nowhere People.' Review of *Janu: C.K. Januvinte Jeevithakatha*, by Bhaskaran. *Infochange India*, August 2003, www.infochan geindia.org/human-rights/39-human-rights/books-a-reports/6004-janu-and-the-nowhere-people. Accessed 29 Oct. 2017.

Nair, Sreekantan C. N. and Sarah Joseph. *Retelling the Ramayana: Voices from Kerala*. Translated by Vasanthi Sankaranarayanan, Oxford UP, 2005.

Namboothiri, Vishnunarayanan, editor. *Vanaparvam*. DC Books, 1983.

Narain, Sunita and Chandra Bhushan. '30 Years of Bhopal Gas Tragedy: A Continuing Disaster.' *Down to Earth*, 15 Dec. 2014, www.downtoearth.org.in/ coverage/30-years-of-bhopal-gas-tragedy-a-continuing-disaster-47634. Accessed 14. Oct. 2017.

Narayan. *Kocharethi*. 1998. DC Books, 2011.

———. *Kocharethi: The Araya Woman*. 2011. Translated by Catherine Thankamma, Oxford UP, 2012.

———. *Ooralikkudi*. 1999. SPCS, 2012.

Nayanar, Vengayil Kunhiraman. 'Vasana Vikruthi.' *Pratilipi*, m.pratilipi.com/ read?id=5920357043142656&ret=/vengayil-kunhiraman-nayanar/vasana-vikruthi. Accessed 06 Dec. 2017.

Nayar, Pramod K. *English Writing and India, 1600–1920: Colonizing Aesthetics.* Routledge, 2008.

———. 'Indigenous Cultures and the Ecology of Protest: Moral Economy and "Knowing Subalternity" in Dalit and Tribal Writing from India.' *Journal of Postcolonial Writing*, vol. 50, no. 3, 2014, pp. 291–303, www.tandfonline.com/doi/abs/10.1080/17449855.2013.815127. Accessed 24 Oct. 2017.

———. *The Postcolonial Studies Dictionary.* Wiley Blackwell, 2015.

Nedungadi, T. M. Appu. *Kundalatha.* Mathrubhumi, 1999.

Neuman, Shirley. '"An Appearance Walking in a Forest Sexes Burn:" Autobiography and the Construction of the Feminine Body.' *Autobiography and Postmodernism*, edited by Kathleen M. Ashley, Leigh Gilmore, and Gerald Peters, U of Massachusetts P, 1994.

Nixon, Rob. 'Environmentalism and Postcolonialism.' *Ecocriticism: The Essential Reader*, edited by Ken Hiltner, Routledge, 2015, pp. 196–210.

———. *Slow Violence and the Environmentalism of the Poor.* Harvard UP, 2011.

Nocella II, Anthony. 'Defining Eco-ability: Social Justice and the Intersectionality of Disability, Nonhuman Animals, and Ecology.' *Disability Studies and the Environmental Humanities: Toward an Eco-Crip Theory*, edited by Sarah Jaquette Ray and Jay Sibara, U of Nebraska P, 2017. *Google Books*, books.google.co.in/books?id=jZ0nDwAAQBAJ&printsec=frontcover#v=onepage&q&f=false. Accessed 28 Oct. 2017.

North, Liisa and Ricardo Grinspun. 'Neo-extractivism and the New Latin American Developmentalism: The Missing Piece of Rural Transformation.' *Third World Quarterly*, vol. 37, no. 8, 2016, pp. 1483–1504.

Notermans, Catrein, Albertina Nugteren, and Suma Sunny. 'The Changing Landscape of Sacred Groves in Kerala (India): A Critical View on the Role of Religion in Nature Conservation.' *Religions*, vol. 7.4, no. 38, 2016, pp. 1–14, doi: 10.3390/rel7040038. Accessed 18 Feb. 2017.

Ogrodnick, Margaret. *Instinct and Intimacy: Political Philosophy and Autobiography in Rousseau.* U of Toronto P, 1999.

Özdağ, Ufuk. 'Keeping Alive the Memory of the Amik: Environmental Aesthetics and Land Restoration.' *The Future of Ecocriticism: New Horizons*, edited by Serpil Oppermann, Ufuk Özdağ, Nevin Özkan, and Scott Slovic, Cambridge Scholars, 2011, pp. 118–135.

Padre, Sri. 'Endosulfan Samaram.' *Endosulfan Bheegaratha*, edited by Babu John, Chintha, 2011, pp. 45–58.

———. *Vishamazhayil Polliya Manassu.* DC Books, 2010.

Palakeel, Thomas. 'Twentieth-Century Malayalam Literature.' *Handbook of Twentieth-Century Literatures of India*, edited by Nalini Natarajan, Greenwood, 1996, pp. 180–206.

Palott, Jaffer. 'Kandalkkadinte Paaristhithika Pradhanyangal.' *Kandalkkadukalkkidayil Ente Jeevitham*, edited by Thaha Madyi, 2002. DC Books, 2010, pp.73–99.

Pandathil, Rajesh and O. P. Raveendran. 'This Tribal Farmer Preserves 40 Indigenous Paddy Seeds and Incurs Rs 30,000 Loss Every Year.' *First Post*, 09 May 2016, www.firstpost.com/india/this-tribal-farmer-preserves-40-indigenous-paddy-seeds-and-incurs-rs-30000-loss-every-year-2771534.html. Accessed 30 Nov. 2016.

Paniker, K. Ayyappa. *A Short History of Malayalam Literature.* Information & Public Relations Department Kerala State, 2006, ia801000.us.archive.org/33/items/ASHORTHISTORYOFMALAYALAMLITERATURE/A%20SHORT%20HISTORY%20OF%20MALAYALAM%20LITERATURE.pdf. Accessed 16 Oct. 2017.

———. 'Modern Malayalam Literature.' *Modern Indian Literature, an Anthology: Surveys and Poems,* edited by K. M. George, vol. 1, Sahitya Akademi, 1992, pp. 231–255.

———. 'Nadevide Makkale.' *Agnipoojayum Mattu Pradhana Kavithakalum,* edited by K. Satchidanandan, DC Books, 2010, pp. 113–116.

———. 'The End of Historiography?' *Frontline,* vol. 16, no. 9, 1999, www.frontline.in/static/html/fl1609/16091110.htm. Accessed 12 Oct. 2017.

Panjikkaran, Mariamma. 'Sarah Joseph A Writer of Women, for Women.' *Kerala Calling,* February 2004, www.kerala.gov.in/documents/10180/adc88e02-5cdb-4b90-8e93-3dd6aeace588. Accessed 12 Oct. 2017.

Papilio Buddha. Directed by Jayan K. Cherian, 2013.

Parajuli, Pramod. 'Coming Home to the Earth Household: Indigenous Communities and Ecological Citizenship in India.' *Indigenous Peoples' Wisdom and Power: Affirming Our Knowledge through Narratives,* edited by Julian Kunnie and Nomalungelo Ivy Goduka, Ashgate, 2006, pp. 175–196.

———. 'Ecological Ethnicity in the Making: Developmentalist Hegemonies and Emergent Identities in India.' *Identities: Global Studies in Culture and Power,* vol. 3, 2010, pp. 14–59, www.tandfonline.com/doi/abs/10.1080/1070289X.1996.9962551. Accessed 09 Dec. 2016.

Parameswaran, K. P. 'Significance of Silent Valley.' *Economic and Political Weekly,* vol. 14, no. 27, 1979, pp. 1117–119. *JSTOR,* www.jstor.org/stable/pdf/4367757.pdf?refreqid=search:8b5cf22a5700b38452d8540794f62778. Accessed 19 Feb. 2018.

Parekh, Bhiku C. *Colonialism, Tradition, and Reform: An Analysis of Gandhi's Political Discourse.* Sage, 1989.

Pariyadath, Jothibai. *Mayilamma: Oru Jeevitham.* 2006. Mathrubhumi Books, 2012.

Passenger. Directed by Ranjith Sankar, 2009.

Pereira, Kiran. 'Sand Mining–The Unexamined Threat to Water Security.' *Envis Centre,* ismenvis.nic.in/Database/SandMining%E2%80%93TheUnexaminedThreattoWaterSecurity_3457.aspx?format=Print. Accessed 09 Aug. 2017.

Perry, Alex. 'Brief History: The Resource Curse.' *Time,* 28 June 2010, content.time.com/time/magazine/article/0,9171,1997460,00.html. Accessed 09 Aug. 2017.

Pezzullo, Phaedra C. *Toxic Tourism: Rhetorics of Pollution, Travel, and Environmental Justice.* U of Alabama P, 2007.

Phillips, Dana. 'Excremental Ecocriticism and the Global Sanitation Crisis.' *Material Ecocriticism,* edited by Serenella Iovino and Serpil Oppermann, Indiana UP, 2014, pp.172–185.

Picou, J. Steven, Brent K. Marshall, and Duane A. Gill. 'Disaster, Litigation, and the Corrosive Community.' *Social Forces,* vol. 82, no. 4, 2004, pp. 1493–1522. *JSTOR,* www.jstor.org/stable/pdf/3598443.pdf. Accessed 19 Feb. 2018.

Pillai, Sreekanteswaram G. Padmanabha. *Sabdatharavali.* SPCS, 2009.

Pillai, Thakazhi Sivasankara. *Kayar.* Samasya Books, 1978.

————. *Randidangazhi*. 1948. DC Books, 2015.

Plumwood, Val. *Feminism and the Mastery of Nature*. Routledge, 1993.

————. 'Shadow Places and the Politics of Dwelling.' *Australian Humanities Review*, vol. 44, 2008, pp. 139–150, www.australianhumanitiesreview.org/arch ive/Issue-March-2008/plumwood.html. Accessed 30 Nov. 2016.

Poduval, P. P. K. 'Paristhithi Vicharam Malayala Kavithayil.' *Harithaniroopanam Malayalathil*, edited by G. Madhusoodanan, Current Books, 2015, pp. 462–463.

————. *Paristhithibodhavum Samskaravum*. Mathrubhumi Books, 2007.

————. *Paristhithikkavithakku Oraamukham*. DC Books, 1995.

Pokkudan, Kallen. *Choottachi: Puzhajeevikalekkurichulla Pokkudante Ormakal*. 2010. DC Books, 2012.

————. *Ente Jeevitham*. Prepared by Sreejith Paithalen. DC Books, 2010.

————. *Kandal Inangal*, edited by Anadan P, Green Books, 2015.

————. *Kandalkkadukalkkidayil Ente Jeevitham*, edited by Thaha Madayi, 2002. DC Books, 2010.

Pottekkatt, S. K. *Vishakanyaka*. 1948. DC Books, 2006.

Potter, Emily. 'Ecological Consciousness in Australian Literature: Outside the Limits of Environmental Crisis.' Hawke Research Institute Working Paper Series, no. 9. www.unisa.edu.au/siteassets/episerver-6-files/documents/eass/hri/working-papers/wp29.pdf. Accessed 10 March 2023.

Powers, Richard. *The Echo Maker*. Vintage Books, 2007.

Prakkanam, Seleena. *Chengara Samaravum Ente Jeevithavum*. Prepared by O. K. Santhosh and M. B. Manoj. DC Books, 2013.

'The Prelude.' *Encyclopædia Britannica*, www.britannica.com/topic/The-Prelude. Accessed 24 Feb. 2016.

Pulido, Laura. *Environmentalism and Economic Justice: Two Chicano Struggles in the Southwest*. U of Arizona P, 1996.

Putul, AlokPrakash. 'Farmers Tackle Pests with Colas.' *BBC*, 03 Nov. 2014, news. bbc.co.uk/2/hi/south_asia/3977351.stm. Accessed 21 Sept. 2015.

'Quarrykku Ethire Oru Gramam Pushthakam Vayikkunnu' [A Village Reads Book to Fight the Quarry]. *Mathrubhumi*, 19 June 2015. http://archives. mathrubhumi.com/ pathanamthitta/news/3657082-local_news-Pathanamthitta-%E0%B4%AA% E0%B4%A4%E0%B5%8D%E0%B4%A4%E0%B4%A8%E0%B4%82%E 0%B4%A4%E0%B4%BF%E0%B4%9F%E0%B5%8D%E0%B4%9F.html. Accessed 04 July 2020.

Rafferty, John P. 'Anthropocene Epoch.' *Encyclopædia Britannica*, www.britann ica.com/science/Anthropocene-Epoch. Accessed 17 Dec. 2017.

Rajasekharan, P. K. 'Bhoomiyum, Bhoopadangalum, Ormmayude Thattakangalum.' *Haritha Niroopanam Malayalathil*, edited by G. Madhusoodanan, Current Books, 2015, pp. 451–456.

Rajasekharan, S. *Paristhithidarsanam Malayala Kavithayil*. Kerala Bhasha Institute, 2010.

Rajendran, S. 'Pesticide Spraying in Kerala: Human Cost and Environmental Loss.' *Economic and Political Weekly*, vol. 37, no. 23, 2002, pp. 2206–2207. JSTOR, www.jstor.org/stable/pdf/4412210.pdf?refreqid=search%3A6bc0cac3e8ae1 9b0947bb8d0e6411ef0. Accessed 19 Feb. 2018.

Ramesh, Randeep. 'Soft-drink Giants Accused over Pesticides.' *The Guardian*, 05 Feb. 2004, www.theguardian.com/world/2004/feb/05/india.randeepramesh. Accessed 13 Nov. 2017.

Rammohan, K. T. 'Caste and Landlessness in Kerala: Signals from Chengara.' *Economic and Political Weekly*, vol. 43, no. 37, 2008, pp. 14–17. *JSTOR*, www. jstor.org/stable/pdf/40277941.pdf?refreqid=search%3Abb02b47e22c308a59 ba1033fea841c14. Accessed 19 Feb. 2018.

Rangarajan, Swarnalatha. 'Women Writing Nature in the Global South: New Forest Texts from Fractured Indian Forests.' *Handbook of Ecocriticism and Cultural Ecology*, edited by Hubert Zapf and De Gruyter, 2016, pp. 438–458.

Ravi Shanker, N. 'Translator's Note.' *Mother Forest: The Unfinished Story of C.K. Janu*, by Bhaskaran. Kali for Women & Women Unlimited, 2004, pp. ix–xii.

Ray, Sarah Jaquette. *The Ecological Other: Environmental Exclusion in American Culture*. U of Arizona P, 2013.

Ray, Sarah Jaquette and Jay Sibara. *Disability Studies and the Environmental Humanities: Toward an Eco-Crip Theory*. U of Nebraska P, 2017. *Google Books*, books.google.co.in/books?id=jZ0nDwAAQBAJ&printsec=frontcover#v= onepage&q&f=false. Accessed 28 Oct. 2017.

Reed, T. V. 'Toward an Environmental Justice Ecocriticism.' *The Environmental Justice Reader: Politics, Poetics, & Pedagogy*, edited by Joni Adamson, Mei Mei Evans, and Rachel Stein, U of Arizona P, 2002, pp. 145–162.

Rishoi, Christy. *From Girl to Woman: American Women's Coming-of-Age Narratives*. State U of New York P, 2003.

Roos, Bonnie and Alex Hunt, editors. *Postcolonial Green: Environmental Politics and World Narratives*. U of Virginia P, 2010.

Rueckert, William. 'Literature and Ecology: An Experiment in Ecocriticism.' *The Ecocriticism Reader: Landmarks in Literary Ecology*, edited by Cheryll Glotfelty and Harold Fromm, U of Georgia P, 1996, pp. 105–123.

Sadasivan, S. N. *A Social History of India*. A.P.H. Publishing, 2000.

Santhosh, V., et al. 'Brick and Tile Clay Mining from the Paddy Lands of Central Kerala (Southwest Coast of India) and Emerging Environmental Issues.' *Environmental Earth Sciences*, vol. 68, no. 7, 2013, pp. 2111–2121, link. springer.com/content/pdf/10.1007/s12665-012-1896-4.pdf. Accessed 09 Aug. 2017.

Sarkar, Sanchar and Swarnalatha Rangarajan. 'Of Devouring Waters and Unforgiving Lands: An Analysis of Premonition Ecology in two Wetland Narratives from West Bengal.' *International Journal of Fear Studies*, vol. 3, no. 1, 2021, pp. 61–73.

Sebastian, Amstrong. 'Kamala Das: The Ecofeminist Pioneer of Kerala.' Diss. Mahatma Gandhi U, 2009. *Shodhganga*, shodhganga.inflibnet.ac.in/handle/ 10603/22756. Accessed 15 Oct. 2017.

Shaji, K. A. 'Case against Coca-Cola under SC/ST Act.' *The Hindu*, 12 June 2016, www.thehindu.com/todays-paper/tp-national/case-against-coca-cola-under-scst-act/article14418202.ece1. Accessed 30 Oct. 2017.

Shiva, Vandana. 'Earth Democracy.' *Navadanya*, www.navdanya.org/earth-democr acy. Accessed 21 Sept. 2015.

———. *Earth Democracy: Justice, Sustainability and Peace*. Zed Books, 2016. *Google Books*, books.google.co.in/books?id=7xNkDgAAQBAJ&printsec= frontcover#v=onepage&q&f=false. Accessed 29 Oct. 2017.

———. 'Ecological Balance in the Era of Globalization.' *The Globalization Reader*, edited by Frank J. Lechner and John Boli, Wiley Blackwell, 2015, pp. 566–574.

———. *Staying Alive: Women, Ecology and Survival in India*. Kali for Women, 1988.

———. *The Violence of Green Revolution: Third World Agriculture, Ecology and Politics*. Zed Books, 1993.

Shiva, Vandana and J. Bandyopadhyay. 'The Evolution, Structure, and Impact of the Chipko Movement.' *Mountain Research and Development*, vol. 6, no. 2, 1986, pp. 133–142.

Shoptaw, John. 'Why Ecopoetry?,' *Poetry*, January 2016. www.poetryfoundation. org/poetrymagazine/articles/70299/why-ecopoetry. Accessed 10 March 2023.

Silko, Leslie Marmon. *Ceremony*. 1977. Penguin Books, 2006.

Simmons, Matthew R. *Twilight in the Desert: The Coming Saudi Oil Shock and the World Economy*. John Wiley & Sons, 2005.

Sinha, Indra. *Animal's People*. Pocket Books, 2007.

Sivasankar, Rajeev. *Kalpramanam*. SPCS, 2014.

Skirble, Roseanne. 'Environmental Writer Turns Words into Action.' *VOA News*, 16 May 2010, web.archive.org/web/20100516032727/http://www1.voanews. com/english/news/american-life/profiles/Environmental-Writer-Turns-Words-into-Action-91461014.html. Accessed 06 Apr. 2017.

Slovic, Scott. 'Editor's Note.' *Interdisciplinary Studies in Literature and Environment*, vol. 19, no. 4, Autumn 2012, pp. 619–621, doi: doi.org/10.1093/ isle/iss132. Accessed 19 Feb. 2018.

———. 'Taking Care: Toward an Ecomasculinist Literary Criticism?' *Eco-man: New Perspectives on Masculinity and Nature*, edited by Mark Allister, U of Virgina P, 2004, pp. 66–80.

———. 'The Third Wave of Ecocriticism: North American Reflections on the Current Phase of the Discipline.' *Ecozone*, vol. 1, no. 1, 2010, pp. 4–10, ecozona. eu/article/download/312/283. Accessed 19 Feb. 2018.

Slovic, Scott, Swarnalatha Rangarajan, and Vidya Sarveswaran, editors. *Ecoambiguity, Community, Development: Toward a Politicized Ecocriticism*. Lexington Books, 2014.

Snyder, Gary. *The Practice of the Wild*. Counterpoint, 1990.

———. *Turtle Island*. New Directions, 1974.

Sreekumar, K. C. 'Ningal Kuzhikkunnu, Njangale Kadaledukkunnu.' Introduction. *Manal Jeevikal*. By G. R. Indugopan. Chintha, 2013, pp. 14–17.

Starke, Linda. *Breaking New Ground: Mining, Minerals and Sustainable Development*. Earthscan, 2002.

Stein, Rachel. 'Activism as Affirmation: Gender and Environmental Justice in Linda Hogan's *Solar Storms* and Barbara Neely's *Blanche Cleans Up*.' *The Environmental Justice Reader: Politics, Poetics and Pedagogy*, edited by Joni Adamson, Mei Mei Evans, and Rachel Stein, U of Arizona P, 2002, pp. 194–212.

Steur, Luisa. 'Adivasis, Communists, and the Rise of Indigenism in Kerala.' *Dialectical Anthropology*, vol. 35, no. 1, 2011, pp. 59–76. *JSTOR*, www.jstor. org/stable/pdf/29790998.pdf. Accessed 19 Feb. 2018.

Sthalam. Directed by Kaviyoor Sivaprasad, 2011.

Sturgeon, Noël. *Ecofeminist Natures: Race, Gender, Feminist Theory, and Political Action*. Routledge, 1997.

Sugathakumari. 'Kaavu Theendalle, Kudivellam Muttum.' *Kaavu Theendalle*. DC Books, 2014, pp. 11–14.

———. "Marathinu Sthuthi." *Sugathakumariyute Kavithakal Sampoornam*. 2006. DC Books, 2011, pp. 502–503.

———. 'Preface.' *Kaavu Theendalle*. By Sugathakumari. DC Books, 2014, p. 07.

Sullivan, Heather I. 'Dirt Theory and Material Ecocriticism.' *Interdisciplinary Studies in Literature and Environment*, vol. 19, no. 3, Summer 2012, pp. 515–531, doi: doi.org/10.1093/isle/iss067. Accessed 19 Feb. 2018.

———. 'Dirty Nature: Ecocriticism and Tales of Extraction–Mining and Solar Power–in Goethe, Hoffmann, Verne, and Eschbach.' *Colloquia Germanica*, vol. 44, no. 2, 2011, pp. 111–131, www.periodicals.narr.de/index.php/colloquia_ge rmanica/article/viewFile/679/657. Accessed 09 Aug. 2017.

———. 'Material Ecocriticism and the Petro-text.' *The Routledge Companion to the Environmental Humanities*. Routledge, 2017, pp. 414–423.

Summerly, John. 'Pepsi and Coca-Cola Used as Pesticide in India Because They're Cheap and Get the Job Done.' *Prevent Disease*, 06 May 2014, preventdisease. com/news/14/050614-Pepsi-and-Coca-Cola-Used-As-Pesticide-In-India.shtml

Surendran, P. 'Haritha Vidyalayam.' *Thiranjedutha Kadhakal (1981–2011)*. DC Books, 2013, pp. 85–89.

———. 'Mahayanam.' *P. Surendrante 5 Novelukal*. DC Books, 2010, pp. 13–58.

Swamy, Raju Narayana. 'Development, Ecology and Livelihood Security: A Study of Paniyas in Wayanad.' Diss. Amrita Vishwa Vidyapeetham, 2011. *Shodhganga*, shodhganga.inflibnet.ac.in/handle/10603/2732. Accessed 15 Oct. 2017.

Sze, Julie. 'From Environmental Justice Literature to the Literature of Environmental Justice.' *The Environmental Justice Reader: Politics, Poetics, & Pedagogy*, edited by Joni Adamson, Mei Mei Evans, and Rachel Stein, U of Arizona P, 2002, pp. 163–180.

Tagore, Rabindranath. *Gitanjali: Song Offerings*. MacMillan, 1913.

Tarter, Jim. 'Some Live More Downstream Than Others: Cancer, Gender and Environmental Justice.' *The Environmental Justice Reader: Politics, Poetics and Pedagogy*, edited by Joni Adamson, Mei Mei Evans, and Rachel Stein, U of Arizona P, 2002, pp. 213–228.

Thanal, Jayakumar C. 'Endosulfan Charithram.' *Endosulfan Bheegaratha*, edited by Babu John, Chintha, 2011, pp. 84–97.

Thankappan, Ranjith. 'Life, History and Politics: Kallen Pokkudan's Two Autobiographies and the Dalit Print Imaginations in Keralam.' *Dalit Literatures in India*, edited by Joshil K. Abraham and Judith Misrahi-Barak, Routledge, 2016, pp. 194–205.

'37% of Western Ghats Ecologically Sensitive: Kasturirangan Panel Report.' *The Times of India*, 18 Apr. 2013, timesofindia.indiatimes.com/india/

37-of-Western-Ghats-ecologically-sensitive-Kasturirangan-panel-report/ articleshow/19607237.cms. Accessed 09 Aug. 2017.

Thoreau, Henry David. *Walden; or, Life in the Woods*. 1854. Dover, 1995.

Trexler, Adam. *Anthropocene Fictions: The Novel in a Time of Climate Change*. U of Virginia P, 2015. *Google Books*, books.google.co.in/books/about/Anthropocene_ Fictions.html?id=GZOdBAAAQBAJ&print sec=frontcover&source=kp_read_ button&redir_esc=y#v=onepage&q&f=false. Accessed 15 Nov. 2017.

'Tribal: Victims of Development Projects–India's Forced Displacement Policy and Practice.' *Development Projects and Tribal Displacement*, socialissuesindia. files.wordpress.com/2012/09/tribal-displacement-in-india.pdf. Accessed 15 Oct. 2016.

Vijayan, O. V. *Khasakkinte Ithihasam*. 1969. DC Books, 2016.

———. *Madhuram Gayathi*. 1990. DC Books, 2014.

———. *Oru Sindoorappottinte Orma*. DC Books, 1987.

———. *The Legends of Khasak*. Penguin Books, 1994.

Vijayan, Roshni. 'Pokkali Rice Cultivation in Kerala.' *Agricultural Update*, vol. 2, no. 3, 2016, pp. 329–333, doi: 10.15740/HAS/AU/11.3/329-333. Accessed 19 Feb. 2018.

V. K. N. *Bovine Bugles*. DC Books, 2004.

Wald, Priscilla. *Contagious: Cultures, Carriers, and the Outbreak Narrative*. Duke UP, 2008.

Wallace, David Foster. *The Infinite Jest*. Abacus, 1996.

Warren, Karen J. *Ecofeminist Phiosophy: A Western Perspective and What It IS and Why It Matters*. Rowman& Littlefield, 2000.

Wheeler, Wendy. *The Whole Creature: Complexity, Biosemiotics and the Evolution of Culture*. Wishart and Lawrence, 2006.

White, Rob. 'Rob White: Resource Extraction Leaves Something Behind: Environmental Justice and Mining.' *International Journal for Crime and Justice*, vol. 2, no. 1, 2013, pp. 50–64, doi: doi.org/10.5204/ijcjsd.v2i1.90. Accessed 19 Feb. 2018.

Wickramasinghe, Deepthi. 'Regreening the Coast: Community-Based Mangrove Conservation and Restoration in Sri Lanka.' *Participatory Mangrove Management in a Changing Climate: Perspectives from the Asia-Pacific*, edited by Rajarshi DasGupta and Rajib Shaw, Springer, 2017, pp. 161–172.

Williams, Michael Stuart. 'Augustine as a Reader of His Christian Contemporaries.' *A Companion to Augustine*, edited by Mark Vessey, Wiley-Blackwell, 2012, pp. 227–239.

Williams, Raymond. *The Country and the City*. Oxford UP, 1973.

Williams, Terry Tempest. *Red: Passion and Patience in the Desert*. Pantheon Books, 2001.

———. *Refuge: An Unnatural History of Family and Place*. Vintage, 1991.

Willow, Anna J. 'Indigenous ExtrACTIVISM in Boreal Canada: Colonial Legacies, Contemporary Struggles and Sovereign Futures.' *Humanities*, vol. 5, no. 3, 2016, doi: 10.3390/h5030055. Accessed 23 Oct. 2017.

Wilson, Edward O. *Consilience: The Unity of Knowledge*. Vintage Books, 1999.

Wilson, Sarah Ruth. "Rape of the Land:' 21st Century Ecofeminism and Environmental Rape Culture.' *Medium*, 27 Feb. 2016, medium.com/@sarahwilsn/rape-of-the-land-21st-century-ecofeminism-and-environmental-rape-culture-c858364174a3. Accessed 18 July 2017.

Wordsworth, William. *The Prelude or The Growth of a Poet's Mind*, edited by Ernest De Selincourt, Oxford UP, 1933.

Yadu, C. R. 'The Land Question and the Mobility of the Marginalized: A Study of Land Inequality in Kerala.' *Agrarian South: Journal of Political Economy*, vol. 4, no. 3, 2015, pp. 1–44. *Academia*, www.academia.edu/25547093/The_Land_Question_and_the_Mobility_of_the_Marginalized_A_Study_of_Land_Inequality_in_Kerala. Accessed 25 Oct. 2017.

Yamashita, Karen. *The Tropic of Orange*. Coffee House, 1997.

Ye, Jingzhong, Jan Douwe van der Ploeg, Sergio Schneider and Teodor Shanin. 'The Incursions of Extractivism: Moving from Dispersed Places to Global Capitalism.' *The Journal of Peasant Studies*, vol. 47, no. 1, 2012, pp. 155–183.

Zacharia, George. *Alternatives Unincorporated: Earth Ethics from the Grassroots*. Routledge, 2014.

Zalasiewicz, Jan, Mark Williams, and Collin N. Waters. 'Anthropocene.' *Key Words for Environmental Studies*, edited by Joni Adamson, William A. Gleason, and David N. Pellow, New York UP, 2016, pp. 14–16.

Index